Pharmacology Exam Success

By Lewis Morris

www.insiderswords.com/pharmacology

ISBN-13: 978-1791318741

Table of Contents

What is "Insider Language"?

Recent research has confirmed what we have known for decades: The strongest students and leaders in industry have a mastered an Insider Language in their subject and field. This Insider language is made up of the technical terms and vocabulary necessary to communicate effectively in classes or the workplace. For those who master it, learning is easier, faster, and much more enjoyable.

Most students who are surveyed report that the greatest challenge to any course of study is learning the vocabulary. When we examine typical college courses, we discover that there is, on average, 250 Insider Terms a student must learn over the course of a semester. Further, most exams rely heavily on this set of words for assessment purposes. The structure of multiple choice exams lends itself perfectly to the testing of this Insider Language. Students who can differentiate between Insider Language terms can handle challenging exam questions with ease and confidence.

From recent research on learning and vocabulary we have learned:

- Your knowledge of any subject is contained in the content-specific words you know. The more of these terms that you know, the easier it is to understand and recall important information; the easier it will be to communicate your ideas to peers, professors, supervisors, and co-workers. The stronger your content-area vocabulary is, the higher your scores will be on your exams and written assignments.

- Students who develop a strong Insider Language perform better on tests, learn faster, retain more information, and express greater satisfaction in learning.

- Familiarizing yourself with subject-area vocabulary before formal study (pre-learning) is the most effective way to learn this language and reap the most benefit.

- The vocabulary on standardized exams come directly from the stated objectives of the test-makers. This means that the vocabulary found on standardized exams is predictable. Our books focus on this vocabulary.

- Most multiple-choice exams are glorified vocabulary quizzes. Think about the format of a multiple-choice question. The question stem is a definition of a term and the choices (known as distractors) are 4 or 5 similar words. Your task is to differentiate between the meanings of those terms and choose the correct word.

- It takes a person several exposures to a new word to be able to use it with confidence in conversation or in writing. You need to process these words several different ways to make them part of your long-term memory.

The goals of this book are:

- To give you an "Insider Language" for your subject.
- Pre-teach the most important words before you set out on a traditional course of review or study.
- Teach you the most important words in your subject area.
- Teach you strategies for learning subject-area words on your own.
- Boost your confidence in your ability to master this language and support you in your study.
- Reduce the stress of studying and provide you with fun activities that work.

How it works:

The secret to mastering Insider Language is through repetition and exposure. We have eleven steps for you to follow:

1. Read the word and definition in the glossary out loud. "See it, Say it"
2. Identify the part of speech the word belongs to such as noun, verb, adverb, or adjective. This will help you group the word and identify similar words.
3. Place the word in context by using it in a sentence. Write this sentence down and read it aloud.
4. Use "Chunking" to group the words. Make a diagram or word cloud using these groups.
5. Make connections to the words by creating analogies.
6. Create mnemonics that help you recognize patterns and orders of words by substituting the words for more memorable items or actions.
7. Examine the morphology of the word, that is, identify the root, prefix, and suffix that make up the word. Identify similar and related words.
8. Complete word games and puzzles such as crosswords and word searches.
9. Complete matching questions that require you to differentiate between related words.
10. Complete Multiple-choice questions containing the words.
11. Create a visual metaphor or "memory cartoon" to make a mental picture of the word and related processes.

By completing this word study process, you will be exposed to the terminology in various ways that will activate your memory and create a lasting understanding of this language.

The strategies in this book are designed to make you an independent expert at learning insider language. These strategies include:

- Verbalizing the word by reading it and its definition aloud ("See It, Say It"). This allows you to make visual, auditory, and speech connections with its meaning.

- Identifying the type of word (Noun, verb, adverb, and adjective). Making this distinction helps you understand how to visualize the word. It helps you "chunk" the words into groups, and gives you clues on how to use the word.

- Place the word in context by using it in a sentence. Write this sentence down and read it aloud. This will give you an example of how the word is used.

- "Chunking". By breaking down the word list into groups of closely related words, you will learn them better and be able to remember them faster. Once you have group the terms, you can then make word clouds using a free online service. These word clouds provide visual cues to remembering the words and their meanings.

- Analogies. By creating analogies for essential words, you will be making connections that you can see on paper. These connections can trigger your memory and activate your ability to use the word in your writing as you begin to use them. Many of these analogies also use visual cues. In a sense, you can make a mental picture from the analogy.

- Mnemonics. A device such as a pattern of letters, ideas, or associations that assists in remembering something. A mnemonic is especially useful for remembering the order of a set of words or the order of a process.

- Morphology. The study of word roots, prefixes, and suffixes. By examining the structure of the words, you will gain insight into other words that are closely related, and learn how to best use the word.

- Visual metaphors. This is the most sophisticated and entertaining strategy for learning vocabulary. Create a "memory cartoon" using one or more of the vocabulary terms. This activity triggers the visual part of your memory and makes fast, permanent, imprints of the word on your memory. By combining the terms in your visual metaphor, you can "chunk" the entire set of vocabulary terms into several visual metaphors and benefit from the brain's tendency to group these terms.

The activities in this book are designed to imprint the words and their meanings in your memory in different ways. By completing each activity, you will gain the necessary exposures to the word to make it a permanent part of your vocabulary. Each activity uses a different part of your memory. The result is that you will be comfortable using these words and be able to tell the difference between closely related words. The activities include:

A. Crossword Puzzles and Word Searches- These are proven to increase test scores and improve comprehension. Students frequently report that they are fun and engaging, while requiring them to analyze the structure and meaning of the words.

B. Matching- This activity is effective because it forces you to differentiate between many closely related terms.

C. Multiple Choice- This classic question format lends itself to vocabulary study perfectly. Most exams are in this format because they are simple to make, easy to score, and are a reliable type of assessment. (Perfect for the Vocabulary Master!) One strategy to use with multiple choice questions that enhance their effectiveness is to cover the answer choices while you read the question. After reading the question, see if you can answer it before looking at the choices. Then look at the choices to see if you match one of them.

Conducting a thorough "word study" of your insider language will take time and effort, but the rewards will be well worth it. By following this guide and completing the exercises thoughtfully, you will become a stronger, more effective, and satisfied student. Best of luck on your mastery of this Insider Language!

Insider Language Strategies

"See It, Say It!" Reading your Insider Language set aloud

"It is better to fail in originality than to succeed in imitation."
-Herman Melville

Reading aloud is the foundation for the development of an Insider Language. It is the single most important thing you can do for vocabulary acquisition. Done correctly, it engages the visual, auditory, and speech centers of the brain and hastens its storage in your long-term memory.

Reading aloud demonstrates the relationship between the printed word and its meaning.

You can read aloud on a higher level than you can initially understand, so reading aloud makes complex ideas more accessible and exposes you to vocabulary and patterns that are not part of your typical speech. Reading aloud helps you understand the complicated text better and makes more challenging text easier to grasp and understand. Reading aloud helps you to develop the "habits of mind" the strongest students use.

Reading aloud will make connections to concepts in the reading that requires you to relate the new vocabulary to things you already know. Go to the glossary at the end of this book and for each word complete the five steps outlined below:

1. Read the word and its definition aloud. Focus on the sound of the word and how it looks on the paper.
2. Read the word aloud again try to say three or four similar words; this will help you build connections to closely related words.
3. Read the word aloud a third time. Try to make a connection to something you have read or heard.
4. Visualize the concept described in the term. Paint a mental picture of the word in use.
5. Try to think of the opposite of the word. Discovering a close antonym will help you place this word in context.

Create a sentence using the word in its proper context

"OPPORTUNITIES DON'T HAPPEN. YOU CREATE THEM." -CHRIS GROSSER

Context means the circumstances that form the setting for an event, statement, or idea, and which it can be fully understood and assessed. Synonyms for context include conditions, factors, situation, background, and setting.

Place the word in context by using it in a sentence. Write this sentence down and read it aloud. By creating sentences, you are practicing using the word correctly. If you strive to make these sentences interesting and creative, they will become more memorable and effective in activating your long-term memory.

Identify the Parts of Speech

"SUCCESS IS NOT FINAL; FAILURE IS NOT FATAL: IT IS THE COURAGE TO CONTINUE THAT COUNTS." -WINSTON S. CHURCHILL

Read through each term in the glossary and make a note of what part of speech each term is. Studying and identifying parts of speech shows us how the words relate to each other. It also helps you create a visualization of each term. Below are brief descriptions of the parts of speech for you to use as a guide.

VERB: A word denoting action, occurrence, or existence. Examples: walk, hop, whisper, sweat, dribbles, feels, sleeps, drink, smile, are, is, was, has.

NOUN: A word that names a person, place, thing, idea, animal, quality, or action. Nouns are the subject of the sentence. Examples: dog, Tom, Florida, CD, pasta, hate, tiger.

ADJECTIVE: A word that modifies, qualifies, or describes nouns and pronouns. Generally, adjectives appear immediately before the words they modify. Examples: smart girl, gifted teacher, old car, red door.

ADVERB: A word that modifies verbs, adjectives and other adverbs. An "ly" ending almost always changes an adjective to an adverb. Examples: ran swiftly, worked slowly, and drifted aimlessly. Many adverbs do not end in "ly." However, all adverbs identify when, where, how, how far, how much, etc. Examples: run hot, lived hard, moved right, study smart.

Chunking

"YOUR POSITIVE ACTION COMBINED WITH POSITIVE THINKING RESULTS IN SUCCESS." SHIV KHERA

Chunking is when you take a set of words and break it down into groups based on a common relationship. Research has shown that our brains learn by chunking information. By grouping your terms, you will be able to recall large sets of these words easily. To help make your chunking go easily use an online word cloud generator to make a set of word clouds representing your chunks.

1. Study the glossary and decide how you want to chunk the set of words. You can group by part of speech, topic, letter of the alphabet, word length, etc. Try to find an easy way to group each term.
2. Once you have your different groups, visit www.wordclouds.com to create a custom word cloud for each group. Print each one of these clouds and post it in a prominent place to serve as constant visual aids for your learning.

Analogies

"CHOOSE THE POSITIVE. YOU HAVE CHOICE, YOU ARE MASTER OF YOUR ATTITUDE, CHOOSE THE POSITIVE, THE CONSTRUCTIVE. OPTIMISM IS A FAITH THAT LEADS TO SUCCESS."– BRUCE LEE

An analogy is a comparison in which an idea or a thing is compared to another thing that is quite different from it. Analogies aim at explaining an idea by comparing it to something that is familiar. Metaphors and similes are tools used to create analogies.

Analogies are useful for learning vocabulary because they require you to analyze a word (or words), and then transfer that analysis to another word. This transfer reinforces the understanding of all the words.

As you analyze the relationships between the analogies you are creating, you will begin to understand the complex relationships between the seemingly unrelated words.

_A__ is to __B_ as __C_ is to __D_

This can be written using colons in place of the terms "is to" and "as."

A:B::C:D

The two items on the left (items A & B) describe a relationship and are separated by a single colon. The two items on the right (items C & D) are shown on the right and are also separated by a colon. Together, both sides are then separated by two colons in the middle, as shown here: Tall: Short :: Skinny: Fat. The relationship used in this analogy is the antonym.

How to create an analogy

Start with the basic formula for an analogy:

____ : ____ :: ____ : ____

Next, we will examine a simple synonym analogy:

automobile : car :: box : crate

The key to figuring out a set of word analogies is determining the relationship between the paired set of words.

Here is a list of the most common types of Analogies and examples

Synonym	Scream : Yell :: Push : Shove
Antonym	Rich : Poor :: Empty : Full
Cause is to Effect	Prosperity : Happiness :: Success : Joy
A Part is to its Whole	Toe : Foot :: Piece : Set
An Object to its Function	Car : Travel :: Read : Learn
A Item is to its Category	Tabby : House Cat :: Doberman : Dog
Word is a symptom of the other	Pain : Fracture :: Wheezing : Allergy
An object and it's description	Glass : Brittle :: Lead : Dense
The word is lacking the second word	Amputee : Limb :: Deaf : Hearing
The first word Hinders the second word	Shackles : Movement :: Stagger : Walk
The first word helps the action of the second	Knife : Bread :: Screwdriver : Screw
This word is made up of the second word	Sweater : Wool :: Jeans : Denim
A word and it's definition	Cede: Break Away :: Abolish : To get rid of

Using words from the glossary, make a set of analogies using each one. As a bonus, use more than one glossary term in a single analogy.

__________________ : _______________ :: ______________________ : _________________

Name the relationship between the words in your analogy:______________________________

__________________ : _______________ :: ___________________ : ____________________

Name the relationship between the words in your analogy:______________________________

__________________ : _______________ :: ______________________ : _________________

Name the relationship between the words in your analogy:______________________________

Mnemonics

"It isn't the mountains ahead to climb that wear you out; it's the pebble in your shoe." -Muhammad Ali

A mnemonic is a learning technique that helps you retain and remember information. Mnemonics are one of the best learning methods for remembering lists or processes in order. Mnemonics make the material more meaningful by adding associations and creating patterns. Interestingly, mnemonics may work better when they utilize absurd, startling, or shocking examples and references. Mnemonics help organize the information so that you can easily retrieve it later. By giving you associations and cues, mnemonics allow you to form a mental structure ordering a list or process to help you remember it better. This mental structure allows you to create a structure of association between items that may not appear to have any relationship. Mnemonics typically use references that are easy to visualize and thus easier to remember. Through visualization of vivid images and references, the information is much easier to imprint into long-term memory. The power of making mnemonics lies in converting dull, inert and uninspiring information into something vibrant and memorable.

How to make simple and effective mnemonics

Some of the best mnemonics help us remember simple rules or lists in order.

Step 1. Take a list of terms you are trying to remember in order. For example, we will use the scientific method:

observation, question, hypothesis, methods, results, and conclusion.

Next, we will replace each word on the list with a new word that starts with the same letter. These new words will together form a vivid sentence that is easy to remember:

Objectionable Queens Haunted Macho Rednecks Creatively.

As silly as the above sentence seems, it is easy to remember, and now we can call on this sentence to remind us of the order of the scientific method.

Visit http://www.mnemonicgenerator.com/ and try typing in a list of words. It is fun to see the mnemonics that it makes and shows how easy it is to make great mnemonics to help your studying.

Using vivid words in your mnemonics allows you to see the sentence you are making. Words that are gross, scary, or name interesting animals are helpful. Profanity is also useful because the shock value can trigger memory. The following are lists of vivid words to use in your mnemonics:

Gross words
Moist, Gurgle, Phlegm, Fetus, Curd, Smear, Squirt, Chunky, Orifice, Maggots, Viscous, Queasy, Bulbous, Pustule, Putrid, Fester, Secrete, Munch, Vomit, Ooze, Dripping, Roaches, Mucus, Stink, Stank, Stunk, Slurp, Pus, Lick, Salty, Tongue, Fart, Flatulence, Hemorrhoid.

Interesting Animals
Aardvark, Baboon, Chicken, Chinchilla, Duck, Dragonfly, Emu, Electric Eel, Frog, Flamingo, Gecko, Hedgehog, Hyena, Iguana, Jackal, Jaguar, Leopard, Lynx, Minnow, Manatee, Mongoose, Neanderthal, Newt, Octopus, Oyster, Pelican, Penguin, Platypus, Quail, Racoon, Rattlesnake, Rhinoceros, Scorpion, Seahorse, Toucan, Turkey, Vulture, Weasel, Woodpecker, Yak, Zebra.

Superhero Words
Diabolical, Activate, Boom, Clutch, Dastardly, Dynamic, Dynamite, Shazam, Kaboom, Zip, Zap, Zoom, Zany, Crushing, Smashing, Exploding, Ripping, Tearing.

Scary Words
Apparition, Bat, Chill, Demon, Eerie, Fangs, Genie, Hell, Lantern, Macabre, Nightmare, Owl, Ogre, Phantasm, Repulsive, Scarecrow, Tarantula, Undead, Vampire, Wraith, Zombie.

There are several types of mnemonics that can help your memory.

1. Images
Visual mnemonics are a type of mnemonic that works by associating an image with characters or objects whose name sounds like the item that must be memorized. This is one of the easiest ways to create effective mnemonics. An example would be to use the shape of numbers to help memorize a long list of them. Numbers can be memorized by their shapes, so that: 0 -looks like an egg; 1 -a pencil, or a candle; 2 -a snake; 3 -an ear; 4 -a sailboat; 5 -a key; 6 -a comet; 7 -a knee; 8 -a snowman; 9 -a comma.

Another type of visual mnemonic is the word-length mnemonic in which the number of letters in each word corresponds to a digit. This simple mnemonic gives pi to seven decimal places:

3.141582 becomes "How I wish I could calculate pi."

Of course, you could use this type of mnemonic to create a longer sentence showing the digits of an important number. Some people have used this type of mnemonic to memorize thousands of digits.

Using the hands is also an important tool for creating visual objects. Making the hands into specific shapes can help us remember the pattern of things or the order of a list of things.

2. Rhyming
Rhyming mnemonics are quick ways to make things memorable. A classic example is a mnemonic for the number of days in each month:
"30 days hath September, April, June, and November.
All the rest have 31
Except February, my dear son.
It has 28, and that is fine
But in Leap Year it has 29."

Another example of a rhyming mnemonic is a common spelling rule:
"I before e except after c
or when sounding like a
in neighbor and weigh."

Use **rhymer.com** to get large lists of rhyming words.

3. Homonym
A homonym is one of a group of words that share the same pronunciation but have different meanings, whether spelled the same or not.

Try saying what you're attempting to remember out loud or very quickly, and see if anything leaps out. If you know other languages, using similar-sounding words from those can be effective.

You could also browse this list of homonyms at http://www.cooper.com/alan/homonym_list.html.

4. Onomatopoeia
An Onomatopeia is a word that phonetically imitates, resembles or suggests the source of the sound that it describes. Are there any noises made by the thing you're trying to memorize? Is it often associated with some other sound? Failing that, just make up a noise that seems to fit.

Achoo, ahem, baa, bam, bark, beep, beep beep, belch, bleat, boo, boo hoo, boom, burp, buzz, chirp, click clack, crash, croak, crunch, cuckoo, dash, drip, ding dong, eek, fizz, flit, flutter, gasp, grrr, ha ha, hee hee, hiccup, hiss, hissing, honk, icky, itchy, jiggly, jangle, knock knock, lush, la la la, mash, meow, moan, murmur, neigh, oink, ouch, plop, pow, quack, quick, rapping, rattle, ribbit, roar, rumble, rustle, scratch, sizzle, skittering, snap crackle pop, splash, splish splash, spurt, swish, swoosh, tap, tapping, tick tock, tinkle, tweet, ugh, vroom, wham, whinny, whip, whooping, woof.

5. Acronyms

An acronym is a word or name formed as an abbreviation from the initial components of a word, such as NATO, which stands for North Atlantic Treaty Organization. If you're trying to memorize something involving letters, this is often a good bet. A lot of famous mnemonics are acronyms, such as ROYGBIV which stands for the order of colors in the light spectrum (Red, Orange, Yellow, Green, Blue, Indigo, and Violet).
A great acronym generator to try is: www.all-acronyms.com.

A different spin on an acronym is a backronym. A **backronym** is a specially constructed phrase that is supposed to be the source of a word that is an acronym. A backronym is constructed by creating a new phrase to fit an already existing word, name, or acronym.

The word is a combination of *backward* and *acronym*, and has been defined as a "reverse acronym." For example, the United States Department of Justice assigns to their Amber Alert program the meaning "**A**merica's **M**issing: **B**roadcast **E**mergency **R**esponse." The process can go either way to make good mnemonics.

Visit: https://arthurdick.com/projects/backronym/ to try out a simple backronym generator.

6. Anagrams

An anagram is a direct word switch or word play, the result of rearranging the letters of a word or phrase to produce a new word or phrase, using all the original letters exactly once; for example, the word anagram can be rearranged into nag-a-ram.

Try re-arranging letters or components and see if anything memorable emerges. Visit http://www.nameacronym.net/ to use a simple anagram generator.

One particularly memorable form of anagram is the spoonerism, where you swap the initial syllables or letters of words to make new phrases. These are usually humorous, and this makes them easier to remember. Here are some examples:

"Is it kisstomary to cuss the bride?" (as opposed to "customary to kiss")
"The Lord is a shoving leopard." (instead of "a loving shepherd")
"A blushing crow." ("crushing blow")
"A well-boiled icicle" ("well-oiled bicycle")
"You were fighting a liar in the quadrangle." ("lighting a fire")
"Is the bean dizzy?" (as opposed to "is the dean busy?")

7. Stories

Make up quick stories or incidents involving the material you want to memorize. For larger chunks of information, the stories can get more elaborate. Structured stories are particularly good for remembering lists or other sequenced information. Have a look at https://en.wikipedia.org/wiki/Method_of_loci for a more advanced memory sequencing technique.

Visual Metaphors

"Limits, like fear, is often an illusion." -Michael Jordan

What is a Metaphor?

A metaphor is a figure of speech that refers to one thing by mentioning another thing. Metaphors provide clarity and identify hidden similarities between two seemingly unrelated ideas. A visual metaphor is an image that creates a link between different ideas.

Visual metaphors help us use our understanding of the world to learn new concepts, skills, and ideas. Visual metaphors help us relate new material to what we already know. Visual metaphors must be clear and simple enough to spark a connection and understanding. Visual metaphors should use familiar things to help you be less fearful of new, complex, or challenging topics. Metaphors trigger a sense of familiarity so that you are more accepting of the new idea. Metaphors work best when you associate a familiar, easy to understand idea with a challenging, obscure, or abstract concept.

How to make a visual metaphor

1. Brainstorm using the words of the concept. Use different fonts, colors, or shapes to represent parts of the concept.

2. Merge these images together

3. Show the process using arrows, accents, etc.

4. Think about the story line your metaphor projects.

Examples of visual metaphors:

A skeleton used to show a framework of something.

A cloud showing an outline.

A bodybuilder whose muscles represent supporting ideas and details.

A sandwich where the meat, tomato, and lettuce represent supporting ideas.

A recipe card to show a process.

Your metaphor should be accurate. It should be complex enough to convey meaning, but simple and clear enough to be easily understood.

Morphology

"SCIENCE IS THE CAPTAIN, AND PRACTICE THE SOLDIERS." LEONARDO DA VINCI

Morphology is the study of the origin, roots, suffixes, and prefixes of the words. Understanding the meaning of prefixes, suffixes, and roots make it easier to decode the meaning of new vocabulary. Having the ability to decode using morphology increases text comprehension when initially reading as well.

The capability of identifying meaningful parts of words (morphemes), including prefixes, suffixes, and roots can be helpful. Identifying morphemes improves decoding accuracy and fluency. Reading speed improves when you can decode larger chunks of text quickly. When you can recognize morphemes in words, you will be better able to make sense of new words in context. Below are charts containing the most common prefixes, suffixes, and root words. Use them to help you decode your vocabulary terms.

Prefixes

Prefix	Meaning	Example words and meanings	
a, ab, abs	away from	absent abdicate	not to be present, to give up an office or throne.
ad, a, ac, af, ag, an, ar, at, as	to, toward	Advance advantage	To move forward To have the upper hand
anti	against	Antidote antisocial antibiotic	To repair poisoning refers to someone who's not social
bi, bis	two	bicycle binary biweekly	two-wheeled cycle two number system every two weeks
circum, cir	around	circumnavigate circle	Travel around the world a figure that goes all around
com, con, co, col	with, together	Complete Complement	To finish To go along with
de	away from, down, the opposite of	depart detour	to go away from to go out of your way
dis, dif, di	apart	dislike dishonest distant	not to like not honest away
En-, em-	Cause to	Entrance	the way in.
epi	upon, on top of	epitaph epilogue epidemic	writing upon a tombstone speech at the end, on top of the rest
equ, equi	equal	equalize equitable	to make equal fair, equal
ex, e, ef	out, from	exit eject exhale	to go out to throw out to breathe out
Fore-	Before	Forewarned	To have prior warning

Prefix	Meaning	Example Words and Meanings	
in, il, ir, im, en	in, into	Infield Imbibe	The inner playing field to take part in
in, il, ig, ir, im	not	inactive ignorant irreversible irritate	not active not knowing not reversible to put into discomfort
inter	between, among	international interact	among nations to mix with
mal, male	bad, ill, wrong	malpractice malfunction	bad practice fail to function, bad function
Mid	Middle	Amidships	In the middle of a ship
mis	wrong, badly	misnomer	The wrong name
mono	one, alone, single	monocle	one lensed glasses
non	not, the reverse of	nonprofit	not making a profit
ob	in front, against, in front of, in the way of	Obsolete	No longer needed
omni	everywhere, all	omnipresent omnipotent	always present, everywhere all powerful
Over	On top	Overdose	Take too much medication
Pre	Before	Preview	Happens before a show.
per	through	Permeable pervasive	to pass through, all encompassing
poly	many	Polygamy polygon	many spouses figure with many sides
post	after	postpone postmortem	to do after after death
pre	before, earlier than	Predict Preview	To know before To view before release
pro	forward, going ahead of, supporting	proceed pro-war promote	to go forward supporting the war to raise or move forward
re	again, back	retell recall reverse	to tell again to call back to go back
se	apart	secede seclude	to withdraw, become apart to stay apart from others
Semi	Half	Semipermeable	Half-permeable

Prefix	Meaning	Example Words and Meanings	
Sub	under, less than	Submarine	under water
super	over, above, greater	superstar superimpose	a start greater than her stars to put over something else
trans	across	transcontinental transverse	across the continent to lie or go across
un, uni	one	unidirectional unanimous unilateral	having one direction sharing one view having one side
un	not	uninterested unhelpful unethical	not interested not helpful not ethical

Roots

Root	Meaning	Example words & meanings	
act, ag	to do, to act	Agent Activity	One who acts as a representative Action
Aqua	Water	Aquamarine	The color of water
Aud	To hear	Auditorium	A place to hear music
apert	open	Aperture	An opening
bas	low	Basement Basement	Something that is low, at the bottom A room that is low
Bio	Living thing	Biological	Living matter
cap, capt, cip, cept, ceive	to take, to hold, to seize	Captive Receive Capable Recipient	One who is held To take Able to take hold of things One who takes hold or receives
ced, cede, ceed, cess	to go, to give in	Precede Access Proceed	To go before Means of going to To go forward
Cogn	Know	Cognitive	Ability to think
cred, credit	to believe	Credible Incredible Credit	Believable Not believable Belief, trust
curr, curs, cours	to run	Current Precursory Recourse	Now in progress, running Running (going) before To run for aid
Cycle	Circle	Lifecycle	The circle of life
dic, dict	to say	Dictionary Indict	A book explaining words (sayings)

Root	Meaning	Examples and meanings	
duc, duct	to lead	Induce Conduct Aqueduct	To lead to action To lead or guide Pipe that leads water somewhere
equ	equal, even	Equality Equanimity	Equal in social, political rights Evenness of mind, tranquility
fac, fact, fic, fect, fy	to make, to do	Facile Fiction Factory Affect	Easy to do Something that is made up Place that makes things To make a change in
fer, ferr	to carry, bring	Defer Referral	To carry away Bring a source for help/information
Gen	Birth	Generate	To create something
graph	write	Monograph Graphite	A writing on a particular subject A form of carbon used for writing
Loc	Place	Location	A place
Mater	Mother	Maternity	Expecting birth
Mem	Recall	Memory	The recall experiences
mit, mis	to send	Admit Missile	To send in Something sent through the air
Nat	Born	Native	Born in a place
par	equal	Parity Disparate	Equality No equal, not alike
Ped	Foot	Podiatrist	Foot doctor
Photo	Light	Photograph	A picture
plic	to fold, to bend, to turn	Complicate Implicate	To fold (mix) together To fold in, to involve
pon, pos, posit, pose	to place	Component Transpose Compose Deposit	A part placed together with others A place across To put many parts into place To place for safekeeping
scrib, script	to write	Describe Transcript Subscription	To write about or tell about A written copy A written signature or document
sequ, secu	to follow	Sequence	In following order

Root	Meaning	Examples and Meanings	
Sign	Mark	Signal	to alert somebody
spec, spect, spic	to appear, to look, to see	Specimen Aspect	An example to look at One way to see something
sta, stat, sist,	to stand, or make stand	Constant	Standing with
stit, sisto	Stable, steady	Status Stable Desist	Social standing Steady (standing) To stand away from
Struct	To build	Construction	To build a thing
tact	to touch	Contact Tactile	To touch together To be able to be touched
ten, tent, tain	to hold	Tenable Retentive Maintain	Able to be held, holding Holding To keep or hold up
tend, tens, tent	to stretch	Extend Tension	To stretch or draw out Stretched
Therm	Temperature	Thermometer	Detects temperature
tract	to draw	Attract Contract	To draw together An agreement drawn up
ven, vent	to come	Convene Advent	To come together A coming
Vis	See	Invisible	Cannot be seen
ver, vert, vers	to turn	Avert Revert Reverse	To turn away To turn back To turn around

Crossword Puzzles

1. Using the Across and Down clues, write the correct words in the numbered grid below.

ACROSS

5. An elevated concentration of potassium in blood.
7. Slowing down of heart rate.
9. Nadolol
10. Action that causes the decomposition or destruction of proteins.
12. Hydralazine
13. A mathematical equation that expresses the equality between two ratios.
14. Permanent black discoloration of skin and mucous membranes caused by prolonged use of silver protein.
15. Occurring in the general circulation, resulting in distribution to most organs.
16. Produces an action that is greater than either of the components can produce alone; synergy.
17. Baldness or hair loss.
18. Abnormally high body temperature.

DOWN

1. Drug that liquefies bronchial secretions.
2. Location within the body where a drug exerts its therapeutic effect, often a specific drug receptor.
3. Defective metabolism of fat.
4. Trandolapril
6. Spread of cancer cells throughout the body, from primary to secondary sites.
8. Substance that kills disease-causing microorganisms on nonliving surfaces.
11. Fluticasone

A. Site of Action	B. Argyria	C. Bradycardia	D. Alopecia	E. Proteolytic
F. Corgard	G. Mavik	H. Flonase	I. Systemic	J. Apresoline
K. Metastasis	L. Disinfectant	M. Mucolytic	N. Hyperthermia	O. Hyperkalemia
P. Proportion	Q. Potentiates	R. Lipodystrophy		

2. Using the Across and Down clues, write the correct words in the numbered grid below.

ACROSS

2. Condition of drug abuse and drug dependence that is characterized by compulsive drug behavior.
4. Plaque formed in the artery wall that remains in the wall.
7. Medical specialty that deals with individuals over 65 years of age.
8. Loss of blood from blood vessels.
11. Chlordiazepoxide
12. Drug that prevents mast cells from releasing histamine and other vasoactive substances.
13. Amount of time it takes for food to travel from the mouth to the anus.
15. Homogeneous mixture of two or more substances.
16. Antibiotic that kills bacteria; chemical that kills or destroys bacteria.
17. Entrance of a drug into the bloodstream from its site of administration.

DOWN

1. Intermediary kind of male germ cell in the production of spermatozoa.
3. Amrinone
5. Neurotransmitter of parasympathetic nerves.
6. Neural pathway connecting different brain areas involved in regulation of behavior and emotion.
9. Inhibits the growth of fungi but does not kill off the fungi.
10. An abrasion of the epidermis usually from a mechanical cause; a scratch.
11. An element similar to sodium that is used in the treatment of mania and bipolar mood disorder.
14. Prefix meaning small.

A. Solution	B. Inocor	C. Librium	D. Bactericidal
E. Hemorrhage	F. Limbic System	G. Spermatogonia	H. Excoriation
I. Stable Plaque	J. Geriatrics	K. Fungistatic	L. Antiallergic
M. Transit Time	N. Lithium	O. Drug Addiction	P. Micro
Q. Drug Absorption	R. Acetylcholine		

3. Using the Across and Down clues, write the correct words in the numbered grid below.

ACROSS

2. Naphazoline
4. Primidone
5. Drug used to induce and maintain sleep.
7. Losartan
11. Molecule that contains purine or pyrimidine bases in combination with sugar.
13. Excessive hair growth on the body.
14. Peptides in the plasma that stimulate cellular growth and have insulin-like activity.
15. Mature sperm cells.
16. Beclomethasone
17. Eszopiclone

DOWN

1. Hydrolysis of glycogen to yield free glucose.
2. Labetalol
3. Condition that causes urine to be excreted; usually associated with large volumes of urine.
6. A persistent abnormal sense of taste.
8. Diazepam
9. Specific cellular structure that a drug binds to and that produces a physiologic effect.
10. Another way to write a fraction when the denominator is 10, 100, 1000, and so on.
12. Group or island of cells.

A. Normodyne	B. Hypertrichosis	C. Beconase	D. Hypnotic	E. Somatomedins
F. Spermatozoa	G. Naphcon	H. Glycogenolysis	I. Receptor	J. Lunesta
K. Diuresis	L. Dysgeusia	M. Nucleoside	N. Valium	O. Islets
P. Cozaar	Q. Mysoline	R. Decimal		

4. Using the Across and Down clues, write the correct words in the numbered grid below.

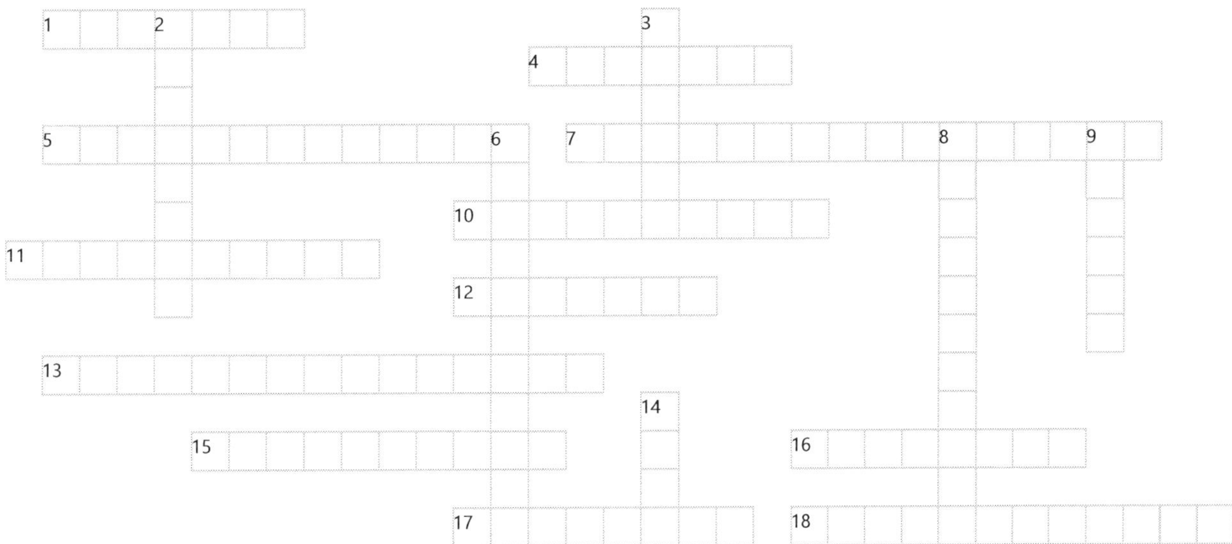

ACROSS

1. Decimal fraction with a denominator of 100.
4. A state of anxiousness and hyperemotionalism that occurs with uncertainty, stress, and fearful situations.
5. General term for undesirable and potentially harmful drug effect.
7. A low platelet count in blood.
10. A thin membrane enclosing a striated (skeletal) muscle fiber.
11. Substance, chemical solution, or drug that kills fungi; chemical that kills or destroys fungi.
12. Process in which water moves across membranes following the movement of sodium ions.
13. Refers to the action of an adrenergic drug or an action that increases sympathetic activity.
15. Joint pain.
16. Condition that causes urine to be excreted; usually associated with large volumes of urine.
17. Valproic
18. A group of cell bodies within the white matter of the cerebrum that helps control body movement

DOWN

2. Colestipol
3. Chlorothiazide
6. Amount of time it takes for food to travel from the mouth to the anus.
8. Cell that synthesizes and releases hydrochloric acid (HCl) into the stomach lumen.
9. Eplerenone
14. A measurement of the amount of drug that is administered.

A. Diuresis
B. Depakene
C. Sarcolemma
D. Inspra
E. Basal Ganglia
F. Colestid
G. Sympathomimetic
H. Dose
I. Adverse Effect
J. Percent
K. Thrombocytopenia
L. Osmosis
M. Diuril
N. Fungicidal
O. Arthralgia
P. Oxyntic Cell
Q. Transit Time
R. Anxiety

5. Using the Across and Down clues, write the correct words in the numbered grid below.

ACROSS

1. Refers to the action of an adrenergic blocking drug or an action that decreases sympathetic activity.
5. A low platelet count in blood.
10. Inhibitory neurotransmitter in the basal ganglia.
11. Oxymetazoline
12. A measurement of the amount of drug that is administered.
13. A thin membrane enclosing a striated (skeletal) muscle fiber.
15. A stiffness and inflexibility of movement.
16. Area of tissue that has died because of a sudden lack of blood supply.
17. Triamterene

DOWN

2. Drug that liquefies bronchial secretions.
3. Cell in the blood, commonly called a platelet, that is necessary for coagulation.
4. Quinapril
6. Condition in which an arterial blood pressure is abnormally low.
7. Condition in which tissues have been damaged, characterized by swelling, pain, heat, and sometimes
8. Arresting of malaria, in which protozoal parasites are eliminated from all tissues.
9. Loss of blood from blood vessels.
13. Suffix denoting the inhibition of, as of microorganisms.
14. Verapamil

A. Accupril	B. Calan	C. Static	D. Dose
E. Thrombocytopenia	F. Sarcolemma	G. Radical Cure	H. Afrin
I. Infarction	J. Thrombocyte	K. Inflammation	L. Mucolytic
M. Hemorrhage	N. Hypotension	O. Rigidity	P. Dopamine
Q. Dyrenium	R. Sympatholytic		

6. Using the Across and Down clues, write the correct words in the numbered grid below.

ACROSS

1. Intensely itching raised areas of skin caused by an allergic reaction; hives.
11. Budesonide
12. Drug used to induce and maintain sleep.
14. Urokinase
15. Open sore in the mucous membranes or mucosal linings of the body.
16. Composed of a protein substance largely found in hair and nails.
17. Normal state of balance among the body's internal organs.

DOWN

2. The rapid breakdown of skeletal muscle due to muscle injury.
3. Flushing of the stomach.
4. Condition that causes individuals to resist acquiring or developing a disease or infection.
5. Higher than normal level of glucose in the blood.
6. Intended or indicated uses for any drug.
7. Tissue containing fat cells; fat.
8. Bedsore.
9. Single-celled organism belonging to the genus Protozoa.
10. A decrease in stool frequency.
12. Chlorthalidone
13. Clopidogrel

A. Adipose Tissue
B. Rhinocort
C. Abbokinase
D. Hypnotic
E. Homeostasis
F. Plavix
G. Drug Indications
H. Urticarial
I. Constipation
J. Hygroton
K. Protozoan
L. Keratinized
M. Hyperglycemia
N. Rhabdomyolysis
O. Gastric Lavage
P. Ulcer
Q. Decubitis Ulcer
R. Immunity

7. Using the Across and Down clues, write the correct words in the numbered grid below.

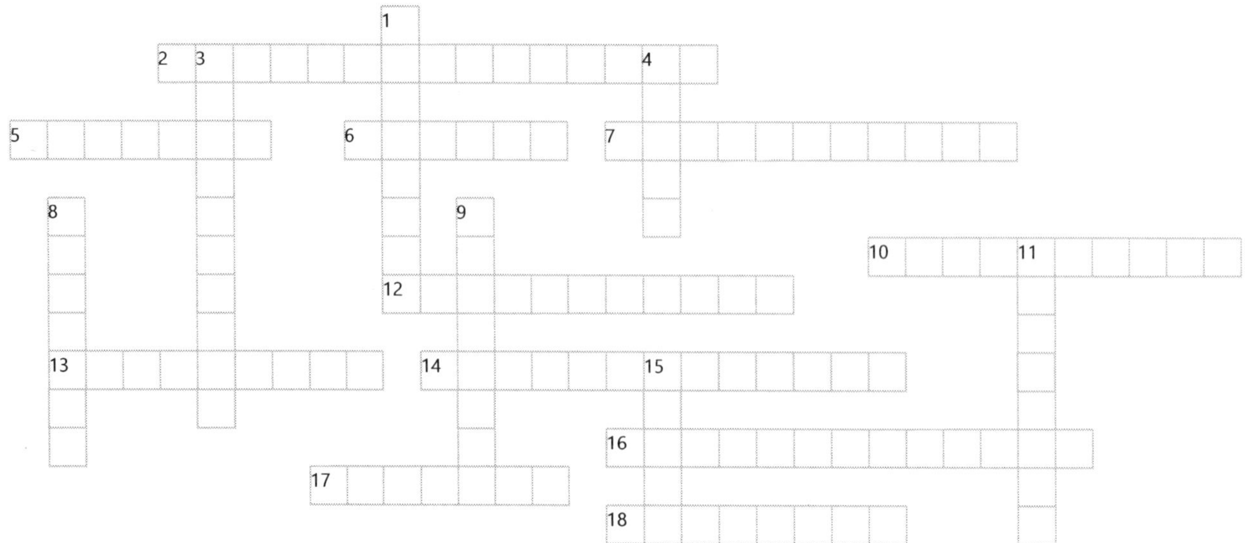

ACROSS

2. Dizziness often caused by a decrease in blood supply to the brain.
5. Abnormal discharge of brain neurons that causes alteration of behavior and motor activity.
6. Natural substance in the body.
7. Amount of time it takes for food to travel from the mouth to the anus.
10. Infection acquired as a result of being in a hospital.
12. Hormone from adrenal medulla that stimulates adrenergic receptors, especially during stress.
13. Moricizine
14. Bacterial enzymes that inactivate penicillin antibiotics.
16. Specialized cells in the hypothalamus that respond to changes in sodium concentration in the blood.
17. Nadolol
18. Polypeptide released within the brain that has specific functions during and after pregnancy.

DOWN

1. Sodium valproate
3. Washing (lavage) of a wound or cavity with large volumes of fluid.
4. Oxazepam
8. A state of anxiousness and hyperemotionalism that occurs with uncertainty, stress, and fearful situations.
9. Loss of voluntary muscle movement; restless leg movement.
11. Largest and uppermost part of the brain that is divided into right and left cerebral hemispheres.
15. Furosemide

A. Irrigation	B. Seizure	C. Cerebrum	D. Osmoreceptors
E. Anxiety	F. Depakote	G. Transit Time	H. Epinephrine
I. Oxytocin	J. Nosocomial	K. Native	L. Corgard
M. Ethmozine	N. Akinesia	O. Serax	P. Lightheadedness
Q. Penicillinase	R. Lasix		

8. Using the Across and Down clues, write the correct words in the numbered grid below.

ACROSS

1. Oxazepam
5. Lovastatin
8. Metolazone
9. Substance, usually large, composed of an indefinite number of amino acids.
13. When drugs (substances) produce the same intensity or spectrum of activity.
14. Refers to drugs or effects that reduce the activity of the parasympathetic nervous system.
15. Protein in red blood cells that transports oxygen to all tissues of the body.
16. Organism in an immature stage of development.
17. CNS depressant drug possessing the barbituric acid ring structure.

DOWN

2. Pertaining to glands that secrete substances directly into the blood.
3. Condition, also called delayed gastric emptying, in which the stomach muscles do not function properly.
4. Dipyridamole
6. Isradipine
7. Excessive urine production; increased urination.
9. Form of mental illness that produces bizarre behavior and deterioration of the personality.
10. Condition characterized by frequent watery stools (usually containing blood and mucus), tenesmus.
11. Drug that attaches to a receptor, does not initiate an action, but blocks an agonist from producing an effect.
12. Substance that has the ability to attach other substances to its surface.

A. Gametocyte
B. Zaroxolyn
C. Psychosis
D. Barbiturate
E. Gastroparesis
F. Polyuria
G. Polypeptide
H. Serax
I. Equipotent
J. Persantine
K. Dynacirc
L. Mevacor
M. Hemoglobin
N. Endocrine
O. Dysentery
P. Adsorbent
Q. Anticholinergic
R. Antagonist

9. Using the Across and Down clues, write the correct words in the numbered grid below.

ACROSS

2. Quinapril
6. A measure of hydration status; the amount of solute per liter of solution.
7. Adverse reaction which results from an exaggerated but otherwise usual pharmacological effect.
10. Not able to continue drug therapy usually because of extreme sensitivity to the side effects.
11. Substance, chemical solution, or drug that kills fungi; chemical that kills or destroys fungi.
13. Zonisamide
14. Joint space into which drug is injected.
15. Condition in which no urine is produced.
16. Number written with both a whole number and a fraction.
17. Time required for the body to reduce the amount of drug in the plasma by one-half.
18. Plaque formed in the artery wall that can break away and obstruct blood flow or form a clot.

DOWN

1. Lisinopril
3. A substance, chemical solution, or drug that kills protozoa.
4. Oxazepam
5. Excessive urine production; increased urination.
8. Irreversible chemical bond that some cancer drugs form with nucleic acids and DNA.
9. Xylometazoline
12. Ramipril

A. Serax	B. Unstable Plaque	C. Protozoacidal	D. Polyuria
E. Accupril	F. Type A Reaction	G. Otrivin	H. Anuria
I. Mixed Number	J. Altace	K. Half Life	L. Osmolarity
M. Alkylation	N. Intolerant	O. Intra Articular	P. Fungicidal
Q. Zestril	R. Zonegran		

10. Using the Across and Down clues, write the correct words in the numbered grid below.

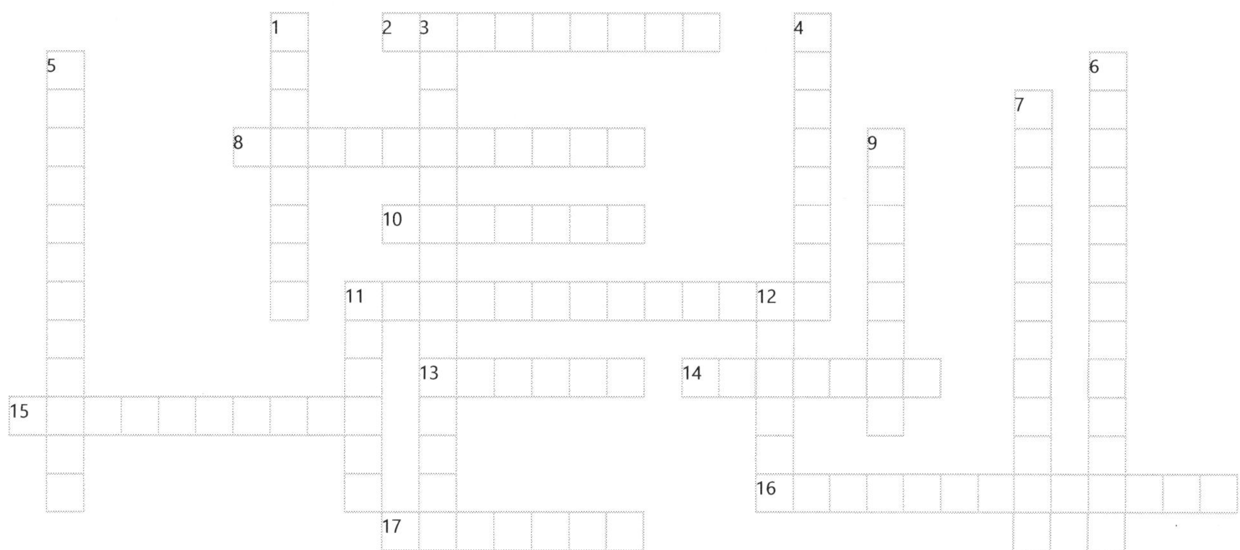

ACROSS

2. Life-threatening; refers to growth of a cancerous tumor.
8. The presence of the plasma protein albumin in the urine.
10. name Nonproprietary name of a drug.
11. Abnormally low level of chloride ions circulating in the blood.
13. Zolpidem
14. Lisinopril
15. Involuntary muscle contraction that is either tonic or clonic.
16. Substance that induces abortion.
17. Aspirin

DOWN

1. Fibric acid
3. Drug that inhibits the growth and proliferation of cancer cells.
4. Single-celled microorganisms, some of which cause disease.
5. Study of the distribution and determinants of diseases in populations.
6. Infection of the skin, hair, or nails caused by a fungus.
7. After a meal.
9. Guanabenz
11. Protrusion of an organ through the tissue usually containing it.
12. Eplerenone

A. Dermatophytic
B. Abortifacient
C. Malignant
D. Hernia
E. Generic
F. Antineoplastic
G. Ambien
H. Ecotrin
I. Bacteria
J. Albuminuria
K. Zestril
L. Trilipix
M. Inspra
N. Postprandial
O. Convulsion
P. Epidemiology
Q. Hypochloremia
R. Wytensin

11. Using the Across and Down clues, write the correct words in the numbered grid below.

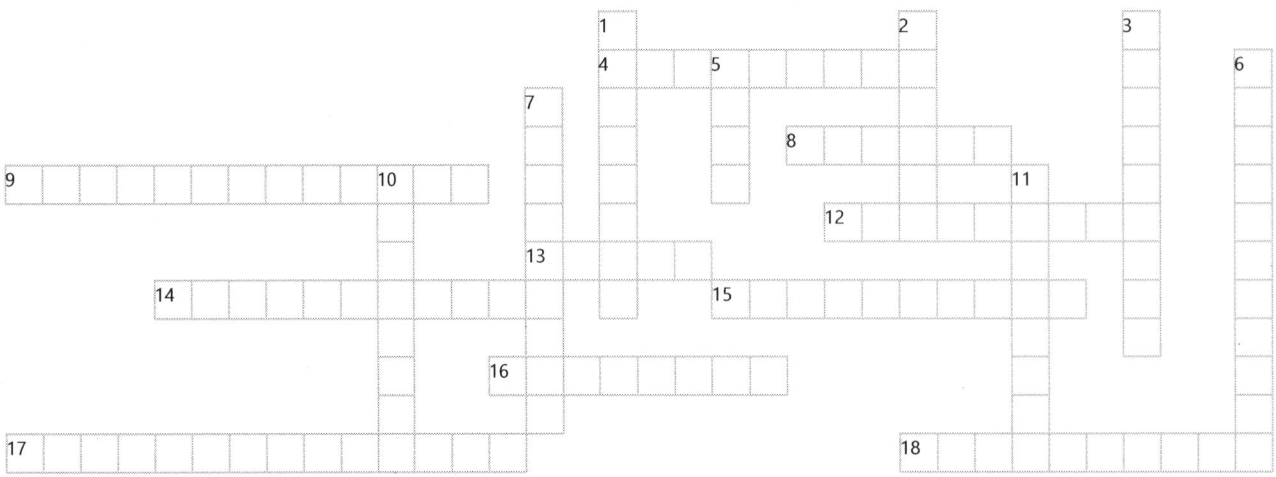

ACROSS

4. Amiodarone
8. Tetrahydrazoline
9. Adverse reaction which is aberrant, and may be due to hypersensitivity or immunologic reactions.
12. Beclomethasone
13. Negatively charged ion.
14. Ability of a substance to produce many different biological responses.
15. The muscular layer of the heart.
16. Tocainide
17. Plaque formed in the artery wall that can break away and obstruct blood flow or form a clot.
18. Inflammatory condition of the skin associated with itching, burning, and edematous vesicular formations.

DOWN

1. Quinapril
2. An inflammation of the hair follicles of the beard or scalp caused by ringworm with swelling and pus.
3. A type of cell formed after macrophages in the artery wall digest LDL cholesterol.
5. A measurement of the amount of drug that is administered.
6. Infection caused by the yeast Candida; also known as moniliasis.
7. Release of an egg from the ovary.
10. It is difficulty getting to sleep or staying asleep, or having non-refreshing sleep for at least 1 month.
11. An abnormal widening or ballooning of a portion of an artery due to weakness in the wall of the blood vessel.

A. Aneurysm
B. Accupril
C. Myocardium
D. Foam Cells
E. Tyzine
F. Dermatitis
G. Tonocard
H. Dose
I. Type B Reaction
J. Candidiasis
K. Vancenase
L. Anion
M. Kerion
N. Cordarone
O. Unstable Plaque
P. Pluripotent
Q. Ovulation
R. Insomnia

12. Using the Across and Down clues, write the correct words in the numbered grid below.

ACROSS

2. Drug that relaxes bronchial smooth muscle and dilates the lower respiratory passages.
6. Hormone released from adrenal cortex that causes the retention of sodium from the kidneys.
9. Procainamide
12. Hormone synthesized and released by the thyroid gland.
13. Ethosuximide
14. Causing a muscle to contract intermittently, resulting in a state of spasms.
15. Substance that causes the removal of mucous secretions from the respiratory system.
16. Dipyridamole
17. The muscular layer of the heart.
18. Study of the distribution and determinants of diseases in populations.

DOWN

1. Generalized seizure that does not involve motor convulsions; also referred to as petit mal.
3. Eplerenone
4. Substance, chemical solution, or drug that kills fungi; chemical that kills or destroys fungi.
5. Atorvastatin
7. Cell that synthesizes and releases hydrochloric acid (HCl) into the stomach lumen.
8. Trandolapril
10. Pertaining to the skin.
11. Abnormal discharge of brain neurons that causes alteration of behavior and motor activity.

A. Inspra
B. Oxyntic Cell
C. Expectorant
D. Fungicidal
E. Zarontin
F. Epidemiology
G. Bronchodilator
H. Myocardium
I. Lipitor
J. Thyroxine
K. Seizure
L. Procanbid
M. Cutaneous
N. Persantine
O. Absence Seizure
P. Spasmogenic
Q. Mavik
R. Aldosterone

13. Using the Across and Down clues, write the correct words in the numbered grid below.

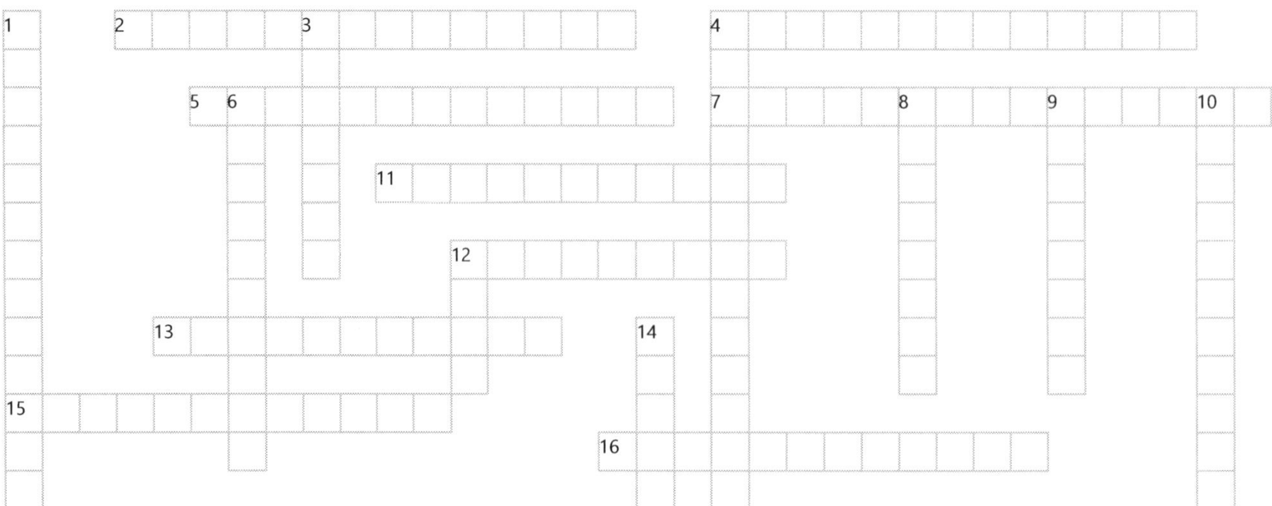

ACROSS

2. Return of the electric potential across a cell membrane to its resting state following depolarization.
4. Neurotransmitter of parasympathetic nerves.
5. Condition, also called delayed gastric emptying, in which the stomach muscles do not function properly.
7. Undesirable interaction of drugs not suitable for combination or administration together.
11. Producing heat.
12. Indigestion.
13. Responsible for bone resorption by binding to bone matrix proteins and releasing enzymes to break down bone.
15. watery substance that is located behind the cornea of the eye and in front of the lens.
16. Normal structures responsible for energy production in cells.

DOWN

1. Bacterial enzymes that inactivate penicillin antibiotics.
3. Substance, usually protein or carbohydrate, that is capable of stimulating an immune response.
4. Process that alters the pH to less than 7.
6. Drug-induced confusion that can cause increased drug consumption.
8. Milrinone
9. Single-celled microorganisms, some of which cause disease.
10. Amount of time it takes for food to travel from the mouth to the anus.
12. A measurement of the amount of drug that is administered.
14. The relationship of one number to another expressed by whole numbers.

A. Gastroparesis
B. Dyspepsia
C. Osteoclasts
D. Bacteria
E. Primacor
F. Calorigenic
G. Repolarization
H. Automatism
I. Aqueous Humor
J. Penicillinase
K. Antigen
L. Incompatibility
M. Dose
N. Acidification
O. Transit Time
P. Ratio
Q. Mitochondria
R. Acetylcholine

14. Using the Across and Down clues, write the correct words in the numbered grid below.

ACROSS

1. Condition characterized by frequent watery stools (usually containing blood and mucus), tenesmus.
4. Process in which water moves across membranes following the movement of sodium ions.
7. watery substance that is located behind the cornea of the eye and in front of the lens.
11. Substance, chemical solution, or drug that kills fungi; chemical that kills or destroys fungi.
12. Unusually high concentration of calcium in the blood.
13. Sodium valproate
14. Suffix meaning cells.
15. Study of the distribution and determinants of diseases in populations.
16. A type of cell formed after macrophages in the artery wall digest LDL cholesterol.
17. Excessive hunger.
18. Condition of reliance on the use of a particular drug.

DOWN

2. Budesonide
3. Levetiracetam
5. Abnormally high body temperature.
6. Pharmacologically active substance obtained from the marijuana plant.
8. Condition in which the color of red blood cells is less than the normal index.
9. Reteplase
10. Beclomethasone

A. Cannabinoid
B. Aqueous Humor
C. Drug Dependence
D. Dysentery
E. Hypochromic
F. Retavase
G. Foam Cells
H. Osmosis
I. Hypercalcemia
J. Hyperthermia
K. Keppra
L. Depakote
M. Vancenase
N. Rhinocort
O. Polyphagia
P. Epidemiology
Q. Fungicidal
R. Cytic

15. Using the Across and Down clues, write the correct words in the numbered grid below.

ACROSS

4. Pertaining to glands that secrete substances directly into the blood.
6. Topiramate
10. Drug effect other than the therapeutic effect that is usually undesirable but not harmful.
11. name Nonproprietary name of a drug.
13. Ability to stimulate and increase immune function.
15. Neuropeptides produced within the CNS that interact with opioid receptors to produce analgesia.
16. Rapid involuntary movement of eyes.
17. Moricizine
18. Increase in muscle tone or contractions causing faster clearance of substances through the GI tract.

DOWN

1. Refers to sedative-hypnotic drugs that do not possess the barbituric acid structure.
2. Drug that relaxes bronchial smooth muscle and dilates the lower respiratory passages.
3. A substance that causes vomiting.
5. An antigen-presenting white blood cell that is found in the skin, mucosa, and lymphoid tissues and that
7. A substance secreted by T cells that signals other immune cells like macrophages to aggregate.
8. Disease process causing destruction of the walls of the alveoli.
9. Telmisartan
12. Substance, usually protein or carbohydrate, that is capable of stimulating an immune response.
14. Estazolam

A. Endocrine
B. Generic
C. Dendritic Cell
D. Nystagmus
E. Emphysema
F. Topamax
G. Immunomodulation
H. Lymphokine
I. Endorphins
J. Nonbarbiturate
K. Ethmozine
L. Micardis
M. Emetogenic
N. Hypermotility
O. Side Effect
P. Bronchodilator
Q. Antigen
R. Prosom

16. Using the Across and Down clues, write the correct words in the numbered grid below.

ACROSS

1. Origin of the pain is in a different location than where the individual feels the pain.
2. Area of the heart from which abnormal impulses originate.
4. A firm, elevated swelling of the skin often pale red in color and itchy; a sign of allergy.
6. Produces an action that is greater than either of the components can produce alone; synergy.
8. Spironolactone
11. A drug that reduces the level of fats in the blood.
14. Inflammation of the walls of the veins, associated with clot formation.
15. Increase in muscle tone or contractions causing faster clearance of substances through the GI tract.
16. Part of a cell that contains enzymes capable of digesting or destroying tissue
17. Elimination of the drug from the body.

DOWN

1. Arresting of malaria, in which protozoal parasites are eliminated from all tissues.
3. Plaque formed in the artery wall that can break away and obstruct blood flow or form a clot.
5. Present continually in a particular geographic region, often in spite of control measures.
7. Composed of a protein substance largely found in hair and nails.
9. Partially digested food and gastric secretions that moves into the duodenum from the stomach by peristalsis.
10. Chlorthalidone
12. pH less than 7.45
13. Hormone secreted by the beta cells of the pancreas to facilitate glucose entry into the cell.

A. Acidosis	B. Radical Cure	C. Potentiates	D. Chime
E. Unstable Plaque	F. Referred Pain	G. Aldactone	H. Hygroton
I. Endemic	J. Ectopic Focus	K. Lysosome	L. Wheal
M. Insulin	N. Thrombophlebitis	O. Drug Excretion	P. Antilipemic Drug
Q. Keratinized	R. Hypermotility		

17. Using the Across and Down clues, write the correct words in the numbered grid below.

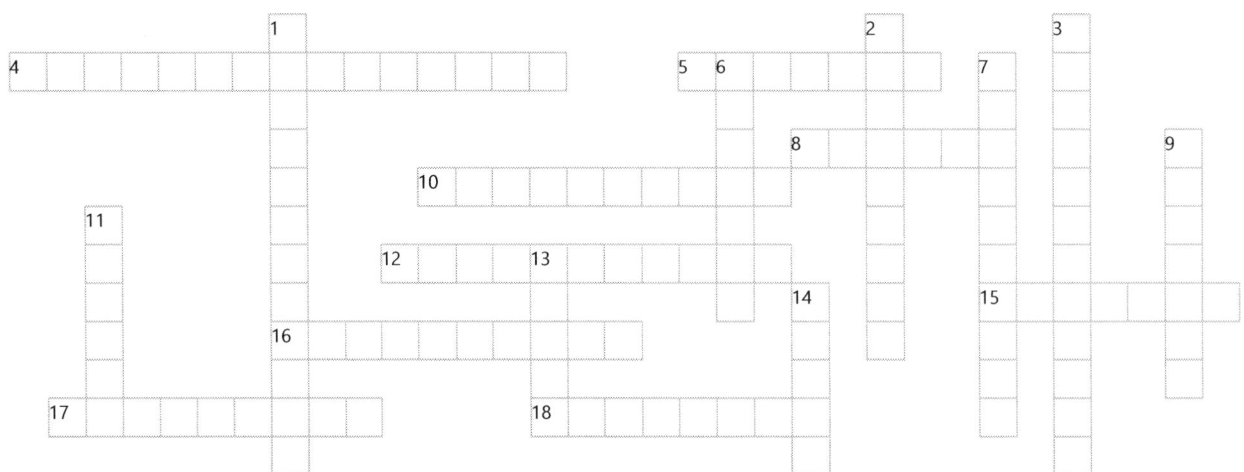

ACROSS

4. When there is an acute deficiency of granulocytes in blood.
5. Minoxidil hypertrichosis
8. Fenofibrate
10. Excessive hunger.
12. Action that causes the decomposition or destruction of proteins.
15. Propranolol
16. It refers to feeling abnormally sleepy during the day.
17. A condition where the concentration of salt (sodium, electrolytes) is less than that found inside the cells.
18. Baldness or hair loss.

DOWN

1. Peptides in the plasma that stimulate cellular growth and have insulin-like activity.
2. Period when cancer cells are not increasing in number.
3. Origin of the pain is in a different location than where the individual feels the pain.
6. Xylometazoline
7. Inflammatory condition of the skin associated with itching, burning, and edematous vesicular formations.
9. Fluticasone
11. A strong sustained muscle contraction.
13. An excessive accumulation of fluid in body tissues.
14. Verapamil

A. Otrivin
B. Tetany
C. Alopecia
D. Dermatitis
E. Flonase
F. Loniten
G. Somatomedins
H. Hypotonic
I. Edema
J. Agranulocytosis
K. Tricor
L. Drowsiness
M. Remission
N. Polyphagia
O. Referred Pain
P. Calan
Q. Inderal
R. Proteolytic

18. Using the Across and Down clues, write the correct words in the numbered grid below.

ACROSS

1. After a meal.
5. Diazoxide
9. A state of anxiousness and hyperemotionalism that occurs with uncertainty, stress, and fearful situations.
10. Major form of psychosis; behavior is inappropriate.
11. Protozoal infection characterized by attacks of chills, fever, and sweating.
12. State in which a substance has accumulated to potentially harmful levels in the body.
13. Methsuximide
14. Molecule that contains purine or pyrimidine bases in combination with sugar.
15. Lisinopril

DOWN

1. Substance, usually large, composed of an indefinite number of amino acids.
2. A lipid substance secreted by glands in the skin to lubricate the skin everywhere but the palms and soles.
3. Inflammatory condition of the skin associated with itching, burning, and edematous vesicular formations.
4. Transmits sensory information from peripheral organs to the central nervous system).
5. Abnormally high degree of acidity (for example, pH less than 1) in the stomach.
6. Clorazepate
7. Increased secretion of growth hormone in childhood, causing excessive growth and height.
8. Compound containing iodine.
10. Abnormal discharge of brain neurons that causes alteration of behavior and motor activity.

A. Tranxene	B. Seizure	C. Malaria	D. Dermatitis	E. Gigantism
F. Nucleoside	G. Afferent Nerve	H. Celontin	I. Iodophor	J. Anxiety
K. Schizophrenia	L. Zestril	M. Sebum	N. Postprandial	O. Hyperstat
P. Polypeptide	Q. Intoxication	R. Hyperacidity		

19. Using the Across and Down clues, write the correct words in the numbered grid below.

ACROSS

1. Substance that induces abortion.
5. A response to a drug which is noxious and unintended.
6. Beclomethasone
8. Diazoxide
11. Formation of ova.
12. An inactive precursor of a drug, converted into its active form in the body by normal metabolic processes.
14. Cell division in which two daughter cells receive the same number of chromosomes as the parent cell.
15. Seizure originating in one area of the brain that may spread to other areas.
16. Joint pain.
17. Flurazepam
18. Chemically altered form of an approved drug that produces similar effects and that is sold illegally.

DOWN

2. Bumetanide
3. A fat formed by three fatty acids into one molecule that supplies energy to muscle cells.
4. The cytoplasm of a striated (skeletal) muscle fiber.
7. A substance secreted by T cells that signals other immune cells like macrophages to aggregate.
9. Methsuximide
10. Natural substance in the body.
13. Fenofibrate

A. Arthralgia
B. Sarcoplasm
C. Designer Drug
D. Hyperstat
E. Vancenase
F. Prodrug
G. Adverse Reaction
H. Lymphokine
I. Triglyceride
J. Abortifacient
K. Tricor
L. Native
M. Bumex
N. Celontin
O. Mitosis
P. Partial Seizure
Q. Oogenesis
R. Dalmane

20. Using the Across and Down clues, write the correct words in the numbered grid below.

ACROSS

2. Silodosin
6. Substance that inhibits secretion of digestive enzymes, hormones, or acid.
9. name Nonproprietary name of a drug.
11. Loss of brain function due to a loss of blood supply.
13. A persistent abnormal sense of taste.
14. Cerivastatin
15. CNS depressant drug possessing the barbituric acid ring structure.
16. Labetalol
17. Phenytoin
18. Increase in the amount of drug metabolizing enzymes after repeated administration of certain drugs.

DOWN

1. Washing with fluids or flushing of a cavity such as the stomach.
3. Furosemide
4. A decrease in stool frequency.
5. An elevated concentration of potassium in blood.
7. Procainamide
8. Guanabenz
10. Triamterene
12. Two different amounts of estrogen hormone are released during the cycle.

A. Normodyne
B. Hyperkalemia
C. Stroke
D. Lasix
E. Enzyme Induction
F. Baycol
G. Lavage
H. Constipation
I. Biphasic
J. Rapaflo
K. Generic
L. Dilantin
M. Dyrenium
N. Antisecretory
O. Barbiturate
P. Wytensin
Q. Dysgeusia
R. Procanbid

21. Using the Across and Down clues, write the correct words in the numbered grid below.

ACROSS

2. Feeling of well-being or elation; feeling good.
4. Muscle spasms, facial grimacing, and other involuntary movements and postures.
6. Active ingredient of the marijuana plant.
7. Permanent black discoloration of skin and mucous membranes caused by prolonged use of silver protein.
8. High levels of insulin in the blood often associated with type 2 diabetes mellitus and insulin resistance.
10. Abnormally high fat (lipid) levels in the plasma.
13. Cell death, due to either programmed cell death or other physiological events.
14. Hormone released by the alpha cells of the pancreas to increase plasma glucose concentration.
15. Lamotrigine
16. Normal structures responsible for energy production in cells.
17. Drug-induced confusion that can cause increased drug consumption.

DOWN

1. Plaque formed in the artery wall that can break away and obstruct blood flow or form a clot.
3. Excessive hunger.
5. Circulating cell that ingests waste products or bacteria in order to remove them from the body.
9. Convulsive muscle contraction characterized by sustained muscular contractions.
11. Moricizine
12. Quazepam
13. A state of anxiousness and hyperemotionalism that occurs with uncertainty, stress, and fearful situations.

A. Phagocyte	B. Tonic	C. Hyperinsulinemia	D. Automatism
E. Mitochondria	F. Apoptosis	G. Lamictal	H. Polyphagia
I. Ethmozine	J. Unstable Plaque	K. Doral	L. Argyria
M. Glucagon	N. Anxiety	O. Dystonia	P. Hyperlipidemia
Q. THC	R. Euphoria		

22. Using the Across and Down clues, write the correct words in the numbered grid below.

ACROSS

1. Preparation in which undissolved solids are dispersed within a liquid.
4. Tiny hairs that line the respiratory tract and continuously move, pushing secretions toward the mouth.
6. The storage form of glucose in humans and animals.
8. Substance that inhibits secretion of digestive enzymes, hormones, or acid.
12. Neuropeptides produced within the CNS that interact with opioid receptors to produce analgesia.
13. Reteplase
14. Substance that causes the removal of mucous secretions from the respiratory system.
15. Chemical substance that produces a change in body function.
16. Indigestion.
17. Substance, chemical solution, or drug that kills microorganisms.

DOWN

1. Drug produced by a chemical process outside the body.
2. Plaque formed in the artery wall that remains in the wall.
3. Valproic
5. Artery that supplies blood flow to the heart.
7. An inactive precursor of a drug, converted into its active form in the body by normal metabolic processes.
9. Complementary or additive.
10. Clonidine
11. Hormone synthesized and released by the thyroid gland.

A. Dyspepsia
B. Glycogen
C. Endorphins
D. Thyroxine
E. Prodrug
F. Drug
G. Expectorant
H. Catapres
I. Synergistic
J. Suspension
K. Retavase
L. Synthetic Drug
M. Microcilia
N. Stable Plaque
O. Antisecretory
P. Germicidal
Q. Coronary Artery
R. Depakene

23. Using the Across and Down clues, write the correct words in the numbered grid below.

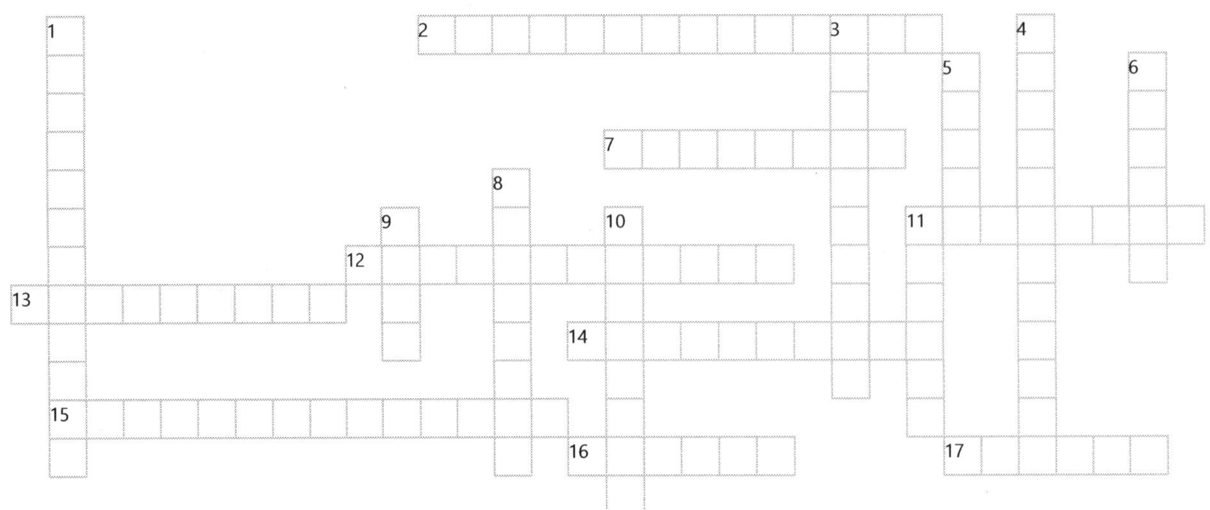

ACROSS

2. Drug usually administered IV that stops a convulsive seizure.
7. Clonazepam
11. Fibric acid
12. Bacteria that retain only the red stain in a gram stain.
13. Condition in which menstruation no longer occurs.
14. Infection in the blood caused by the yeast Candida.
15. Joint space into which drug is injected.
16. Bisoprolol
17. Suffix denoting the inhibition of, as of microorganisms.

DOWN

1. Drug that prevents mast cells from releasing histamine and other vasoactive substances.
3. Edema and swelling beneath the skin.
4. Low blood glucose level.
5. Simvastatin
6. Protrusion of an organ through the tissue usually containing it.
8. Zonisamide
9. Chemical substance that produces a change in body function.
10. Clonidine
11. A strong sustained muscle contraction.

A. Static	B. Klonopin	C. Menopause	D. Candidemia	E. Hernia
F. Drug	G. Trilipix	H. Antiallergic	I. Tetany	J. Gram Negative
K. Zonegran	L. Catapres	M. Zocor	N. Zebeta	O. Anticonvulsant
P. Intra Articular	Q. Angioedema	R. Hypoglycemia		

24. Using the Across and Down clues, write the correct words in the numbered grid below.

ACROSS

3. Opening in a hollow organ, such as a break in the intestinal wall.
5. Clots that jam a blood vessel; formed by the action of platelets and other coagulation factors in the blood.
8. Drug used to induce and maintain sleep.
9. Neurotransmitter of parasympathetic nerves.
13. Low blood glucose level.
14. Atorvastatin
15. Lovastatin
16. Having normal thyroid gland function.
17. Washing with fluids or flushing of a cavity such as the stomach.
18. Lamotrigine

DOWN

1. Simvastatin
2. Ability of a substance to produce many different biological responses.
4. A thick-walled structure in which parasitic protozoal sex cells develop for transfer to new hosts.
6. A firm, elevated swelling of the skin often pale red in color and itchy; a sign of allergy.
7. Torsemide
10. An element similar to sodium that is used in the treatment of mania and bipolar mood disorder.
11. Nadolol
12. Substance, usually protein or carbohydrate, that is capable of stimulating an immune response.

A. Demadex
B. Zocor
C. Hypnotic
D. Corgard
E. Lamictal
F. Euthyroid
G. Lavage
H. Thromboembolism
I. Lipitor
J. Perforation
K. Lithium
L. Wheal
M. Mevacor
N. Antigen
O. Acetylcholine
P. Hypoglycemia
Q. Oocyst
R. Pluripotent

25. Using the Across and Down clues, write the correct words in the numbered grid below.

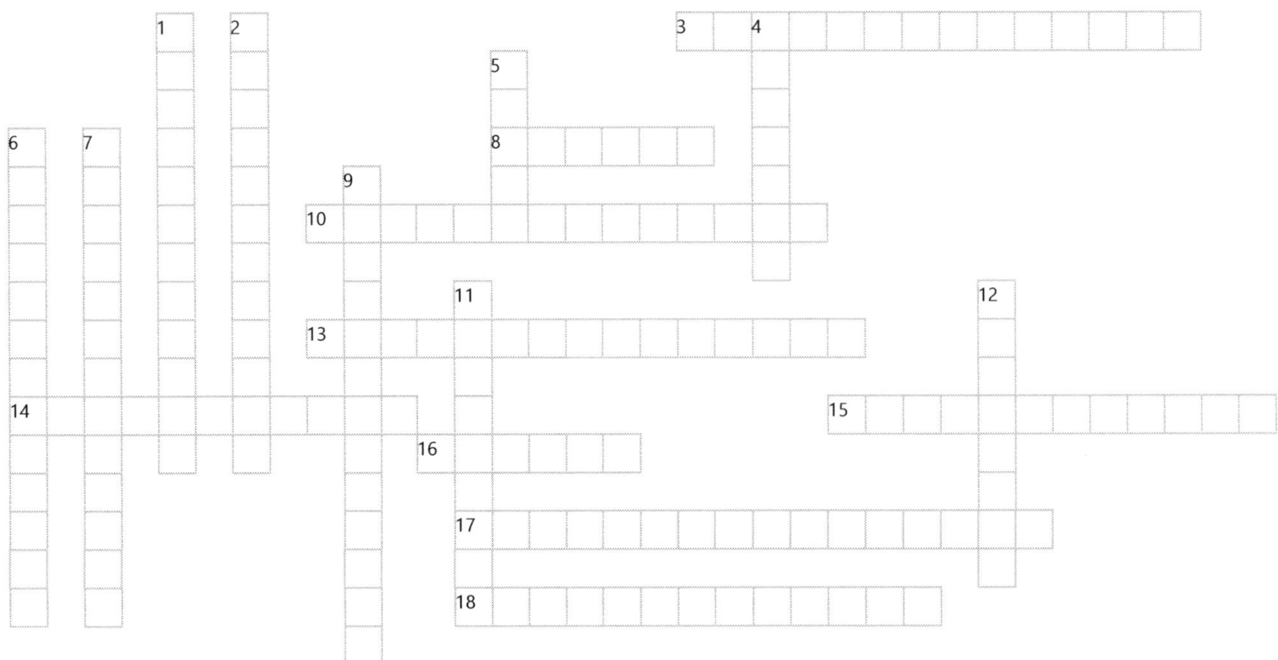

ACROSS

3. Bedsore.
8. Tenecteplase
10. Abnormally high level of chloride ions circulating in the blood.
13. The amount of drug required to produce the desired change in the disease or condition.
14. Ion in solution, such as sodium, potassium, or chloride, that is capable of mediating conduction.
15. A decrease in stool frequency.
16. Bisoprolol
17. Hardening or fibrosis of the arteries; accumulation of fatty deposits in the walls of arteries.
18. Type of tablet or pill with a coating that enables it to pass through the stomach without being dissolved.

DOWN

1. Abnormally high degree of acidity (for example, pH less than 1) in the stomach.
2. Condition in which tissues have been damaged, characterized by swelling, pain, heat, and sometimes
4. Condition of long duration, usually months or years.
5. Suffix meaning cells.
6. Drug that is effective against a wide variety of both gram-positive and gram-negative pathogenic bacteria.
7. Generalized-type seizure characterized by a sudden loss of muscle tone.
9. Drug produced by a chemical process outside the body.
11. Beclomethasone
12. Single-celled microorganisms, some of which cause disease.

A. Hyperacidity
B. Enteric Coated
C. Vancenase
D. Tnkase
E. Hyperchloremia
F. Zebeta
G. Atonic Seizure
H. Decubitis Ulcer
I. Constipation
J. Bacteria
K. Cytic
L. Chronic
M. Therapeutic Dose
N. Broad Spectrum
O. Synthetic Drug
P. Electrolyte
Q. Inflammation
R. Arteriosclerosis

26. Using the Across and Down clues, write the correct words in the numbered grid below.

ACROSS

1. Name that defines the chemical composition of a drug.
3. Origin of the pain is in a different location than where the individual feels the pain.
6. Decrease in the number of circulating lymphocytes.
8. Tetrahydrazoline
10. A measurement of the amount of drug that is administered.
12. Amiloride
13. Involuntary muscle contraction that is either tonic or clonic.
14. Clorazepate
15. Washing with fluids or flushing of a cavity such as the stomach.
16. Inadequate secretion of glucocorticoids and mineralocorticoids.
17. Twitchings of muscle fiber groups.

DOWN

2. Type of tablet or pill with a coating that enables it to pass through the stomach without being dissolved.
4. Eject from the mouth; spit.
5. Distortion of sensory perception; usually associated with the use of LSD.
6. Digoxin
7. Male sex hormone responsible for the development of male characteristics.
9. Condition of long duration, usually months or years.
11. A lipid substance secreted by glands in the skin to lubricate the skin everywhere but the palms and soles.

A. Enteric Coated	B. Addisons Disease	C. Lavage	D. Expectorate
E. Androgen	F. Tranxene	G. Fasciculation	H. Tyzine
I. Midamor	J. Referred Pain	K. Convulsion	L. Lymphopenia
M. Lanoxin	N. Chronic	O. Sebum	P. Chemical Name
Q. Synesthesia	R. Dose		

27. Using the Across and Down clues, write the correct words in the numbered grid below.

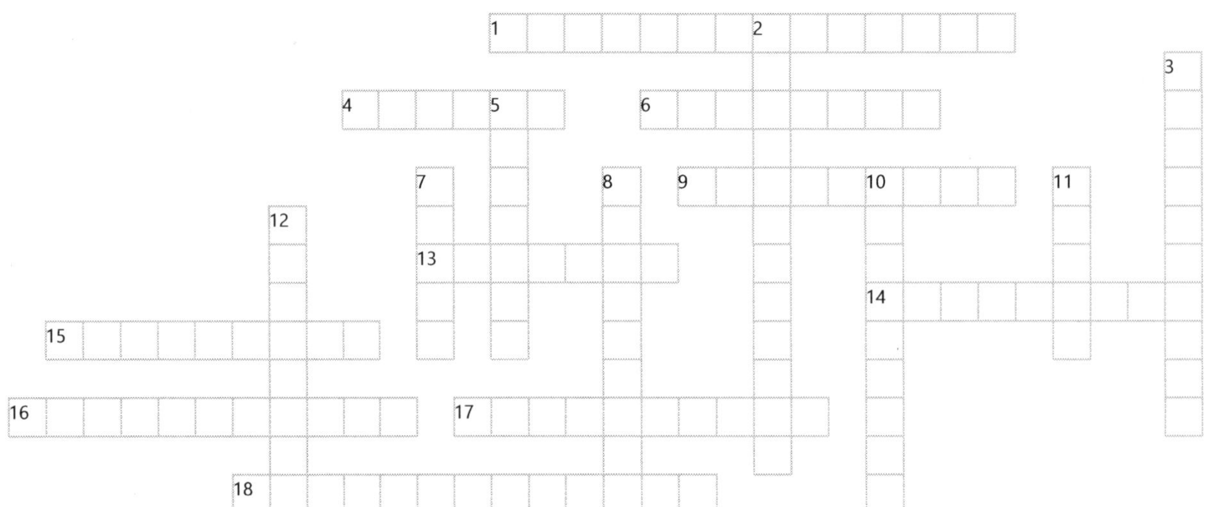

ACROSS

1. Class of drugs used to treat anxiety and sleep disorders.
4. Washing with fluids or flushing of a cavity such as the stomach.
6. An abnormal widening or ballooning of a portion of an artery due to weakness in the wall of the blood vessel.
9. Generalized seizures that are usually brief and often confined to one part of the body.
13. Amlodipine
14. Substance that is soothing to mucous membranes or skin.
15. Life-threatening; refers to growth of a cancerous tumor.
16. Generalized seizure characterized by full body tonic and clonic motor convulsions and loss of consciousness.
17. Preparation in which undissolved solids are dispersed within a liquid.
18. Infection of the skin, hair, or nails caused by a fungus.

DOWN

2. watery substance that is located behind the cornea of the eye and in front of the lens.
3. A mathematical equation that expresses the equality between two ratios.
5. name Nonproprietary name of a drug.
7. Alprazolam
8. Substance that has the ability to attach other substances to its surface.
10. Formation of ova.
11. Trandolapril
12. Sodium valproate

A. Aqueous Humor	B. Emollient	C. Aneurysm	D. Myoclonic
E. Lavage	F. Generic	G. Xanax	H. Depakote
I. Mavik	J. Malignant	K. Adsorbent	L. Suspension
M. Norvasc	N. Oogenesis	O. Dermatophytic	P. Tonic Clonic
Q. Proportion	R. Benzodiazepine		

28. Using the Across and Down clues, write the correct words in the numbered grid below.

ACROSS

1. Peptides in the plasma that stimulate cellular growth and have insulin-like activity.
3. Protein in red blood cells that transports oxygen to all tissues of the body.
9. Error introduced into a study by its design rather than due to random variation.
11. Stage of sleep characterized by rapid eye movement (REM) and dreaming.
13. An abnormal decrease in the number of circulating white blood cells.
14. Process of discharging the contents of the intestines as feces.
15. Space around the brain and spinal cord that contains the cerebrospinal fluid.
16. Chemical action of a substance to bond permanently to a metal ion.
17. Pharmacologically active substance obtained from the marijuana plant.
18. Compound that contains acetic acid.

DOWN

2. Chest pain or discomfort that occurs when the heart muscle does not get enough blood and oxygen.
4. Abnormality in blood.
5. Substance that is soothing to mucous membranes or skin.
6. Ethacrynic acid
7. A painful burning feeling behind the sternum that occurs when stomach acid backs up into the esophagus.
8. Drug effect other than the therapeutic effect that is usually undesirable but not harmful.
10. Inflammation of a vein.
12. A measurement of the amount of drug that is administered.

A. Acetate	B. Hemoglobin	C. Side Effect	D. Heartburn
E. Somatomedins	F. Angina	G. Defecation	H. Cannabinoid
I. Leucopenia	J. Systematic Error	K. Intrathecal	L. Blood Dyscrasia
M. Edecrin	N. Emollient	O. Dose	P. Rem Sleep
Q. Phlebitis	R. Chelate		

29. Using the Across and Down clues, write the correct words in the numbered grid below.

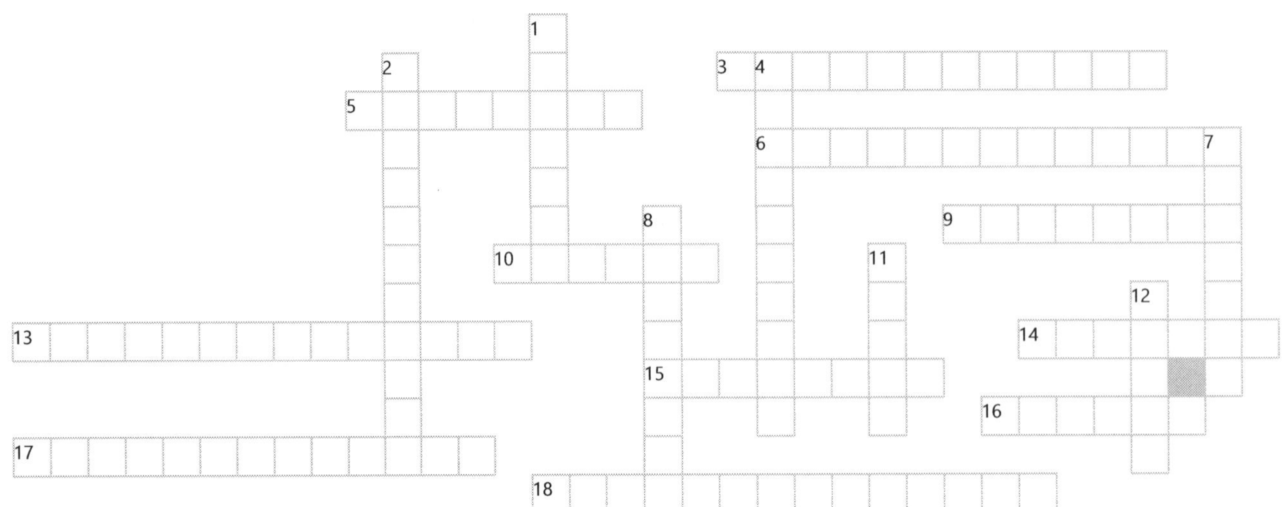

ACROSS

3. Substance that kills disease-causing microorganisms on nonliving surfaces.
5. Largest and uppermost part of the brain that is divided into right and left cerebral hemispheres.
6. Hormone secreted by the anterior pituitary that binds to a receptor on another endocrine gland.
9. Clorazepate
10. Lack of coordination of muscle movements.
13. Abnormality in blood.
14. Any disease caused by a fungus.
15. Clot formed by the action of coagulation factors and circulating blood cells.
16. Condition in which no urine is produced.
17. Drug produced by a chemical process outside the body.
18. Excessive hair growth on the body.

DOWN

1. Decimal fraction with a denominator of 100.
2. Bottom number of a fraction; shows the number of parts in a whole.
4. Chemical mediator produced by immune cells that increases immune function.
7. Ethacrynic acid
8. Alkaloid drug in tobacco that stimulates ganglionic receptors.
11. A lipid substance secreted by glands in the skin to lubricate the skin everywhere but the palms and soles.
12. Gemfibrozil

A. Interferon	B. Percent	C. Denominator	D. Anuria
E. Tranxene	F. Tropic Hormone	G. Blood Dyscrasia	H. Thrombus
I. Mycosis	J. Edecrin	K. Cerebrum	L. Disinfectant
M. Nicotine	N. Lopid	O. Synthetic Drug	P. Ataxia
Q. Hypertrichosis	R. Sebum		

30. Using the Across and Down clues, write the correct words in the numbered grid below.

ACROSS

5. Drug that relaxes bronchial smooth muscle and dilates the lower respiratory passages.
6. Nicotinic acid
9. Drug that is effective against a wide variety of both gram-positive and gram-negative pathogenic bacteria.
14. Unusually high concentration of calcium in the blood.
15. Number written with both a whole number and a fraction.
16. Adverse reaction which results from an exaggerated but otherwise usual pharmacological effect.
17. Appearance of blood or red blood cells in the urine.
18. Infection acquired as a result of being in a hospital.

DOWN

1. Inadequate secretion of glucocorticoids and mineralocorticoids.
2. Substance, usually protein or carbohydrate, that is capable of stimulating an immune response.
3. Abnormally low level of chloride ions circulating in the blood.
4. General term for undesirable and potentially harmful drug effect.
7. After a meal.
8. When drugs (substances) produce the same intensity or spectrum of activity.
10. Permanent black discoloration of skin and mucous membranes caused by prolonged use of silver protein.
11. A type of cell formed after macrophages in the artery wall digest LDL cholesterol.
12. Method of staining and identifying bacteria.
13. Having normal thyroid gland function.

A. Mixed Number
B. Argyria
C. Hypercalcemia
D. Broad Spectrum
E. Bronchodilator
F. Addisons Disease
G. Nicobid
H. Postprandial
I. Gram Stain
J. Equipotent
K. Nosocomial
L. Type A Reaction
M. Antigen
N. Hematuria
O. Hypochloremia
P. Foam Cells
Q. Euthyroid
R. Adverse Effect

1. Using the Across and Down clues, write the correct words in the numbered grid below.

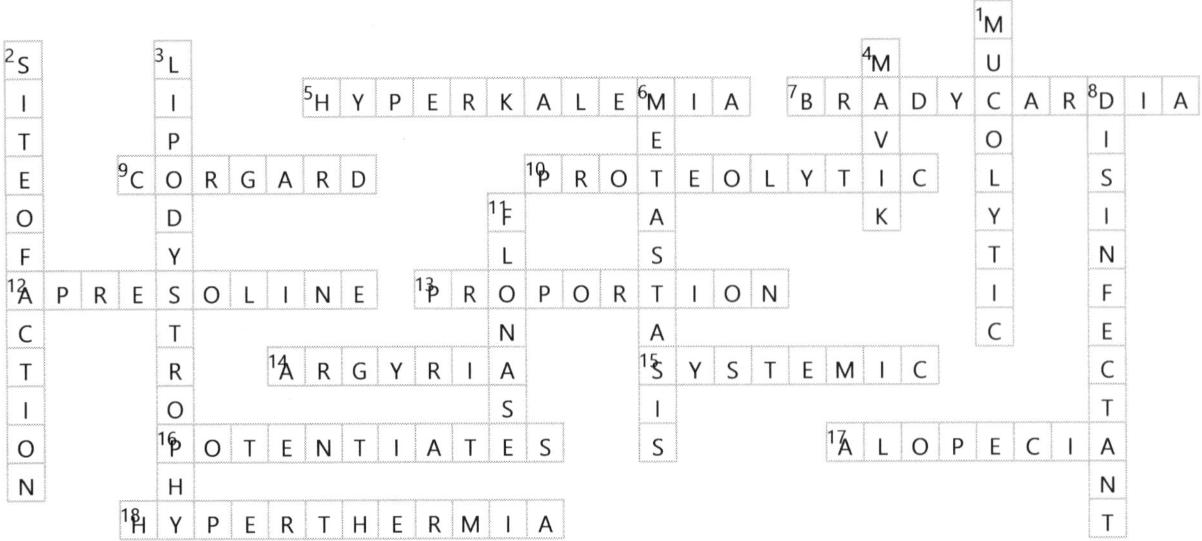

ACROSS

5. An elevated concentration of potassium in blood.
7. Slowing down of heart rate.
9. Nadolol
10. Action that causes the decomposition or destruction of proteins.
12. Hydralazine
13. A mathematical equation that expresses the equality between two ratios.
14. Permanent black discoloration of skin and mucous membranes caused by prolonged use of silver protein.
15. Occurring in the general circulation, resulting in distribution to most organs.
16. Produces an action that is greater than either of the components can produce alone; synergy.
17. Baldness or hair loss.
18. Abnormally high body temperature.

DOWN

1. Drug that liquefies bronchial secretions.
2. Location within the body where a drug exerts its therapeutic effect, often a specific drug receptor.
3. Defective metabolism of fat.
4. Trandolapril
6. Spread of cancer cells throughout the body, from primary to secondary sites.
8. Substance that kills disease-causing microorganisms on nonliving surfaces.
11. Fluticasone

A. Site of Action	B. Argyria	C. Bradycardia	D. Alopecia	E. Proteolytic
F. Corgard	G. Mavik	H. Flonase	I. Systemic	J. Apresoline
K. Metastasis	L. Disinfectant	M. Mucolytic	N. Hyperthermia	O. Hyperkalemia
P. Proportion	Q. Potentiates	R. Lipodystrophy		

2. Using the Across and Down clues, write the correct words in the numbered grid below.

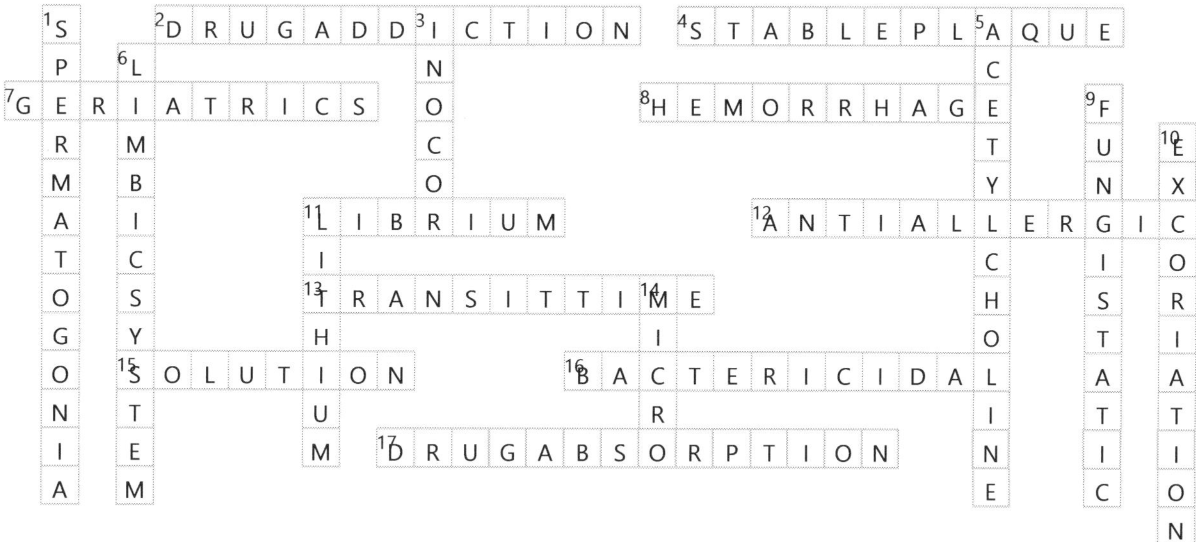

ACROSS

2. Condition of drug abuse and drug dependence that is characterized by compulsive drug behavior.
4. Plaque formed in the artery wall that remains in the wall.
7. Medical specialty that deals with individuals over 65 years of age.
8. Loss of blood from blood vessels.
11. Chlordiazepoxide
12. Drug that prevents mast cells from releasing histamine and other vasoactive substances.
13. Amount of time it takes for food to travel from the mouth to the anus.
15. Homogeneous mixture of two or more substances.
16. Antibiotic that kills bacteria; chemical that kills or destroys bacteria.
17. Entrance of a drug into the bloodstream from its site of administration.

DOWN

1. Intermediary kind of male germ cell in the production of spermatozoa.
3. Amrinone
5. Neurotransmitter of parasympathetic nerves.
6. Neural pathway connecting different brain areas involved in regulation of behavior and emotion.
9. Inhibits the growth of fungi but does not kill off the fungi.
10. An abrasion of the epidermis usually from a mechanical cause; a scratch.
11. An element similar to sodium that is used in the treatment of mania and bipolar mood disorder.
14. Prefix meaning small.

A. Solution	B. Inocor	C. Librium	D. Bactericidal
E. Hemorrhage	F. Limbic System	G. Spermatogonia	H. Excoriation
I. Stable Plaque	J. Geriatrics	K. Fungistatic	L. Antiallergic
M. Transit Time	N. Lithium	O. Drug Addiction	P. Micro
Q. Drug Absorption	R. Acetylcholine		

3. Using the Across and Down clues, write the correct words in the numbered grid below.

ACROSS

2. Naphazoline
4. Primidone
5. Drug used to induce and maintain sleep.
7. Losartan
11. Molecule that contains purine or pyrimidine bases in combination with sugar.
13. Excessive hair growth on the body.
14. Peptides in the plasma that stimulate cellular growth and have insulin-like activity.
15. Mature sperm cells.
16. Beclomethasone
17. Eszopiclone

DOWN

1. Hydrolysis of glycogen to yield free glucose.
2. Labetalol
3. Condition that causes urine to be excreted; usually associated with large volumes of urine.
6. A persistent abnormal sense of taste.
8. Diazepam
9. Specific cellular structure that a drug binds to and that produces a physiologic effect.
10. Another way to write a fraction when the denominator is 10, 100, 1000, and so on.
12. Group or island of cells.

A. Normodyne
B. Hypertrichosis
C. Beconase
D. Hypnotic
E. Somatomedins
F. Spermatozoa
G. Naphcon
H. Glycogenolysis
I. Receptor
J. Lunesta
K. Diuresis
L. Dysgeusia
M. Nucleoside
N. Valium
O. Islets
P. Cozaar
Q. Mysoline
R. Decimal

4. Using the Across and Down clues, write the correct words in the numbered grid below.

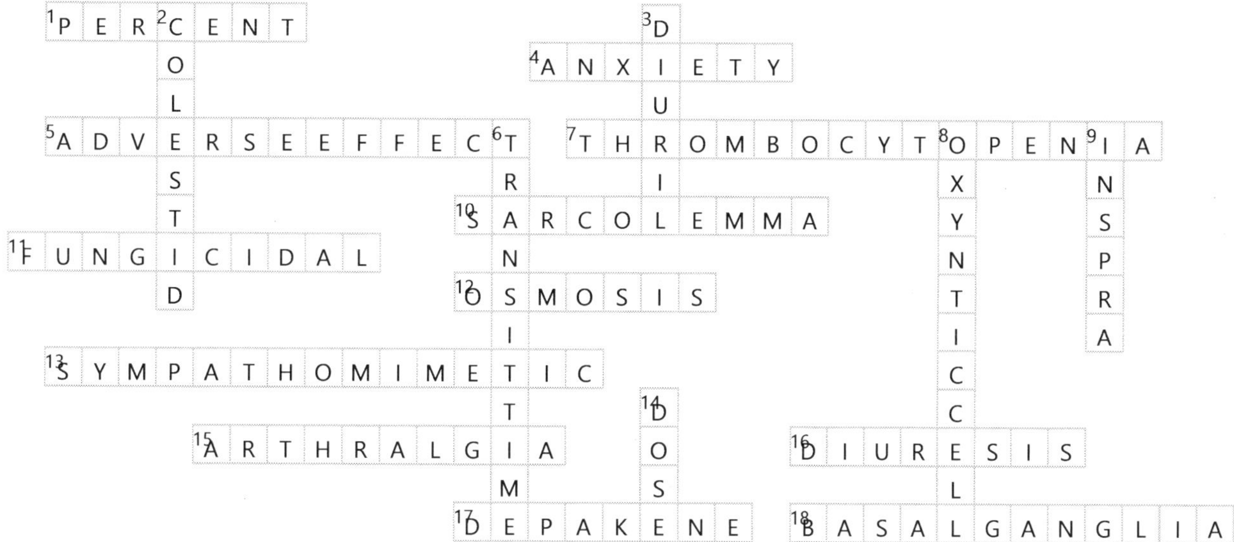

ACROSS

1. Decimal fraction with a denominator of 100.
4. A state of anxiousness and hyperemotionalism that occurs with uncertainty, stress, and fearful situations.
5. General term for undesirable and potentially harmful drug effect.
7. A low platelet count in blood.
10. A thin membrane enclosing a striated (skeletal) muscle fiber.
11. Substance, chemical solution, or drug that kills fungi; chemical that kills or destroys fungi.
12. Process in which water moves across membranes following the movement of sodium ions.
13. Refers to the action of an adrenergic drug or an action that increases sympathetic activity.
15. Joint pain.
16. Condition that causes urine to be excreted; usually associated with large volumes of urine.
17. Valproic
18. A group of cell bodies within the white matter of the cerebrum that helps control body movement

DOWN

2. Colestipol
3. Chlorothiazide
6. Amount of time it takes for food to travel from the mouth to the anus.
8. Cell that synthesizes and releases hydrochloric acid (HCl) into the stomach lumen.
9. Eplerenone
14. A measurement of the amount of drug that is administered.

A. Diuresis	B. Depakene	C. Sarcolemma	D. Inspra
E. Basal Ganglia	F. Colestid	G. Sympathomimetic	H. Dose
I. Adverse Effect	J. Percent	K. Thrombocytopenia	L. Osmosis
M. Diuril	N. Fungicidal	O. Arthralgia	P. Oxyntic Cell
Q. Transit Time	R. Anxiety		

5. Using the Across and Down clues, write the correct words in the numbered grid below.

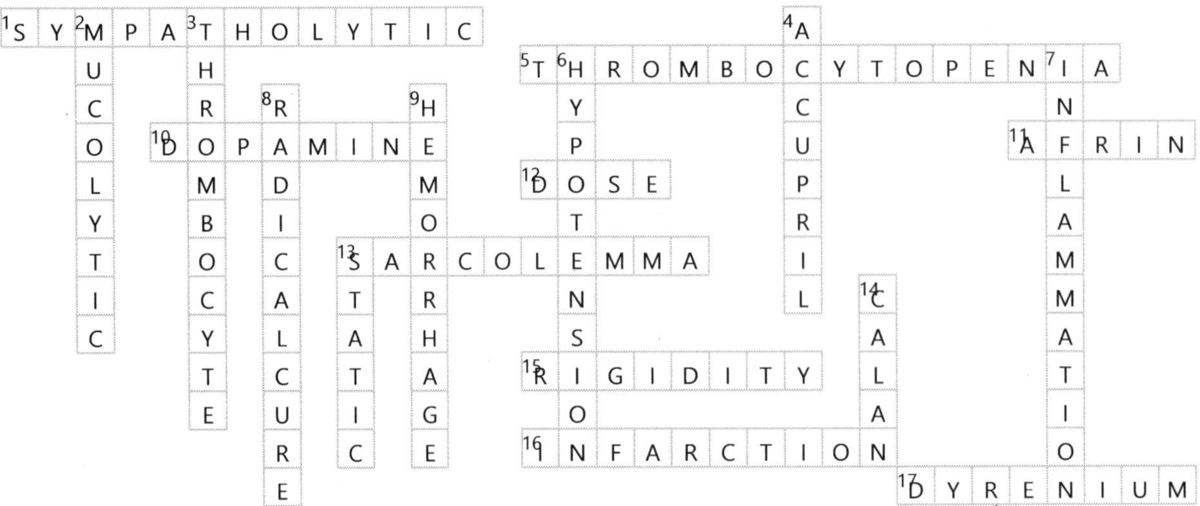

ACROSS

1. Refers to the action of an adrenergic blocking drug or an action that decreases sympathetic activity.
5. A low platelet count in blood.
10. Inhibitory neurotransmitter in the basal ganglia.
11. Oxymetazoline
12. A measurement of the amount of drug that is administered.
13. A thin membrane enclosing a striated (skeletal) muscle fiber.
15. A stiffness and inflexibility of movement.
16. Area of tissue that has died because of a sudden lack of blood supply.
17. Triamterene

DOWN

2. Drug that liquefies bronchial secretions.
3. Cell in the blood, commonly called a platelet, that is necessary for coagulation.
4. Quinapril
6. Condition in which an arterial blood pressure is abnormally low.
7. Condition in which tissues have been damaged, characterized by swelling, pain, heat, and sometimes
8. Arresting of malaria, in which protozoal parasites are eliminated from all tissues.
9. Loss of blood from blood vessels.
13. Suffix denoting the inhibition of, as of microorganisms.
14. Verapamil

A. Accupril	B. Calan	C. Static	D. Dose
E. Thrombocytopenia	F. Sarcolemma	G. Radical Cure	H. Afrin
I. Infarction	J. Thrombocyte	K. Inflammation	L. Mucolytic
M. Hemorrhage	N. Hypotension	O. Rigidity	P. Dopamine
Q. Dyrenium	R. Sympatholytic		

6. Using the Across and Down clues, write the correct words in the numbered grid below.

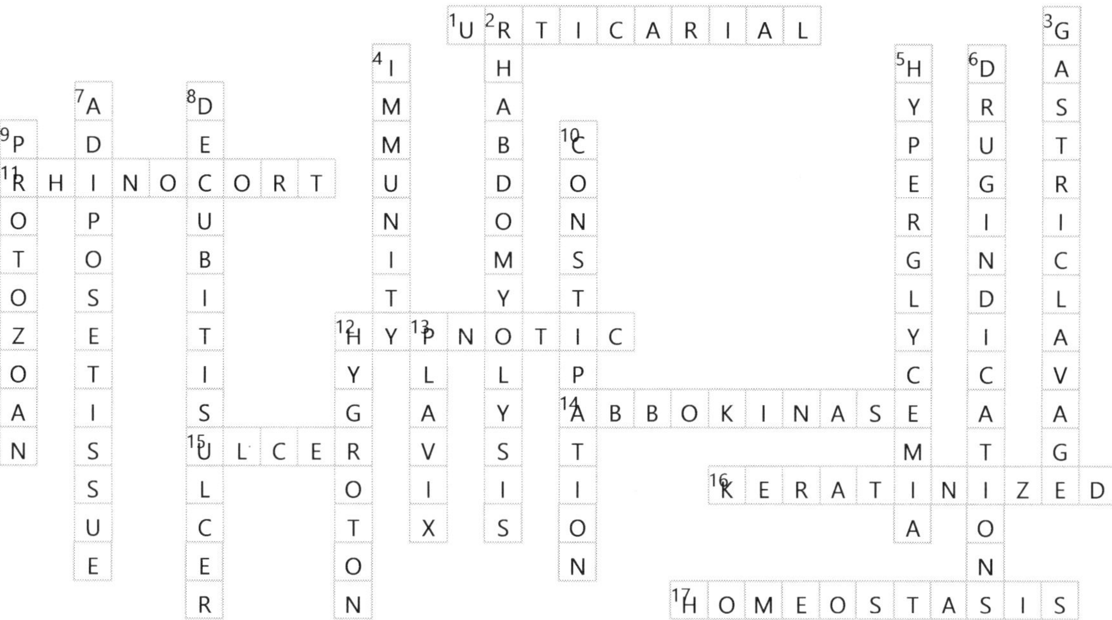

ACROSS

1. Intensely itching raised areas of skin caused by an allergic reaction; hives.
11. Budesonide
12. Drug used to induce and maintain sleep.
14. Urokinase
15. Open sore in the mucous membranes or mucosal linings of the body.
16. Composed of a protein substance largely found in hair and nails.
17. Normal state of balance among the body's internal organs.

DOWN

2. The rapid breakdown of skeletal muscle due to muscle injury.
3. Flushing of the stomach.
4. Condition that causes individuals to resist acquiring or developing a disease or infection.
5. Higher than normal level of glucose in the blood.
6. Intended or indicated uses for any drug.
7. Tissue containing fat cells; fat.
8. Bedsore.
9. Single-celled organism belonging to the genus Protozoa.
10. A decrease in stool frequency.
12. Chlorthalidone
13. Clopidogrel

A. Adipose Tissue
B. Rhinocort
C. Abbokinase
D. Hypnotic
E. Homeostasis
F. Plavix
G. Drug Indications
H. Urticarial
I. Constipation
J. Hygroton
K. Protozoan
L. Keratinized
M. Hyperglycemia
N. Rhabdomyolysis
O. Gastric Lavage
P. Ulcer
Q. Decubitis Ulcer
R. Immunity

7. Using the Across and Down clues, write the correct words in the numbered grid below.

ACROSS

2. Dizziness often caused by a decrease in blood supply to the brain.
5. Abnormal discharge of brain neurons that causes alteration of behavior and motor activity.
6. Natural substance in the body.
7. Amount of time it takes for food to travel from the mouth to the anus.
10. Infection acquired as a result of being in a hospital.
12. Hormone from adrenal medulla that stimulates adrenergic receptors, especially during stress.
13. Moricizine
14. Bacterial enzymes that inactivate penicillin antibiotics.
16. Specialized cells in the hypothalamus that respond to changes in sodium concentration in the blood.
17. Nadolol
18. Polypeptide released within the brain that has specific functions during and after pregnancy.

DOWN

1. Sodium valproate
3. Washing (lavage) of a wound or cavity with large volumes of fluid.
4. Oxazepam
8. A state of anxiousness and hyperemotionalism that occurs with uncertainty, stress, and fearful situations.
9. Loss of voluntary muscle movement; restless leg movement.
11. Largest and uppermost part of the brain that is divided into right and left cerebral hemispheres.
15. Furosemide

A. Irrigation	B. Seizure	C. Cerebrum	D. Osmoreceptors
E. Anxiety	F. Depakote	G. Transit Time	H. Epinephrine
I. Oxytocin	J. Nosocomial	K. Native	L. Corgard
M. Ethmozine	N. Akinesia	O. Serax	P. Lightheadedness
Q. Penicillinase	R. Lasix		

8. Using the Across and Down clues, write the correct words in the numbered grid below.

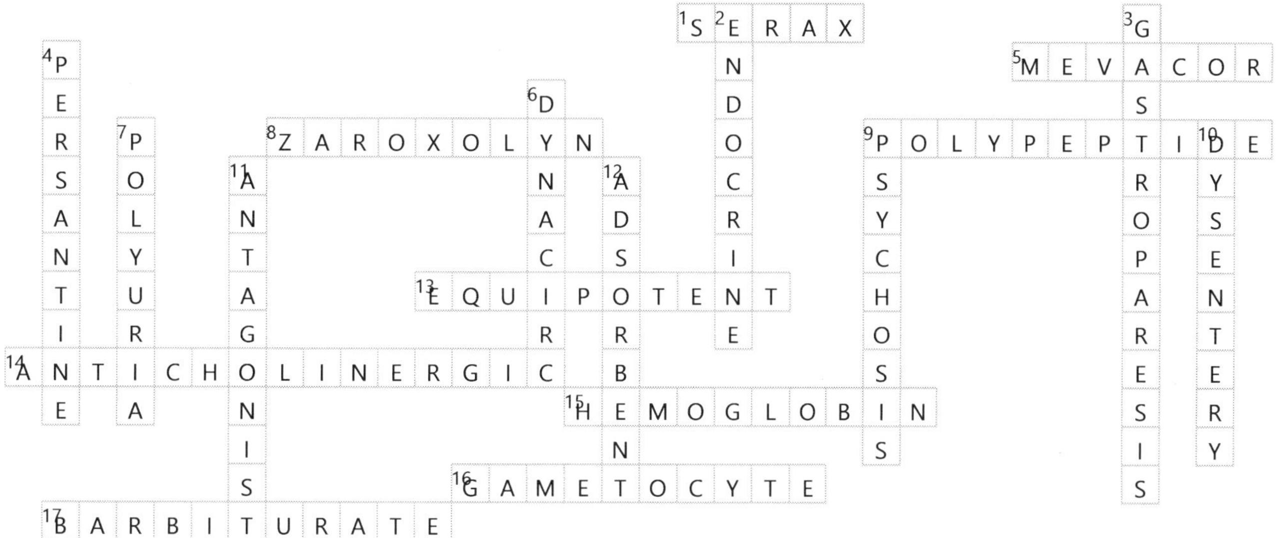

ACROSS

1. Oxazepam
5. Lovastatin
8. Metolazone
9. Substance, usually large, composed of an indefinite number of amino acids.
13. When drugs (substances) produce the same intensity or spectrum of activity.
14. Refers to drugs or effects that reduce the activity of the parasympathetic nervous system.
15. Protein in red blood cells that transports oxygen to all tissues of the body.
16. Organism in an immature stage of development.
17. CNS depressant drug possessing the barbituric acid ring structure.

DOWN

2. Pertaining to glands that secrete substances directly into the blood.
3. Condition, also called delayed gastric emptying, in which the stomach muscles do not function properly.
4. Dipyridamole
6. Isradipine
7. Excessive urine production; increased urination.
9. Form of mental illness that produces bizarre behavior and deterioration of the personality.
10. Condition characterized by frequent watery stools (usually containing blood and mucus), tenesmus.
11. Drug that attaches to a receptor, does not initiate an action, but blocks an agonist from producing an effect.
12. Substance that has the ability to attach other substances to its surface.

A. Gametocyte
B. Zaroxolyn
C. Psychosis
D. Barbiturate
E. Gastroparesis
F. Polyuria
G. Polypeptide
H. Serax
I. Equipotent
J. Persantine
K. Dynacirc
L. Mevacor
M. Hemoglobin
N. Endocrine
O. Dysentery
P. Adsorbent
Q. Anticholinergic
R. Antagonist

9. Using the Across and Down clues, write the correct words in the numbered grid below.

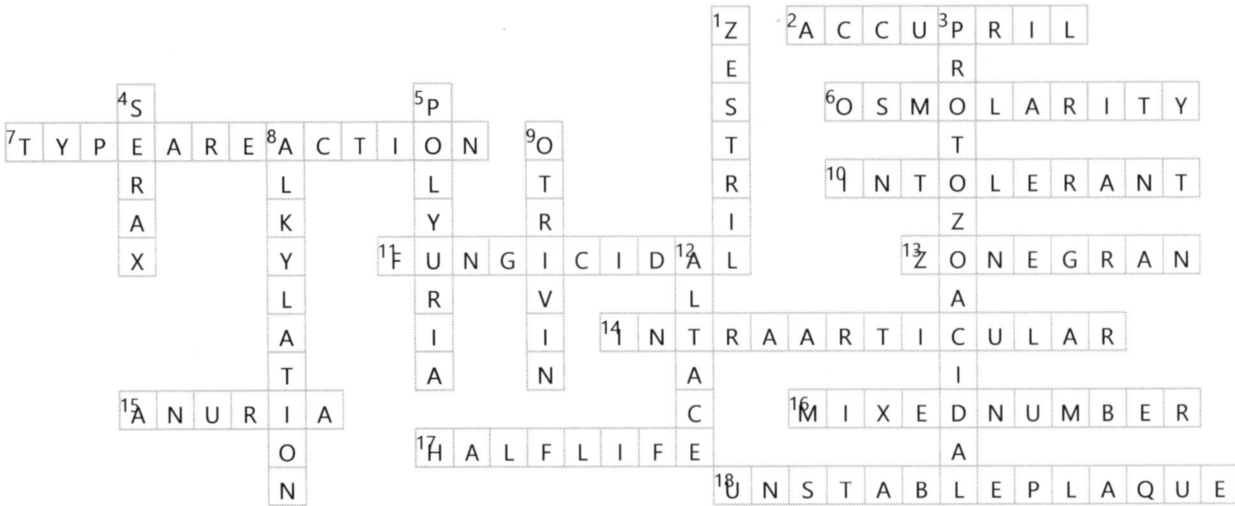

ACROSS

2. Quinapril
6. A measure of hydration status; the amount of solute per liter of solution.
7. Adverse reaction which results from an exaggerated but otherwise usual pharmacological effect.
10. Not able to continue drug therapy usually because of extreme sensitivity to the side effects.
11. Substance, chemical solution, or drug that kills fungi; chemical that kills or destroys fungi.
13. Zonisamide
14. Joint space into which drug is injected.
15. Condition in which no urine is produced.
16. Number written with both a whole number and a fraction.
17. Time required for the body to reduce the amount of drug in the plasma by one-half.
18. Plaque formed in the artery wall that can break away and obstruct blood flow or form a clot.

DOWN

1. Lisinopril
3. A substance, chemical solution, or drug that kills protozoa.
4. Oxazepam
5. Excessive urine production; increased urination.
8. Irreversible chemical bond that some cancer drugs form with nucleic acids and DNA.
9. Xylometazoline
12. Ramipril

A. Serax	B. Unstable Plaque	C. Protozoacidal	D. Polyuria
E. Accupril	F. Type A Reaction	G. Otrivin	H. Anuria
I. Mixed Number	J. Altace	K. Half Life	L. Osmolarity
M. Alkylation	N. Intolerant	O. Intra Articular	P. Fungicidal
Q. Zestril	R. Zonegran		

10. Using the Across and Down clues, write the correct words in the numbered grid below.

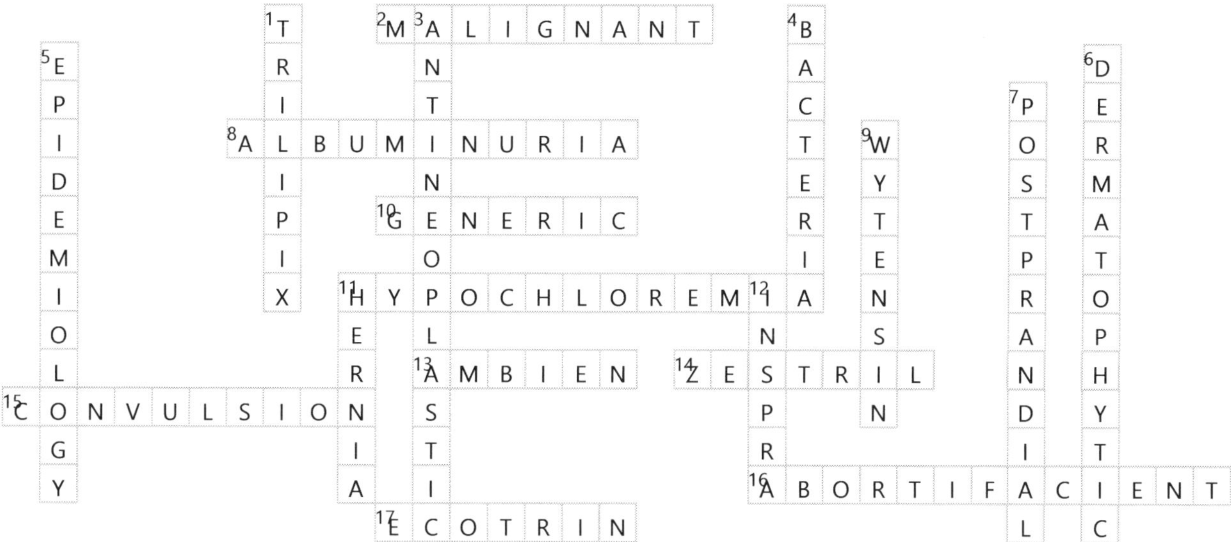

ACROSS

2. Life-threatening; refers to growth of a cancerous tumor.
8. The presence of the plasma protein albumin in the urine.
10. name Nonproprietary name of a drug.
11. Abnormally low level of chloride ions circulating in the blood.
13. Zolpidem
14. Lisinopril
15. Involuntary muscle contraction that is either tonic or clonic.
16. Substance that induces abortion.
17. Aspirin

DOWN

1. Fibric acid
3. Drug that inhibits the growth and proliferation of cancer cells.
4. Single-celled microorganisms, some of which cause disease.
5. Study of the distribution and determinants of diseases in populations.
6. Infection of the skin, hair, or nails caused by a fungus.
7. After a meal.
9. Guanabenz
11. Protrusion of an organ through the tissue usually containing it.
12. Eplerenone

A. Dermatophytic	B. Abortifacient	C. Malignant	D. Hernia	E. Generic
F. Antineoplastic	G. Ambien	H. Ecotrin	I. Bacteria	J. Albuminuria
K. Zestril	L. Trilipix	M. Inspra	N. Postprandial	O. Convulsion
P. Epidemiology	Q. Hypochloremia	R. Wytensin		

11. Using the Across and Down clues, write the correct words in the numbered grid below.

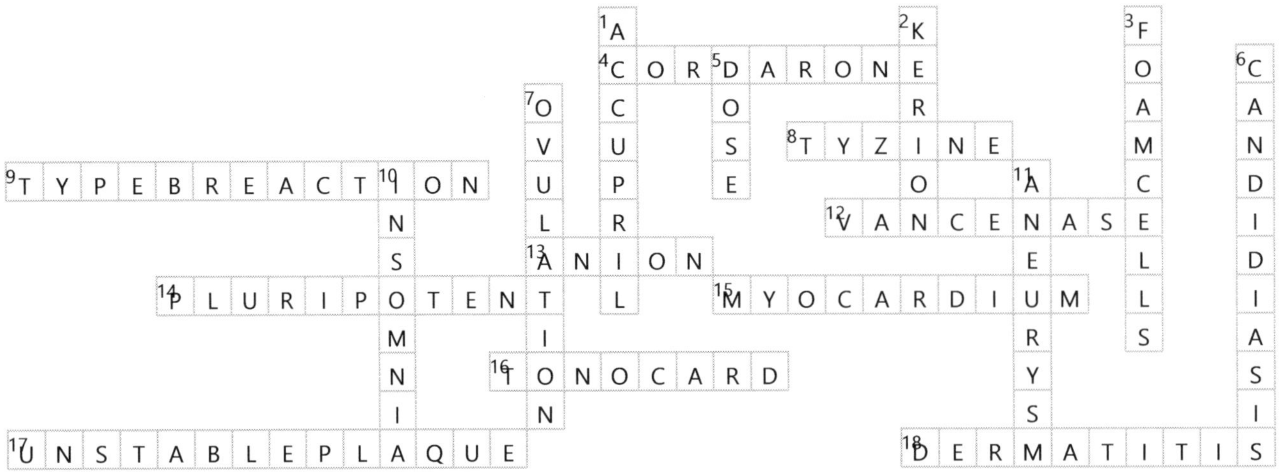

ACROSS

4. Amiodarone
8. Tetrahydrazoline
9. Adverse reaction which is aberrant, and may be due to hypersensitivity or immunologic reactions.
12. Beclomethasone
13. Negatively charged ion.
14. Ability of a substance to produce many different biological responses.
15. The muscular layer of the heart.
16. Tocainide
17. Plaque formed in the artery wall that can break away and obstruct blood flow or form a clot.
18. Inflammatory condition of the skin associated with itching, burning, and edematous vesicular formations.

DOWN

1. Quinapril
2. An inflammation of the hair follicles of the beard or scalp caused by ringworm with swelling and pus.
3. A type of cell formed after macrophages in the artery wall digest LDL cholesterol.
5. A measurement of the amount of drug that is administered.
6. Infection caused by the yeast Candida; also known as moniliasis.
7. Release of an egg from the ovary.
10. It is difficulty getting to sleep or staying asleep, or having non-refreshing sleep for at least 1 month.
11. An abnormal widening or ballooning of a portion of an artery due to weakness in the wall of the blood vessel.

A. Aneurysm
B. Accupril
C. Myocardium
D. Foam Cells
E. Tyzine
F. Dermatitis
G. Tonocard
H. Dose
I. Type B Reaction
J. Candidiasis
K. Vancenase
L. Anion
M. Kerion
N. Cordarone
O. Unstable Plaque
P. Pluripotent
Q. Ovulation
R. Insomnia

12. Using the Across and Down clues, write the correct words in the numbered grid below.

ACROSS

2. Drug that relaxes bronchial smooth muscle and dilates the lower respiratory passages.
6. Hormone released from adrenal cortex that causes the retention of sodium from the kidneys.
9. Procainamide
12. Hormone synthesized and released by the thyroid gland.
13. Ethosuximide
14. Causing a muscle to contract intermittently, resulting in a state of spasms.
15. Substance that causes the removal of mucous secretions from the respiratory system.
16. Dipyridamole
17. The muscular layer of the heart.
18. Study of the distribution and determinants of diseases in populations.

DOWN

1. Generalized seizure that does not involve motor convulsions; also referred to as petit mal.
3. Eplerenone
4. Substance, chemical solution, or drug that kills fungi; chemical that kills or destroys fungi.
5. Atorvastatin
7. Cell that synthesizes and releases hydrochloric acid (HCl) into the stomach lumen.
8. Trandolapril
10. Pertaining to the skin.
11. Abnormal discharge of brain neurons that causes alteration of behavior and motor activity.

A. Inspra	B. Oxyntic Cell	C. Expectorant	D. Fungicidal
E. Zarontin	F. Epidemiology	G. Bronchodilator	H. Myocardium
I. Lipitor	J. Thyroxine	K. Seizure	L. Procanbid
M. Cutaneous	N. Persantine	O. Absence Seizure	P. Spasmogenic
Q. Mavik	R. Aldosterone		

13. Using the Across and Down clues, write the correct words in the numbered grid below.

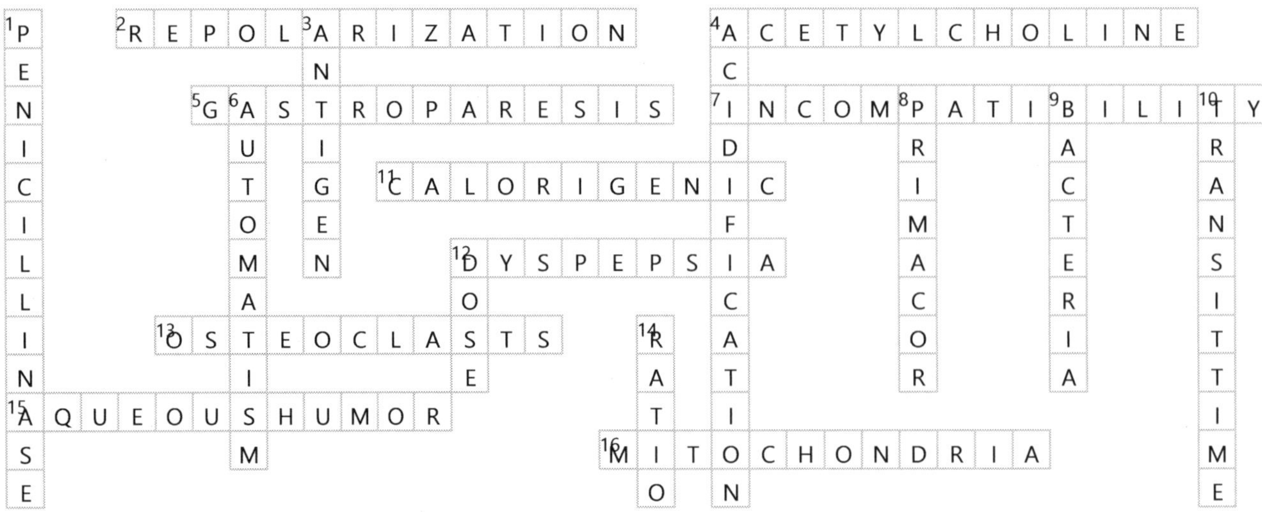

ACROSS

2. Return of the electric potential across a cell membrane to its resting state following depolarization.
4. Neurotransmitter of parasympathetic nerves.
5. Condition, also called delayed gastric emptying, in which the stomach muscles do not function properly.
7. Undesirable interaction of drugs not suitable for combination or administration together.
11. Producing heat.
12. Indigestion.
13. Responsible for bone resorption by binding to bone matrix proteins and releasing enzymes to break down bone.
15. watery substance that is located behind the cornea of the eye and in front of the lens.
16. Normal structures responsible for energy production in cells.

DOWN

1. Bacterial enzymes that inactivate penicillin antibiotics.
3. Substance, usually protein or carbohydrate, that is capable of stimulating an immune response.
4. Process that alters the pH to less than 7.
6. Drug-induced confusion that can cause increased drug consumption.
8. Milrinone
9. Single-celled microorganisms, some of which cause disease.
10. Amount of time it takes for food to travel from the mouth to the anus.
12. A measurement of the amount of drug that is administered.
14. The relationship of one number to another expressed by whole numbers.

A. Gastroparesis
B. Dyspepsia
C. Osteoclasts
D. Bacteria
E. Primacor
F. Calorigenic
G. Repolarization
H. Automatism
I. Aqueous Humor
J. Penicillinase
K. Antigen
L. Incompatibility
M. Dose
N. Acidification
O. Transit Time
P. Ratio
Q. Mitochondria
R. Acetylcholine

14. Using the Across and Down clues, write the correct words in the numbered grid below.

ACROSS

1. Condition characterized by frequent watery stools (usually containing blood and mucus), tenesmus.
4. Process in which water moves across membranes following the movement of sodium ions.
7. watery substance that is located behind the cornea of the eye and in front of the lens.
11. Substance, chemical solution, or drug that kills fungi; chemical that kills or destroys fungi.
12. Unusually high concentration of calcium in the blood.
13. Sodium valproate
14. Suffix meaning cells.
15. Study of the distribution and determinants of diseases in populations.
16. A type of cell formed after macrophages in the artery wall digest LDL cholesterol.
17. Excessive hunger.
18. Condition of reliance on the use of a particular drug.

DOWN

2. Budesonide
3. Levetiracetam
5. Abnormally high body temperature.
6. Pharmacologically active substance obtained from the marijuana plant.
8. Condition in which the color of red blood cells is less than the normal index.
9. Reteplase
10. Beclomethasone

A. Cannabinoid	B. Aqueous Humor	C. Drug Dependence	D. Dysentery
E. Hypochromic	F. Retavase	G. Foam Cells	H. Osmosis
I. Hypercalcemia	J. Hyperthermia	K. Keppra	L. Depakote
M. Vancenase	N. Rhinocort	O. Polyphagia	P. Epidemiology
Q. Fungicidal	R. Cytic		

15. Using the Across and Down clues, write the correct words in the numbered grid below.

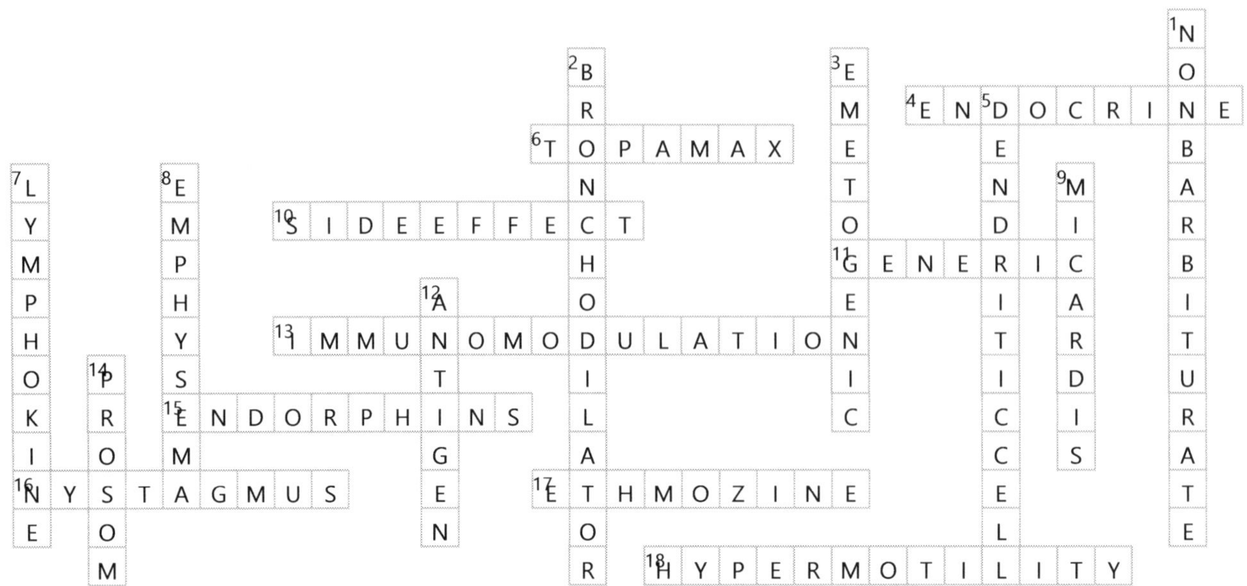

ACROSS

4. Pertaining to glands that secrete substances directly into the blood.
6. Topiramate
10. Drug effect other than the therapeutic effect that is usually undesirable but not harmful.
11. name Nonproprietary name of a drug.
13. Ability to stimulate and increase immune function.
15. Neuropeptides produced within the CNS that interact with opioid receptors to produce analgesia.
16. Rapid involuntary movement of eyes.
17. Moricizine
18. Increase in muscle tone or contractions causing faster clearance of substances through the GI tract.

DOWN

1. Refers to sedative-hypnotic drugs that do not possess the barbituric acid structure.
2. Drug that relaxes bronchial smooth muscle and dilates the lower respiratory passages.
3. A substance that causes vomiting.
5. An antigen-presenting white blood cell that is found in the skin, mucosa, and lymphoid tissues and that
7. A substance secreted by T cells that signals other immune cells like macrophages to aggregate.
8. Disease process causing destruction of the walls of the alveoli.
9. Telmisartan
12. Substance, usually protein or carbohydrate, that is capable of stimulating an immune response.
14. Estazolam

A. Endocrine
B. Generic
C. Dendritic Cell
D. Nystagmus
E. Emphysema
F. Topamax
G. Immunomodulation
H. Lymphokine
I. Endorphins
J. Nonbarbiturate
K. Ethmozine
L. Micardis
M. Emetogenic
N. Hypermotility
O. Side Effect
P. Bronchodilator
Q. Antigen
R. Prosom

16. Using the Across and Down clues, write the correct words in the numbered grid below.

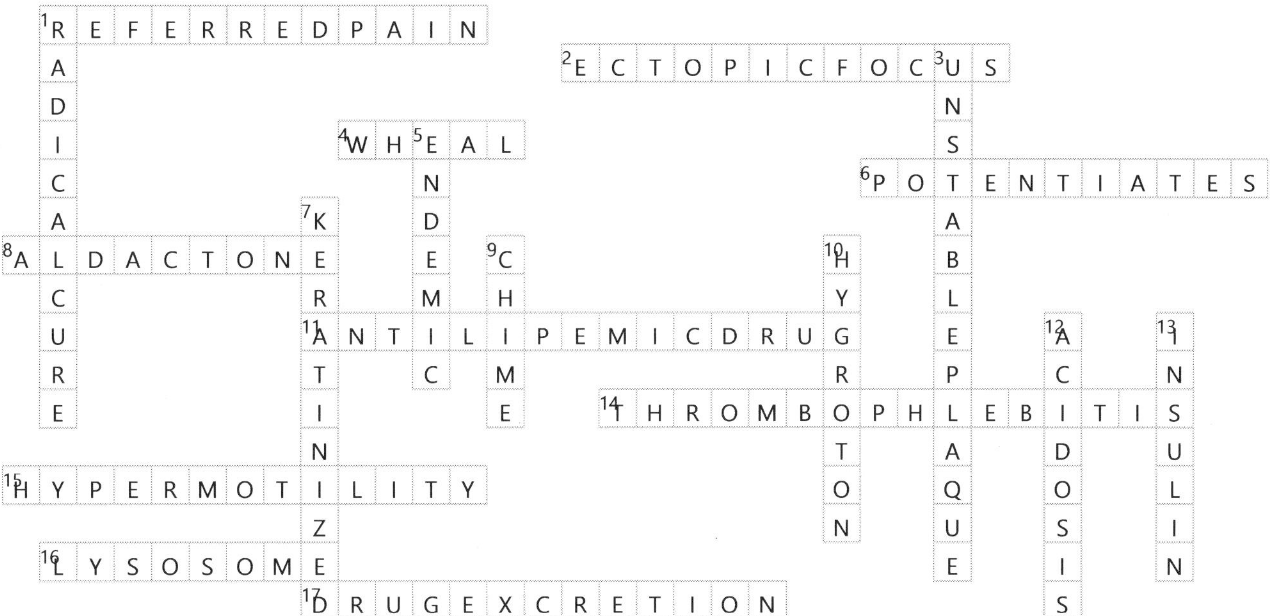

ACROSS

1. Origin of the pain is in a different location than where the individual feels the pain.
2. Area of the heart from which abnormal impulses originate.
4. A firm, elevated swelling of the skin often pale red in color and itchy; a sign of allergy.
6. Produces an action that is greater than either of the components can produce alone; synergy.
8. Spironolactone
11. A drug that reduces the level of fats in the blood.
14. Inflammation of the walls of the veins, associated with clot formation.
15. Increase in muscle tone or contractions causing faster clearance of substances through the GI tract.
16. Part of a cell that contains enzymes capable of digesting or destroying tissue
17. Elimination of the drug from the body.

DOWN

1. Arresting of malaria, in which protozoal parasites are eliminated from all tissues.
3. Plaque formed in the artery wall that can break away and obstruct blood flow or form a clot.
5. Present continually in a particular geographic region, often in spite of control measures.
7. Composed of a protein substance largely found in hair and nails.
9. Partially digested food and gastric secretions that moves into the duodenum from the stomach by peristalsis.
10. Chlorthalidone
12. pH less than 7.45
13. Hormone secreted by the beta cells of the pancreas to facilitate glucose entry into the cell.

A. Acidosis	B. Radical Cure	C. Potentiates	D. Chime
E. Unstable Plaque	F. Referred Pain	G. Aldactone	H. Hygroton
I. Endemic	J. Ectopic Focus	K. Lysosome	L. Wheal
M. Insulin	N. Thrombophlebitis	O. Drug Excretion	P. Antilipemic Drug
Q. Keratinized	R. Hypermotility		

17. Using the Across and Down clues, write the correct words in the numbered grid below.

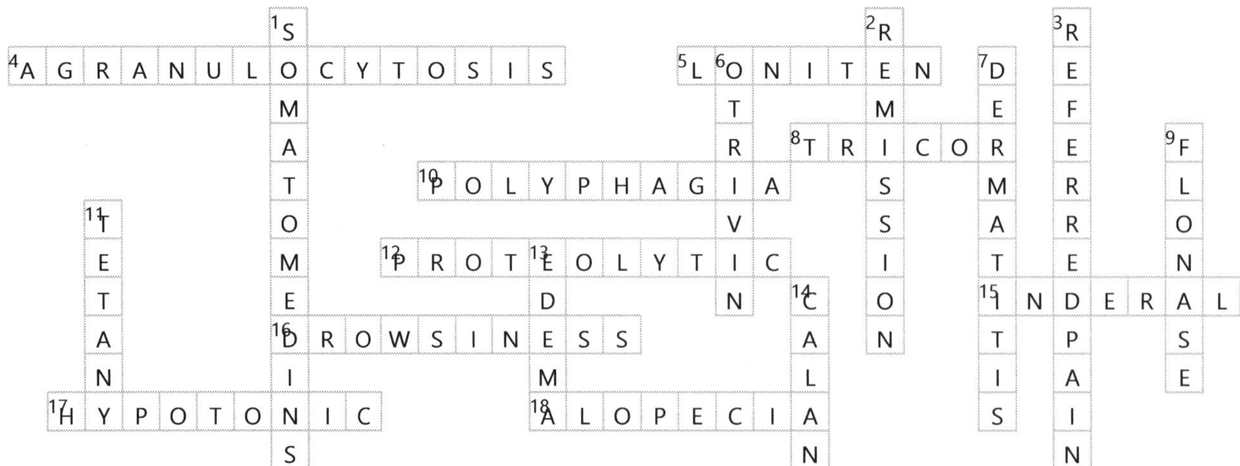

ACROSS

4. When there is an acute deficiency of granulocytes in blood.
5. Minoxidil hypertrichosis
8. Fenofibrate
10. Excessive hunger.
12. Action that causes the decomposition or destruction of proteins.
15. Propranolol
16. It refers to feeling abnormally sleepy during the day.
17. A condition where the concentration of salt (sodium, electrolytes) is less than that found inside the cells.
18. Baldness or hair loss.

DOWN

1. Peptides in the plasma that stimulate cellular growth and have insulin-like activity.
2. Period when cancer cells are not increasing in number.
3. Origin of the pain is in a different location than where the individual feels the pain.
6. Xylometazoline
7. Inflammatory condition of the skin associated with itching, burning, and edematous vesicular formations.
9. Fluticasone
11. A strong sustained muscle contraction.
13. An excessive accumulation of fluid in body tissues.
14. Verapamil

A. Otrivin
B. Tetany
C. Alopecia
D. Dermatitis
E. Flonase
F. Loniten
G. Somatomedins
H. Hypotonic
I. Edema
J. Agranulocytosis
K. Tricor
L. Drowsiness
M. Remission
N. Polyphagia
O. Referred Pain
P. Calan
Q. Inderal
R. Proteolytic

18. Using the Across and Down clues, write the correct words in the numbered grid below.

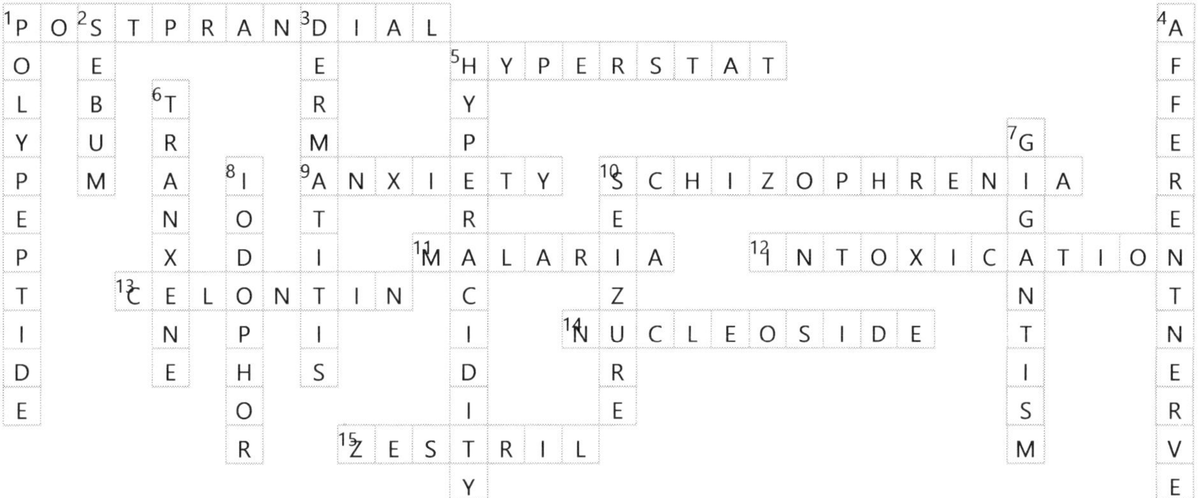

ACROSS

1. After a meal.
5. Diazoxide
9. A state of anxiousness and hyperemotionalism that occurs with uncertainty, stress, and fearful situations.
10. Major form of psychosis; behavior is inappropriate.
11. Protozoal infection characterized by attacks of chills, fever, and sweating.
12. State in which a substance has accumulated to potentially harmful levels in the body.
13. Methsuximide
14. Molecule that contains purine or pyrimidine bases in combination with sugar.
15. Lisinopril

DOWN

1. Substance, usually large, composed of an indefinite number of amino acids.
2. A lipid substance secreted by glands in the skin to lubricate the skin everywhere but the palms and soles.
3. Inflammatory condition of the skin associated with itching, burning, and edematous vesicular formations.
4. Transmits sensory information from peripheral organs to the central nervous system).
5. Abnormally high degree of acidity (for example, pH less than 1) in the stomach.
6. Clorazepate
7. Increased secretion of growth hormone in childhood, causing excessive growth and height.
8. Compound containing iodine.
10. Abnormal discharge of brain neurons that causes alteration of behavior and motor activity.

A. Tranxene	B. Seizure	C. Malaria	D. Dermatitis	E. Gigantism
F. Nucleoside	G. Afferent Nerve	H. Celontin	I. Iodophor	J. Anxiety
K. Schizophrenia	L. Zestril	M. Sebum	N. Postprandial	O. Hyperstat
P. Polypeptide	Q. Intoxication	R. Hyperacidity		

19. Using the Across and Down clues, write the correct words in the numbered grid below.

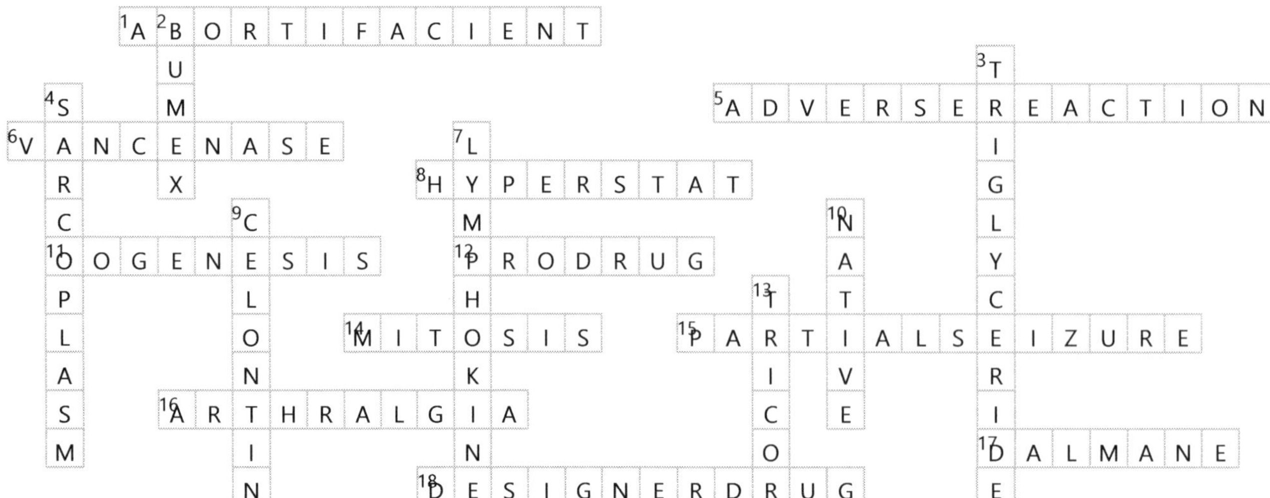

ACROSS

1. Substance that induces abortion.
5. A response to a drug which is noxious and unintended.
6. Beclomethasone
8. Diazoxide
11. Formation of ova.
12. An inactive precursor of a drug, converted into its active form in the body by normal metabolic processes.
14. Cell division in which two daughter cells receive the same number of chromosomes as the parent cell.
15. Seizure originating in one area of the brain that may spread to other areas.
16. Joint pain.
17. Flurazepam
18. Chemically altered form of an approved drug that produces similar effects and that is sold illegally.

DOWN

2. Bumetanide
3. A fat formed by three fatty acids into one molecule that supplies energy to muscle cells.
4. The cytoplasm of a striated (skeletal) muscle fiber.
7. A substance secreted by T cells that signals other immune cells like macrophages to aggregate.
9. Methsuximide
10. Natural substance in the body.
13. Fenofibrate

A. Arthralgia	B. Sarcoplasm	C. Designer Drug	D. Hyperstat
E. Vancenase	F. Prodrug	G. Adverse Reaction	H. Lymphokine
I. Triglyceride	J. Abortifacient	K. Tricor	L. Native
M. Bumex	N. Celontin	O. Mitosis	P. Partial Seizure
Q. Oogenesis	R. Dalmane		

20. Using the Across and Down clues, write the correct words in the numbered grid below.

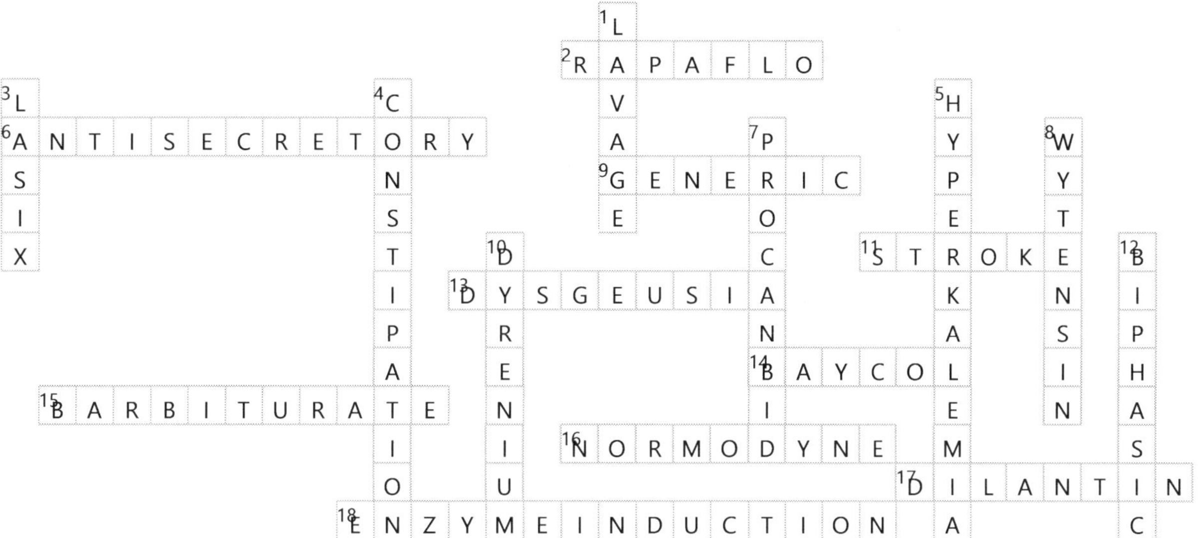

ACROSS

2. Silodosin
6. Substance that inhibits secretion of digestive enzymes, hormones, or acid.
9. name Nonproprietary name of a drug.
11. Loss of brain function due to a loss of blood supply.
13. A persistent abnormal sense of taste.
14. Cerivastatin
15. CNS depressant drug possessing the barbituric acid ring structure.
16. Labetalol
17. Phenytoin
18. Increase in the amount of drug metabolizing enzymes after repeated administration of certain drugs.

DOWN

1. Washing with fluids or flushing of a cavity such as the stomach.
3. Furosemide
4. A decrease in stool frequency.
5. An elevated concentration of potassium in blood.
7. Procainamide
8. Guanabenz
10. Triamterene
12. Two different amounts of estrogen hormone are released during the cycle.

A. Normodyne	B. Hyperkalemia	C. Stroke	D. Lasix
E. Enzyme Induction	F. Baycol	G. Lavage	H. Constipation
I. Biphasic	J. Rapaflo	K. Generic	L. Dilantin
M. Dyrenium	N. Antisecretory	O. Barbiturate	P. Wytensin
Q. Dysgeusia	R. Procanbid		

21. Using the Across and Down clues, write the correct words in the numbered grid below.

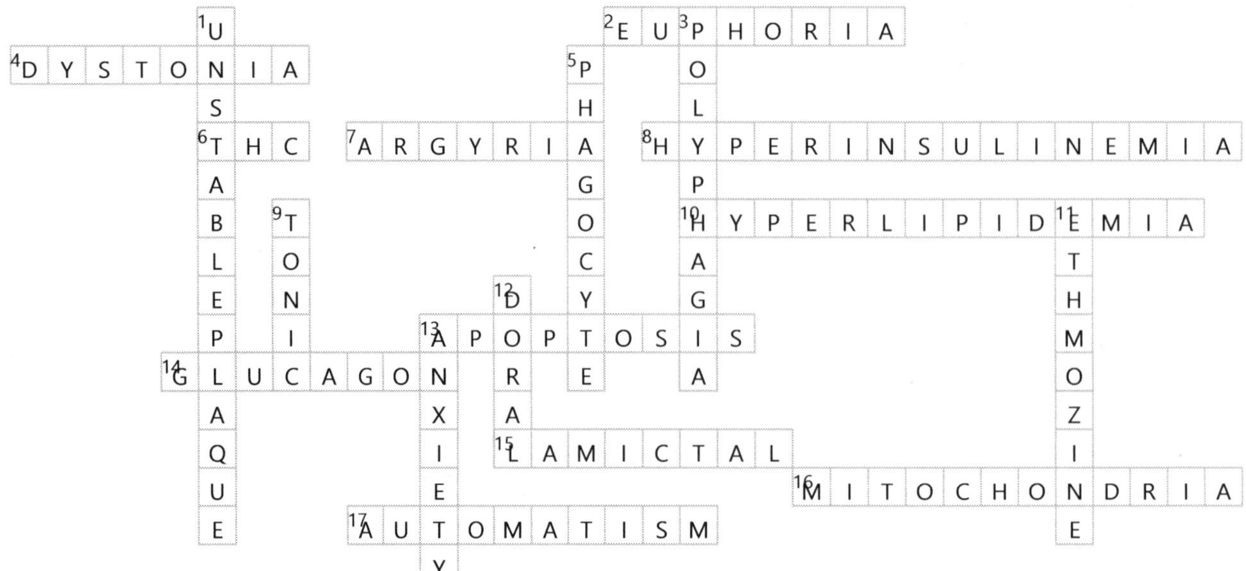

ACROSS

2. Feeling of well-being or elation; feeling good.
4. Muscle spasms, facial grimacing, and other involuntary movements and postures.
6. Active ingredient of the marijuana plant.
7. Permanent black discoloration of skin and mucous membranes caused by prolonged use of silver protein.
8. High levels of insulin in the blood often associated with type 2 diabetes mellitus and insulin resistance.
10. Abnormally high fat (lipid) levels in the plasma.
13. Cell death, due to either programmed cell death or other physiological events.
14. Hormone released by the alpha cells of the pancreas to increase plasma glucose concentration.
15. Lamotrigine
16. Normal structures responsible for energy production in cells.
17. Drug-induced confusion that can cause increased drug consumption.

DOWN

1. Plaque formed in the artery wall that can break away and obstruct blood flow or form a clot.
3. Excessive hunger.
5. Circulating cell that ingests waste products or bacteria in order to remove them from the body.
9. Convulsive muscle contraction characterized by sustained muscular contractions.
11. Moricizine
12. Quazepam
13. A state of anxiousness and hyperemotionalism that occurs with uncertainty, stress, and fearful situations.

A. Phagocyte
B. Tonic
C. Hyperinsulinemia
D. Automatism
E. Mitochondria
F. Apoptosis
G. Lamictal
H. Polyphagia
I. Ethmozine
J. Unstable Plaque
K. Doral
L. Argyria
M. Glucagon
N. Anxiety
O. Dystonia
P. Hyperlipidemia
Q. THC
R. Euphoria

22. Using the Across and Down clues, write the correct words in the numbered grid below.

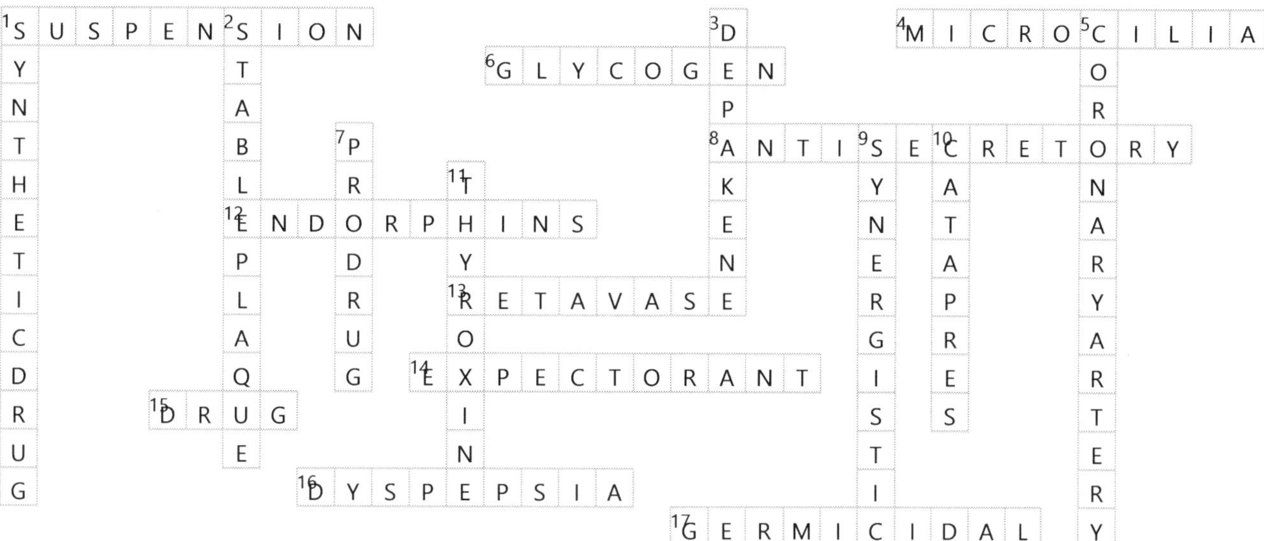

ACROSS

1. Preparation in which undissolved solids are dispersed within a liquid.
4. Tiny hairs that line the respiratory tract and continuously move, pushing secretions toward the mouth.
6. The storage form of glucose in humans and animals.
8. Substance that inhibits secretion of digestive enzymes, hormones, or acid.
12. Neuropeptides produced within the CNS that interact with opioid receptors to produce analgesia.
13. Reteplase
14. Substance that causes the removal of mucous secretions from the respiratory system.
15. Chemical substance that produces a change in body function.
16. Indigestion.
17. Substance, chemical solution, or drug that kills microorganisms.

DOWN

1. Drug produced by a chemical process outside the body.
2. Plaque formed in the artery wall that remains in the wall.
3. Valproic
5. Artery that supplies blood flow to the heart.
7. An inactive precursor of a drug, converted into its active form in the body by normal metabolic processes.
9. Complementary or additive.
10. Clonidine
11. Hormone synthesized and released by the thyroid gland.

A. Dyspepsia
B. Glycogen
C. Endorphins
D. Thyroxine
E. Prodrug
F. Drug
G. Expectorant
H. Catapres
I. Synergistic
J. Suspension
K. Retavase
L. Synthetic Drug
M. Microcilia
N. Stable Plaque
O. Antisecretory
P. Germicidal
Q. Coronary Artery
R. Depakene

23. Using the Across and Down clues, write the correct words in the numbered grid below.

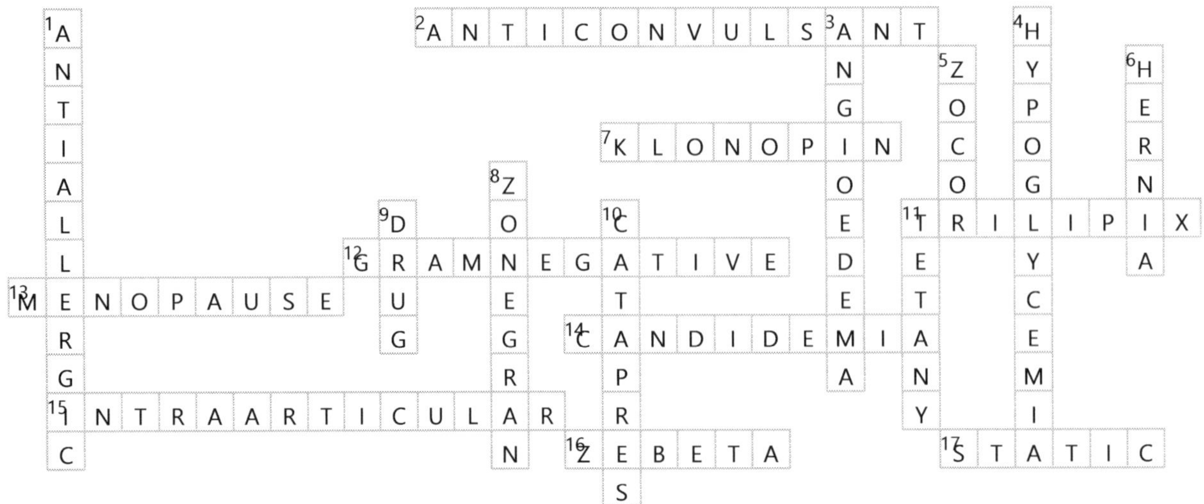

ACROSS

2. Drug usually administered IV that stops a convulsive seizure.
7. Clonazepam
11. Fibric acid
12. Bacteria that retain only the red stain in a gram stain.
13. Condition in which menstruation no longer occurs.
14. Infection in the blood caused by the yeast Candida.
15. Joint space into which drug is injected.
16. Bisoprolol
17. Suffix denoting the inhibition of, as of microorganisms.

DOWN

1. Drug that prevents mast cells from releasing histamine and other vasoactive substances.
3. Edema and swelling beneath the skin.
4. Low blood glucose level.
5. Simvastatin
6. Protrusion of an organ through the tissue usually containing it.
8. Zonisamide
9. Chemical substance that produces a change in body function.
10. Clonidine
11. A strong sustained muscle contraction.

A. Static	B. Klonopin	C. Menopause	D. Candidemia	E. Hernia
F. Drug	G. Trilipix	H. Antiallergic	I. Tetany	J. Gram Negative
K. Zonegran	L. Catapres	M. Zocor	N. Zebeta	O. Anticonvulsant
P. Intra Articular	Q. Angioedema	R. Hypoglycemia		

24. Using the Across and Down clues, write the correct words in the numbered grid below.

ACROSS

3. Opening in a hollow organ, such as a break in the intestinal wall.
5. Clots that jam a blood vessel; formed by the action of platelets and other coagulation factors in the blood.
8. Drug used to induce and maintain sleep.
9. Neurotransmitter of parasympathetic nerves.
13. Low blood glucose level.
14. Atorvastatin
15. Lovastatin
16. Having normal thyroid gland function.
17. Washing with fluids or flushing of a cavity such as the stomach.
18. Lamotrigine

DOWN

1. Simvastatin
2. Ability of a substance to produce many different biological responses.
4. A thick-walled structure in which parasitic protozoal sex cells develop for transfer to new hosts.
6. A firm, elevated swelling of the skin often pale red in color and itchy; a sign of allergy.
7. Torsemide
10. An element similar to sodium that is used in the treatment of mania and bipolar mood disorder.
11. Nadolol
12. Substance, usually protein or carbohydrate, that is capable of stimulating an immune response.

A. Demadex
B. Zocor
C. Hypnotic
D. Corgard
E. Lamictal
F. Euthyroid
G. Lavage
H. Thromboembolism
I. Lipitor
J. Perforation
K. Lithium
L. Wheal
M. Mevacor
N. Antigen
O. Acetylcholine
P. Hypoglycemia
Q. Oocyst
R. Pluripotent

25. Using the Across and Down clues, write the correct words in the numbered grid below.

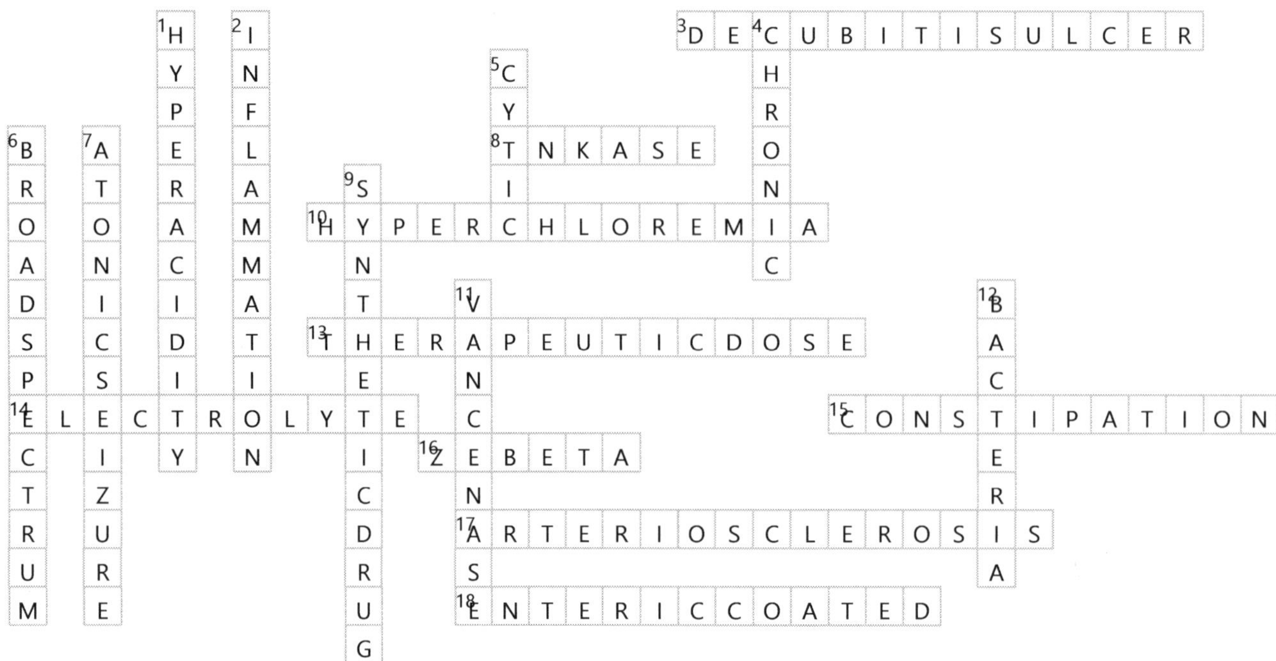

ACROSS

3. Bedsore.
8. Tenecteplase
10. Abnormally high level of chloride ions circulating in the blood.
13. The amount of drug required to produce the desired change in the disease or condition.
14. Ion in solution, such as sodium, potassium, or chloride, that is capable of mediating conduction.
15. A decrease in stool frequency.
16. Bisoprolol
17. Hardening or fibrosis of the arteries; accumulation of fatty deposits in the walls of arteries.
18. Type of tablet or pill with a coating that enables it to pass through the stomach without being dissolved.

DOWN

1. Abnormally high degree of acidity (for example, pH less than 1) in the stomach.
2. Condition in which tissues have been damaged, characterized by swelling, pain, heat, and sometimes
4. Condition of long duration, usually months or years.
5. Suffix meaning cells.
6. Drug that is effective against a wide variety of both gram-positive and gram-negative pathogenic bacteria.
7. Generalized-type seizure characterized by a sudden loss of muscle tone.
9. Drug produced by a chemical process outside the body.
11. Beclomethasone
12. Single-celled microorganisms, some of which cause disease.

A. Hyperacidity	B. Enteric Coated	C. Vancenase	D. Tnkase
E. Hyperchloremia	F. Zebeta	G. Atonic Seizure	H. Decubitis Ulcer
I. Constipation	J. Bacteria	K. Cytic	L. Chronic
M. Therapeutic Dose	N. Broad Spectrum	O. Synthetic Drug	P. Electrolyte
Q. Inflammation	R. Arteriosclerosis		

26. Using the Across and Down clues, write the correct words in the numbered grid below.

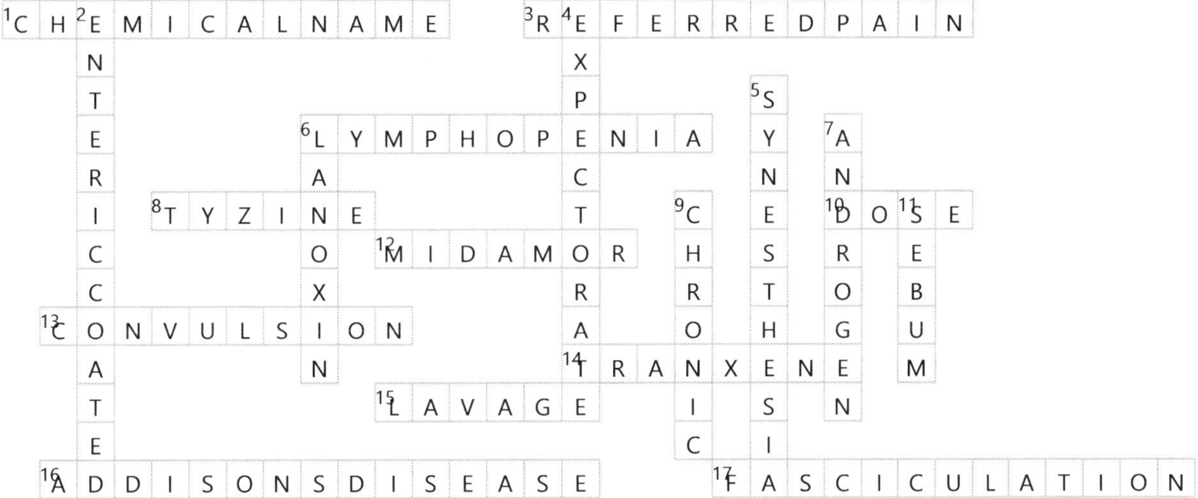

ACROSS

1. Name that defines the chemical composition of a drug.
3. Origin of the pain is in a different location than where the individual feels the pain.
6. Decrease in the number of circulating lymphocytes.
8. Tetrahydrazoline
10. A measurement of the amount of drug that is administered.
12. Amiloride
13. Involuntary muscle contraction that is either tonic or clonic.
14. Clorazepate
15. Washing with fluids or flushing of a cavity such as the stomach.
16. Inadequate secretion of glucocorticoids and mineralocorticoids.
17. Twitchings of muscle fiber groups.

DOWN

2. Type of tablet or pill with a coating that enables it to pass through the stomach without being dissolved.
4. Eject from the mouth; spit.
5. Distortion of sensory perception; usually associated with the use of LSD.
6. Digoxin
7. Male sex hormone responsible for the development of male characteristics.
9. Condition of long duration, usually months or years.
11. A lipid substance secreted by glands in the skin to lubricate the skin everywhere but the palms and soles.

A. Enteric Coated	B. Addisons Disease	C. Lavage	D. Expectorate
E. Androgen	F. Tranxene	G. Fasciculation	H. Tyzine
I. Midamor	J. Referred Pain	K. Convulsion	L. Lymphopenia
M. Lanoxin	N. Chronic	O. Sebum	P. Chemical Name
Q. Synesthesia	R. Dose		

27. Using the Across and Down clues, write the correct words in the numbered grid below.

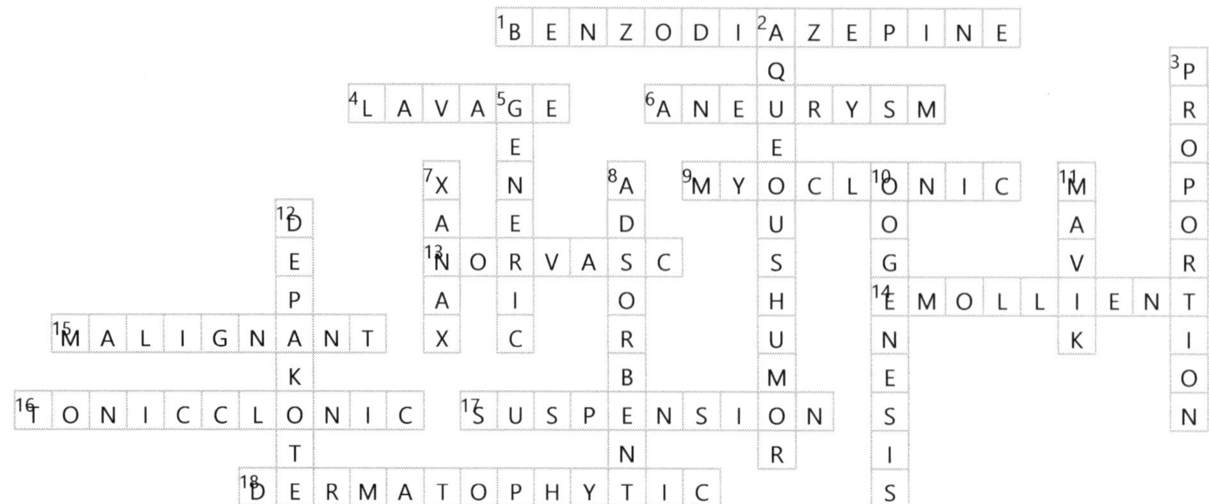

ACROSS

1. Class of drugs used to treat anxiety and sleep disorders.
4. Washing with fluids or flushing of a cavity such as the stomach.
6. An abnormal widening or ballooning of a portion of an artery due to weakness in the wall of the blood vessel.
9. Generalized seizures that are usually brief and often confined to one part of the body.
13. Amlodipine
14. Substance that is soothing to mucous membranes or skin.
15. Life-threatening; refers to growth of a cancerous tumor.
16. Generalized seizure characterized by full body tonic and clonic motor convulsions and loss of consciousness.
17. Preparation in which undissolved solids are dispersed within a liquid.
18. Infection of the skin, hair, or nails caused by a fungus.

DOWN

2. watery substance that is located behind the cornea of the eye and in front of the lens.
3. A mathematical equation that expresses the equality between two ratios.
5. name Nonproprietary name of a drug.
7. Alprazolam
8. Substance that has the ability to attach other substances to its surface.
10. Formation of ova.
11. Trandolapril
12. Sodium valproate

A. Aqueous Humor
B. Emollient
C. Aneurysm
D. Myoclonic
E. Lavage
F. Generic
G. Xanax
H. Depakote
I. Mavik
J. Malignant
K. Adsorbent
L. Suspension
M. Norvasc
N. Oogenesis
O. Dermatophytic
P. Tonic Clonic
Q. Proportion
R. Benzodiazepine

28. Using the Across and Down clues, write the correct words in the numbered grid below.

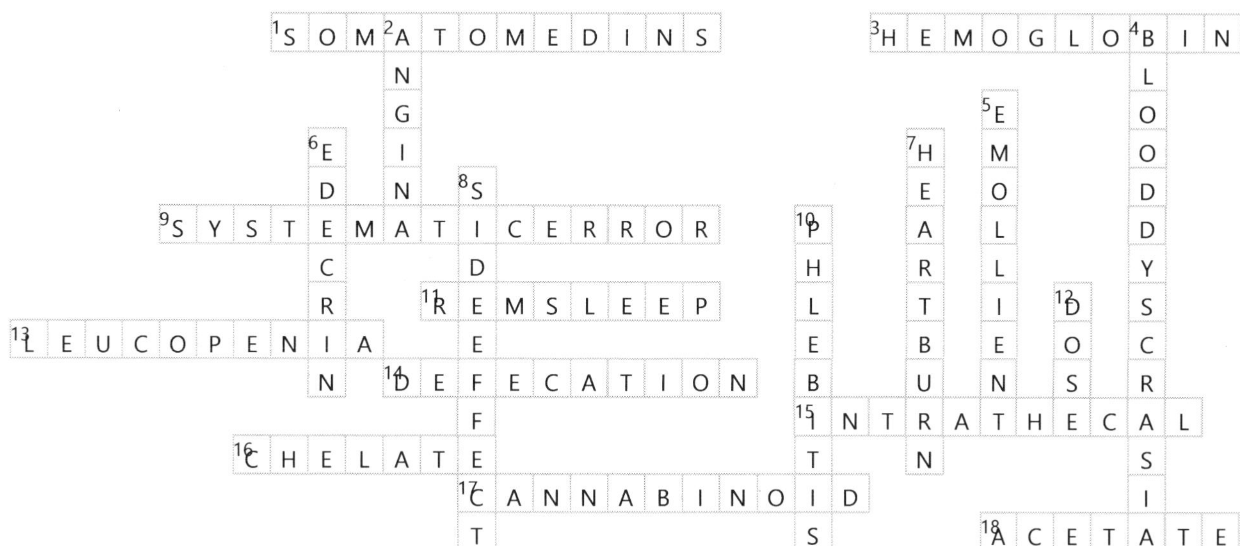

ACROSS

1. Peptides in the plasma that stimulate cellular growth and have insulin-like activity.
3. Protein in red blood cells that transports oxygen to all tissues of the body.
9. Error introduced into a study by its design rather than due to random variation.
11. Stage of sleep characterized by rapid eye movement (REM) and dreaming.
13. An abnormal decrease in the number of circulating white blood cells.
14. Process of discharging the contents of the intestines as feces.
15. Space around the brain and spinal cord that contains the cerebrospinal fluid.
16. Chemical action of a substance to bond permanently to a metal ion.
17. Pharmacologically active substance obtained from the marijuana plant.
18. Compound that contains acetic acid.

DOWN

2. Chest pain or discomfort that occurs when the heart muscle does not get enough blood and oxygen.
4. Abnormality in blood.
5. Substance that is soothing to mucous membranes or skin.
6. Ethacrynic acid
7. A painful burning feeling behind the sternum that occurs when stomach acid backs up into the esophagus.
8. Drug effect other than the therapeutic effect that is usually undesirable but not harmful.
10. Inflammation of a vein.
12. A measurement of the amount of drug that is administered.

A. Acetate	B. Hemoglobin	C. Side Effect	D. Heartburn
E. Somatomedins	F. Angina	G. Defecation	H. Cannabinoid
I. Leucopenia	J. Systematic Error	K. Intrathecal	L. Blood Dyscrasia
M. Edecrin	N. Emollient	O. Dose	P. Rem Sleep
Q. Phlebitis	R. Chelate		

29. Using the Across and Down clues, write the correct words in the numbered grid below.

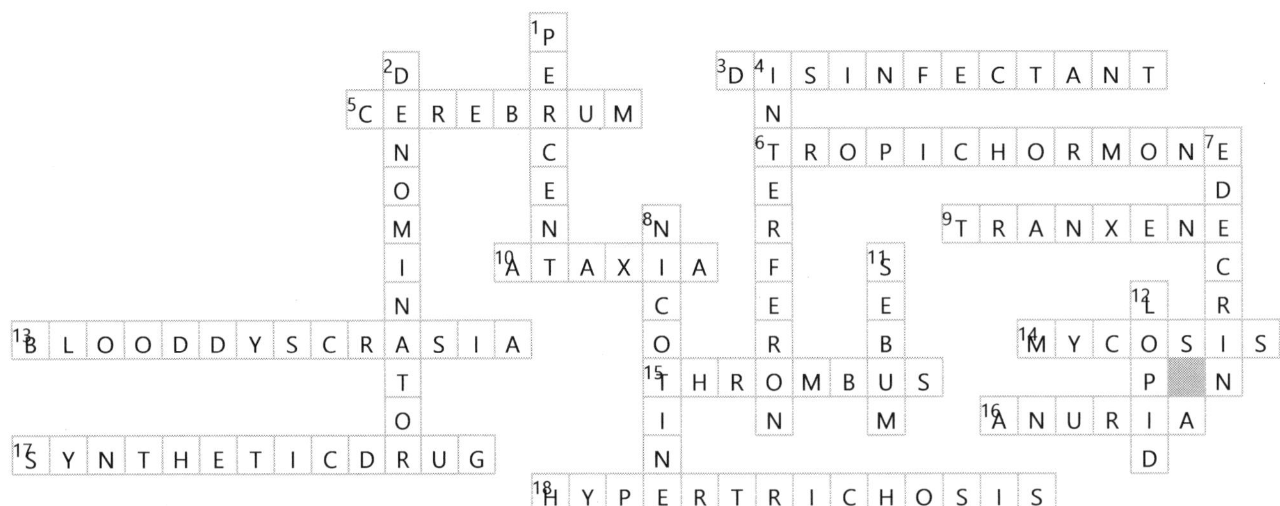

ACROSS

3. Substance that kills disease-causing microorganisms on nonliving surfaces.
5. Largest and uppermost part of the brain that is divided into right and left cerebral hemispheres.
6. Hormone secreted by the anterior pituitary that binds to a receptor on another endocrine gland.
9. Clorazepate
10. Lack of coordination of muscle movements.
13. Abnormality in blood.
14. Any disease caused by a fungus.
15. Clot formed by the action of coagulation factors and circulating blood cells.
16. Condition in which no urine is produced.
17. Drug produced by a chemical process outside the body.
18. Excessive hair growth on the body.

DOWN

1. Decimal fraction with a denominator of 100.
2. Bottom number of a fraction; shows the number of parts in a whole.
4. Chemical mediator produced by immune cells that increases immune function.
7. Ethacrynic acid
8. Alkaloid drug in tobacco that stimulates ganglionic receptors.
11. A lipid substance secreted by glands in the skin to lubricate the skin everywhere but the palms and soles.
12. Gemfibrozil

A. Interferon
B. Percent
C. Denominator
D. Anuria
E. Tranxene
F. Tropic Hormone
G. Blood Dyscrasia
H. Thrombus
I. Mycosis
J. Edecrin
K. Cerebrum
L. Disinfectant
M. Nicotine
N. Lopid
O. Synthetic Drug
P. Ataxia
Q. Hypertrichosis
R. Sebum

30. Using the Across and Down clues, write the correct words in the numbered grid below.

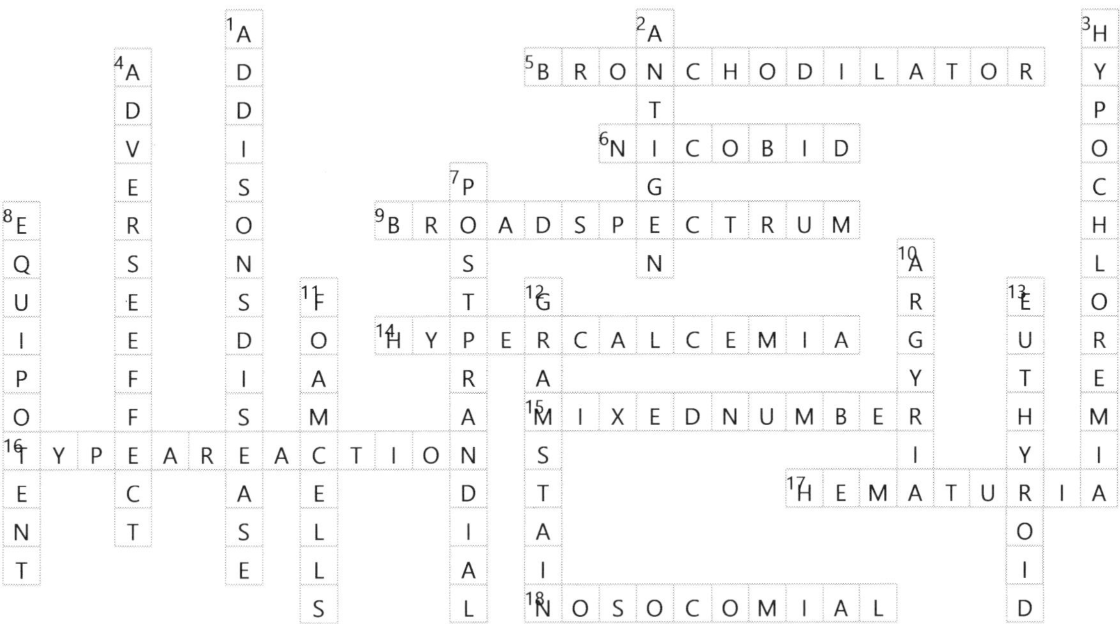

ACROSS

5. Drug that relaxes bronchial smooth muscle and dilates the lower respiratory passages.
6. Nicotinic acid
9. Drug that is effective against a wide variety of both gram-positive and gram-negative pathogenic bacteria.
14. Unusually high concentration of calcium in the blood.
15. Number written with both a whole number and a fraction.
16. Adverse reaction which results from an exaggerated but otherwise usual pharmacological effect.
17. Appearance of blood or red blood cells in the urine.
18. Infection acquired as a result of being in a hospital.

DOWN

1. Inadequate secretion of glucocorticoids and mineralocorticoids.
2. Substance, usually protein or carbohydrate, that is capable of stimulating an immune response.
3. Abnormally low level of chloride ions circulating in the blood.
4. General term for undesirable and potentially harmful drug effect.
7. After a meal.
8. When drugs (substances) produce the same intensity or spectrum of activity.
10. Permanent black discoloration of skin and mucous membranes caused by prolonged use of silver protein.
11. A type of cell formed after macrophages in the artery wall digest LDL cholesterol.
12. Method of staining and identifying bacteria.
13. Having normal thyroid gland function.

A. Mixed Number
E. Bronchodilator
I. Gram Stain
M. Antigen
Q. Euthyroid

B. Argyria
F. Addisons Disease
J. Equipotent
N. Hematuria
R. Adverse Effect

C. Hypercalcemia
G. Nicobid
K. Nosocomial
O. Hypochloremia

D. Broad Spectrum
H. Postprandial
L. Type A Reaction
P. Foam Cells

Multiple Choice

From the words provided for each clue, provide the letter of the word which best matches the clue.

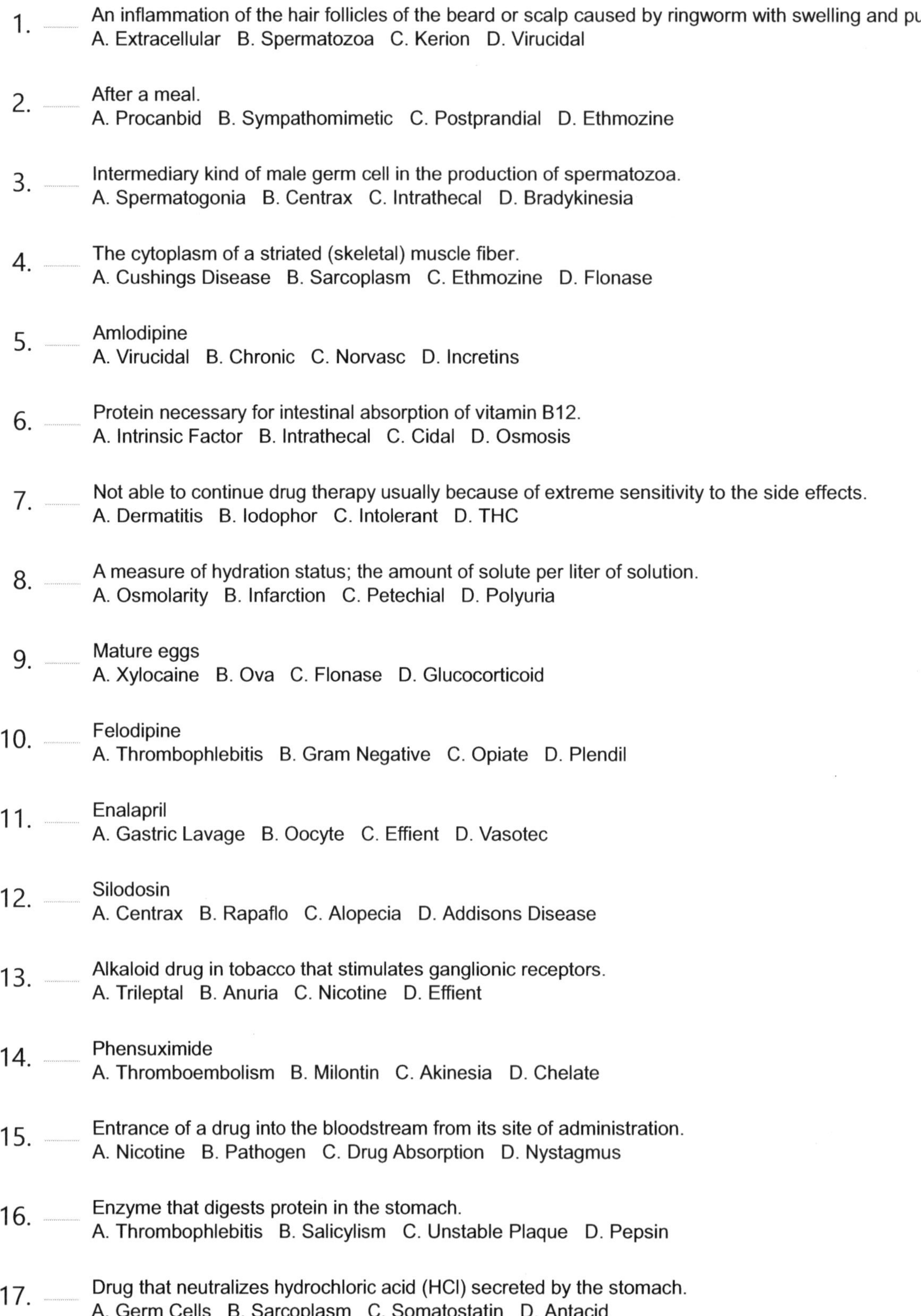

1. ______ An inflammation of the hair follicles of the beard or scalp caused by ringworm with swelling and pus.
   A. Extracellular B. Spermatozoa C. Kerion D. Virucidal

2. ______ After a meal.
   A. Procanbid B. Sympathomimetic C. Postprandial D. Ethmozine

3. ______ Intermediary kind of male germ cell in the production of spermatozoa.
   A. Spermatogonia B. Centrax C. Intrathecal D. Bradykinesia

4. ______ The cytoplasm of a striated (skeletal) muscle fiber.
   A. Cushings Disease B. Sarcoplasm C. Ethmozine D. Flonase

5. ______ Amlodipine
   A. Virucidal B. Chronic C. Norvasc D. Incretins

6. ______ Protein necessary for intestinal absorption of vitamin B12.
   A. Intrinsic Factor B. Intrathecal C. Cidal D. Osmosis

7. ______ Not able to continue drug therapy usually because of extreme sensitivity to the side effects.
   A. Dermatitis B. Iodophor C. Intolerant D. THC

8. ______ A measure of hydration status; the amount of solute per liter of solution.
   A. Osmolarity B. Infarction C. Petechial D. Polyuria

9. ______ Mature eggs
   A. Xylocaine B. Ova C. Flonase D. Glucocorticoid

10. ______ Felodipine
    A. Thrombophlebitis B. Gram Negative C. Opiate D. Plendil

11. ______ Enalapril
    A. Gastric Lavage B. Oocyte C. Effient D. Vasotec

12. ______ Silodosin
    A. Centrax B. Rapaflo C. Alopecia D. Addisons Disease

13. ______ Alkaloid drug in tobacco that stimulates ganglionic receptors.
    A. Trileptal B. Anuria C. Nicotine D. Effient

14. ______ Phensuximide
    A. Thromboembolism B. Milontin C. Akinesia D. Chelate

15. ______ Entrance of a drug into the bloodstream from its site of administration.
    A. Nicotine B. Pathogen C. Drug Absorption D. Nystagmus

16. ______ Enzyme that digests protein in the stomach.
    A. Thrombophlebitis B. Salicylism C. Unstable Plaque D. Pepsin

17. ______ Drug that neutralizes hydrochloric acid (HCl) secreted by the stomach.
    A. Germ Cells B. Sarcoplasm C. Somatostatin D. Antacid

18. .... Substance, chemical solution, or drug that kills viruses.
A. Virucidal B. Intrathecal C. Xylocaine D. Procanbid

19. .... Bedsore.
A. Decubitis Ulcer B. Determinant C. Oogenesis D. Hypnotic

20. .... Absorption of drug through the mucous membranes lining the oral cavity.
A. Intra Articular B. Infarction C. Polypeptide D. Buccal Absorption

21. .... Substance, chemical solution, or drug that kills microorganisms.
A. Addisons Disease B. Germ Cells C. Lipitor D. Germicidal

22. .... Origin of the pain is in a different location than where the individual feels the pain.
A. Referred Pain B. Emesis C. Parietal Cell D. Lotensin

23. .... Rapid involuntary movement of eyes.
A. Tonic B. Penicillinase C. Rigidity D. Nystagmus

24. .... Substance that induces abortion.
A. Lactation B. Barbital C. Intolerant D. Abortifacient

25. .... Phenytoin
A. Dilantin B. Mixed Number C. Synesthesia D. Type B Reaction

26. .... watery substance that is located behind the cornea of the eye and in front of the lens.
A. Ambien B. Sarcoplasm C. Aqueous Humor D. Chromic

27. .... Flushing of the stomach.
A. Type B Reaction B. Pepsin C. Constipation D. Gastric Lavage

28. .... A group of gastrointestinal hormones that increase the amount of insulin released.
A. Nitrostat B. Ambien C. Incretins D. Afrin

29. .... Atorvastatin
A. Extracellular B. Chelate C. Lipitor D. Ascites

30. .... Excessive urine production; increased urination.
A. Librium B. Keratinized C. Thrombophlebitis D. Polyuria

31. .... Pain resulting from a damaged nervous system or damaged nerve cells.
A. Vasotec B. Osmolarity C. Neuropathic Pain D. Benzodiazepine

32. .... A mathematical equation that expresses the equality between two ratios.
A. Flonase B. Nystagmus C. Proportion D. THC

33. .... Excess fluid in the space between the tissues lining the abdomen and abdominal organs.
A. Akinesia B. Atonic Seizure C. Ascites D. Decubitis Ulcer

34. .... Condition in which there is no outward evidence (symptom) that an infection is present.
A. Somatostatin B. Asymptomatic C. Polydipsia D. Mysoline

35. .... Verapamil
A. Calan B. Infarction C. Bradykinesia D. Benzodiazepine

36. .... Increased blood flow to a body part like the eye; engorgement.
A. Synesthesia B. Naphcon C. Hyperemia D. Dermatitis

37. .... Slowed body movements.
A. Dyspepsia B. Cerebellum C. Polyuria D. Bradykinesia

38. .... A painful open sore in the mouth or upper throat; also known as a canker sore.
A. Aphthous Ulcer B. Dyspepsia C. Barbital D. Naphcon

39. .... Responsible for bone resorption by binding to bone matrix proteins and releasing enzymes to break down bone.
A. Vasotec B. Somatostatin C. Afrin D. Osteoclasts

40. .... Ethosuximide
A. Gram Stain B. Diplopia C. Intrathecal D. Zarontin

41. .... Enables another hormone to fully function.
A. Permissive B. Dermatitis C. Pravachol D. Potency

42. .... Hormone synthesized and released by the thyroid gland.
A. Chelate B. Geriatrics C. Thyroxine D. Dermatitis

43. .... Substance dissolved in a solvent; usually present in a lesser amount.
A. Immunomodulation B. Osteoclasts C. Lipitor D. Solute

44. .... Drug derived from opium and producing the same pharmacological effects as opium.
A. Tenex B. Static C. Opiate D. Hypophosphatemia

45. .... Oxcarbamazepine
A. Lysosome B. Trileptal C. Hypertension D. Circadian Rhythm

46. .... Hormone released from adrenal cortex that causes the retention of sodium from the kidneys.
A. Hypotonic B. Geriatrics C. Aldosterone D. Gram Negative

47. .... Number written with both a whole number and a fraction.
A. Gastric Lavage B. Mixed Number C. Hyperemia D. Cardiac Output

48. .... Increase in muscle tone or contractions causing faster clearance of substances through the GI tract.
A. Hypermotility B. Infarction C. Gram Negative D. Ecotrin

49. .... Clopidogrel
A. Plavix B. Hemolytic Anemia C. Mitochondria D. Tonic

50. .... Any disease caused by a fungus.
A. Rigidity B. Mycosis C. Lipitor D. Procanbid

51. .... Fluticasone
A. Flonase B. Hyperchlorhydria C. Apoptosis D. Endorphins

52. .... The amount of blood pumped per minute by the heart.
A. Cardiac Output B. Circadian Rhythm C. Ascites D. Polypeptide

53. .... Opening in a hollow organ, such as a break in the intestinal wall.
A. Extracellular B. Perforation C. Dyspepsia D. Static

54. ______ Naphazoline
A. Convulsion B. Naphcon C. Mitochondria D. Analgesia

55. ______ Chemical substance that produces a change in body function.
A. Drug B. Mitosis C. Iodophor D. Fraction

56. ______ Undesirable interaction of drugs not suitable for combination or administration together.
A. Constipation B. Carcinogenic C. Incompatibility D. Sarcoplasm

57. ______ Molecule that contains purine or pyrimidine bases in combination with sugar.
A. Glycogenolysis B. Hypertension C. Nucleoside D. Fungicidal

58. ______ Feeling of well-being or elation; feeling good.
A. Ethmozine B. Euphoria C. Hypertension D. Oocyte

59. ______ Inadequate secretion of glucocorticoids and mineralocorticoids.
A. Addisons Disease B. Extracellular C. Antagonist D. Virucidal

60. ______ Oxymetazoline
A. Afrin B. Osmolarity C. Potency D. Fungicidal

61. ______ Tightening or contraction of muscles in the blood vessels, which decreases blood flow through the vessels.
A. Diuril B. Designer Drug C. Vasoconstriction D. Trileptal

62. ______ Involuntary muscle contraction that is either tonic or clonic.
A. Oocyte B. Diuresis C. Drug D. Convulsion

63. ______ Levetiracetam
A. Incompatibility B. Chromic C. Keppra D. Addisons Disease

64. ______ Mature sperm cells.
A. Aphthous Ulcer B. Pravachol C. Spermatozoa D. Hyperchlorhydria

65. ______ Condition in which no urine is produced.
A. Native B. Lipitor C. Static D. Anuria

66. ______ Adverse reaction which is aberrant, and may be due to hypersensitivity or immunologic reactions.
A. Dyspepsia B. Synesthesia C. Carcinogenic D. Type B Reaction

67. ______ Active ingredient of the marijuana plant.
A. Ecotrin B. THC C. Receptor D. Ticlid

68. ______ Refers to the action of an adrenergic drug or an action that increases sympathetic activity.
A. Constipation B. Sympathomimetic C. Depakote D. Norepinephrine

69. ______ A type of cell formed after macrophages in the artery wall digest LDL cholesterol.
A. Hypoxia B. Polypeptide C. Solute D. Foam Cells

70. ______ Condition that causes urine to be excreted; usually associated with large volumes of urine.
A. Diuresis B. Apoptosis C. Malaria D. Spermatogonia

71. ______ Refers to nerves of the ANS that originate from the thoracolumbar portion of the spinal cord.
A. Sympathetic B. Glucocorticoid C. Endorphins D. Osmolarity

72. ______ A substance capable of producing an allergic reaction.
A. Keratinized B. Native C. Allergen D. Rigidity

73. ______ Neuropeptides produced within the CNS that interact with opioid receptors to produce analgesia.
A. Endorphins B. THC C. Capoten D. Analgesia

74. ______ Drug used to induce and maintain sleep.
A. Hypnotic B. Hypotonic C. Iodophor D. Plendil

75. ______ Substance, usually large, composed of an indefinite number of amino acids.
A. Vasotec B. Cidal C. Polypeptide D. Constipation

76. ______ Plaque formed in the artery wall that can break away and obstruct blood flow or form a clot.
A. Pravachol B. Oxyntic Cell C. Incompatibility D. Unstable Plaque

77. ______ Cell division in which two daughter cells receive the same number of chromosomes as the parent cell.
A. Decubitis Ulcer B. Mitosis C. Osmosis D. Gram Stain

78. ______ Disease of severe symptoms, which could be fatal if left untreated.
A. Pernicious B. Fraction C. Benzodiazepine D. Immunomodulation

79. ______ Convulsive muscle contraction characterized by sustained muscular contractions.
A. Aqueous Humor B. Tonic C. Dystonia D. Drug Absorption

80. ______ The presence of the plasma protein albumin in the urine.
A. Albuminuria B. Ecotrin C. Somatostatin D. Spermatogonia

81. ______ Method of staining and identifying bacteria.
A. Unstable Plaque B. Plavix C. Gram Stain D. Oxytocin

82. ______ Condition of long duration, usually months or years.
A. Hypophosphatemia B. Thrombophlebitis C. Chronic D. Circadian Rhythm

83. ______ Baldness or hair loss.
A. Alopecia B. Spermatozoa C. Foam Cells D. Barbital

84. ______ Measure of the strength, or concentration, of a drug required to produce a specific effect.
A. Germicidal B. Postprandial C. Apoptosis D. Potency

85. ______ Refers to venous return, the amount of blood returning to the heart that must be pumped.
A. Preload B. Nitrostat C. Referred Pain D. Sympathomimetic

86. ______ Chlorothiazide
A. Nystagmus B. Decubitis Ulcer C. Plendil D. Diuril

87. ______ A decrease in stool frequency.
A. Hemolytic Anemia B. Spermatogonia C. Constipation D. Keratinized

88. ______ Medical specialty that deals with individuals over 65 years of age.
A. Plendil B. Geriatrics C. Antagonist D. Sympathomimetic

89. ______ Lidocaine
A. Androgen B. Hemolytic Anemia C. Albuminuria D. Xylocaine

90. ______ Abnormally high degree of acidity (for example, pH less than 1) in the stomach.
A. Hyperacidity B. Ova C. Naphcon D. Neuropathic Pain

91. ______ Area of tissue that has died because of a sudden lack of blood supply.
A. Cidal B. Zaroxolyn C. Infarction D. Hypophosphatemia

92. ______ Normal salt concentration of most body fluids; a salt concentration of 0.9 percent.
A. Preload B. Geriatrics C. Isotonic D. Ecotrin

93. ______ Joint space into which drug is injected.
A. Pathogen B. Addisons Disease C. Intra Articular D. Chronic

94. ______ Defective metabolism of fat.
A. Drug B. Akinesia C. Lipodystrophy D. Bradykinesia

95. ______ Abnormally high blood pressure.
A. Extracellular B. Designer Drug C. Unstable Plaque D. Hypertension

96. ______ Studies with control groups, namely case-control studies, cohort studies, and randomized clinical trials.
A. Osmosis B. Determinant C. Analytic Studies D. Kerion

97. ______ Chlordiazepoxide
A. Mitochondria B. Naphcon C. Librium D. Iodophor

98. ______ Area outside the cell.
A. Glycogenolysis B. Extracellular C. Pepsin D. Rapaflo

99. ______ Mental state characterized by depressed mood, with feelings of frustration and hopelessness.
A. Depression B. Chromic C. Mixed Number D. Geriatrics

100. ______ Class of drugs used to treat anxiety and sleep disorders.
A. Benzodiazepine B. Plendil C. Thromboembolism D. Cerebellum

From the words provided for each clue, provide the letter of the word which best matches the clue.

101. ______ A group of microorganisms with a membrane-bound nucleus that includes yeasts and molds.
A. Fungus B. Hyperstat C. Edecrin D. Vancenase

102. ______ Nicardipine
A. Cardene B. Hyperstat C. Somatotropin D. Allergen

103. ______ Permanent black discoloration of skin and mucous membranes caused by prolonged use of silver protein.
A. Cardiac Glycoside B. Argyria C. Rhinocort D. Cholelithiasis

104. ______ Drug usually administered IV that stops a convulsive seizure.
A. Anticonvulsant B. Triglyceride C. Topamax D. Candidiasis

105. ______ Candesartan
A. Ambien B. Vasoconstriction C. Atacand D. Oligospermia

106. ______ High levels of insulin in the blood often associated with type 2 diabetes mellitus and insulin resistance.
A. Homeostasis B. Hyperinsulinemia C. Euphoria D. Spermatogenesis

107. .... Chlordiazepoxide
A. Myocardium B. Lotensin C. Librium D. Hematinic

108. .... Formation of spermatozoa.
A. Sympathetic B. Digitalization C. Ulcerogenic D. Spermatogenesis

109. .... Prefix meaning small.
A. Micro B. Expectorant C. Homeostasis D. Lanoxin

110. .... Muscle spasms, facial grimacing, and other involuntary movements and postures.
A. Opiate B. Dystonia C. Somatotropin D. Antipyresis

111. .... Atorvastatin
A. Emetogenic B. Argyria C. Lipitor D. Mysoline

112. .... Digoxin
A. Lotensin B. Micro C. Cardene D. Lanoxin

113. .... Specific cellular structure that a drug binds to and that produces a physiologic effect.
A. Micro B. Receptor C. Convulsion D. Bias

114. .... Action that causes the decomposition or destruction of proteins.
A. Evacuation B. Pharmacology C. Alopecia D. Proteolytic

115. .... Protein necessary for intestinal absorption of vitamin B12.
A. Intrinsic Factor B. Candidemia C. Hyperinsulinemia D. Lipitor

116. .... Study of drugs.
A. Hypertrichosis B. Antagonistic C. Myocardium D. Pharmacology

117. .... Indigestion.
A. Dyspepsia B. Electrolyte C. Cardiac Glycoside D. Analytic Studies

118. .... Suffix denoting the inhibition of, as of microorganisms.
A. Automatism B. Tetany C. Spermatogenesis D. Static

119. .... Amrinone
A. Acidification B. Cardene C. Tyzine D. Inocor

120. .... The muscular layer of the heart.
A. Cardiac Glycoside B. Vasoconstriction C. Anticonvulsant D. Myocardium

121. .... Disease of the muscles.
A. Remission B. Myopathy C. Morphology D. Bias

122. .... Elimination of the drug from the body.
A. Repolarization B. Drug Excretion C. Osmoreceptors D. Chemical Name

123. .... Generalized seizure that does not involve motor convulsions; also referred to as petit mal.
A. Remission B. Normodyne C. Absence Seizure D. Intrathecal

124. .... Reduced sperm count.
A. Menopause B. Drug Dependence C. Oligospermia D. Solute

125. .... Bacterial enzymes that inactivate penicillin antibiotics.
A. Penicillinase B. Somatotropin C. Automatism D. Analytic Studies

126. .... Disease that involves the development and reproduction of abnormal cells.
A. Cancer B. Antipyresis C. Edema D. Emetogenic

127. .... Plaque formed in the artery wall that remains in the wall.
A. Drug Dependence B. Absence Seizure C. Stable Plaque D. Postpartum

128. .... Flushing of the stomach.
A. Immunity B. Gastric Lavage C. Remission D. Thrombophlebitis

129. .... Name that defines the chemical composition of a drug.
A. Chemical Name B. Basal Ganglia C. Lipodystrophy D. Mucolytic

130. .... Milrinone
A. Euthyroid B. Myocardium C. Intrathecal D. Primacor

131. .... A fat formed by three fatty acids into one molecule that supplies energy to muscle cells.
A. Triglyceride B. Depakene C. Thrombophlebitis D. Prosom

132. .... Excessive hair growth on the body.
A. Allergen B. Bone Mass C. Digitalization D. Hypertrichosis

133. .... Substance that is soothing to mucous membranes or skin.
A. Evacuation B. Emollient C. Acidification D. Myocardium

134. .... Tightening or contraction of muscles in the blood vessels, which decreases blood flow through the vessels.
A. Vasoconstriction B. Euphoria C. Keppra D. Atacand

135. .... Lack of coordination of muscle movements.
A. Ataxia B. Gabitril C. Rem Sleep D. Oogenesis

136. .... Pertaining to glands that secrete substances directly into the blood.
A. Endocrine B. Postpartum C. Dyspepsia D. Glycogen

137. .... Azelastine
A. Topamax B. Cholelithiasis C. Hyperemia D. Astelin

138. .... Prefix meaning large.
A. Allergen B. Cytic C. Micro D. Mega

139. .... CNS depressant drug possessing the barbituric acid ring structure.
A. Barbiturate B. Osmoreceptors C. Intrathecal D. Hematinic

140. .... Counteract; oppose.
A. Hyperglycemia B. Antagonistic C. Evacuation D. Hypertrichosis

141. .... Drug-induced confusion that can cause increased drug consumption.
A. Automatism B. Incretins C. Emetogenic D. Dermatophytic

142. .... Ticlopidine
A. Basal Ganglia B. Ticlid C. Librium D. Proteolytic

143. .... A substance secreted by T cells that signals other immune cells like macrophages to aggregate.
A. Dermatophytic B. Lymphokine C. Dynacirc D. Myopathy

144. .... Diazoxide
A. Solute B. Hyperstat C. Evacuation D. Tetany

145. .... Drug obtained from plants of the genus Digitalis.
A. Cardiac Glycoside B. Analytic Studies C. Persantine D. Ulcerogenic

146. .... Antibacterial drug obtained from other microorganisms.
A. Evacuation B. Antibiotic C. Convulsion D. Drug Excretion

147. .... Benazepril
A. Lavage B. Synaptic Knob C. Lotensin D. Pepsin

148. .... Studies with control groups, namely case-control studies, cohort studies, and randomized clinical trials.
A. Cutaneous B. Analytic Studies C. Thrombophlebitis D. Mega

149. .... Part of the brain that coordinates body movements and posture and helps maintain body equilibrium.
A. Convulsion B. Cerebellum C. Stable Plaque D. Mucolytic

150. .... An inflammation of the hair follicles of the beard or scalp caused by ringworm with swelling and pus.
A. Kerion B. Somatotropin C. Opiate D. Keppra

151. .... Having the ability to cause mutations.
A. Dermatophytic B. Rem Sleep C. Mutagenic D. Selective

152. .... Ethacrynic acid
A. Ovulation B. Cushings Disease C. Proarrhythmia D. Edecrin

153. .... Doxazosin
A. Depakene B. Cardura C. Limbic System D. Isotonic

154. .... Partially digested food and gastric secretions that moves into the duodenum from the stomach by peristalsis.
A. Selective B. Antibiotic C. Chelate D. Chime

155. .... Alprazolam
A. Xanax B. Postpartum C. Prostaglandin D. Electrolyte

156. .... Infection caused by the yeast Candida; also known as moniliasis.
A. Candidiasis B. Repolarization C. Bias D. Tyzine

157. .... Any disease caused by a fungus.
A. Spasmogenic B. Hernia C. Mycosis D. Tonic

158. .... Indapamide
A. Lozol B. Cancer C. Stroke Volume D. Angina

159. .... Flecainide
A. Tambocor B. Expectorant C. Mysoline D. Automatism

160. .... Homogeneous mixture of two or more substances.
A. Ambien B. Solution C. Cardura D. Gabitril

161. ______ Higher than normal level of glucose in the blood.
A. Antipyresis B. Hyperglycemia C. Restoril D. Digitalization

162. ______ Condition that causes individuals to resist acquiring or developing a disease or infection.
A. Halcion B. Immunity C. Solute D. Lozol

163. ______ Ion in solution, such as sodium, potassium, or chloride, that is capable of mediating conduction.
A. Lavage B. Electrolyte C. Argyria D. Allergen

164. ______ The storage form of glucose in humans and animals.
A. Glycogen B. Euphoria C. Cushings Disease D. Pharmacology

165. ______ Stage of sleep characterized by rapid eye movement (REM) and dreaming.
A. Rem Sleep B. Heart Rate C. Argyria D. Analytic Studies

166. ______ Normal state of balance among the body's internal organs.
A. Homeostasis B. Ulcerogenic C. Lipitor D. Gabitril

167. ______ Specialized cells in the hypothalamus that respond to changes in sodium concentration in the blood.
A. Synthetic Drug B. Cardura C. Osmoreceptors D. Astelin

168. ______ Inference tending to produce results that depart systematically from the true values.
A. Bias B. Lightheadedness C. Sterilization D. Oxytocin

169. ______ A substance that causes vomiting.
A. Mucolytic B. Tetany C. Emetogenic D. Seizure

170. ______ Refers to the action of an adrenergic blocking drug or an action that decreases sympathetic activity.
A. Sympatholytic B. Gabitril C. Postpartum D. Solute

171. ______ Beclomethasone
A. Vancenase B. Morphology C. Psychosis D. Lotensin

172. ______ Origin of the pain is in a different location than where the individual feels the pain.
A. Edecrin B. Incretins C. Referred Pain D. Minipress

173. ______ Increased blood flow to a body part like the eye; engorgement.
A. Cardene B. Hyperemia C. Cancer D. Ticlid

174. ______ Substance dissolved in a solvent; usually present in a lesser amount.
A. Ratio B. Cerebellum C. Alopecia D. Solute

175. ______ The relationship of one number to another expressed by whole numbers.
A. Intoxication B. Ratio C. Hyperinsulinemia D. Mysoline

176. ______ Can stimulate uterine and intestinal muscle contractions and may cause pain by stimulating nerve endings.
A. Prostaglandin B. Keppra C. Tambocor D. Afferent Nerve

177. ______ Valproic
A. Renin B. Basal Ganglia C. Depakene D. Lipitor

178. ______ Refers to nerves of the ANS that originate from the thoracolumbar portion of the spinal cord.
A. Limbic System B. Sympathetic C. Atacand D. Spermatogenesis

179. .... Nitroglycerine
A. Fungus B. Sympatholytic C. Nitrostat D. Postpartum

180. .... Condition associated with an increased production of ketone bodies as a result of fat metabolism.
A. Ketosis B. Argyria C. Inflammation D. Convulsion

181. .... Condition of long duration, usually months or years.
A. Intrathecal B. Evacuation C. Mycosis D. Chronic

182. .... Excess secretion of adenocorticotropic hormone (ACTH).
A. Cancer B. Cushings Disease C. Cathartic D. Topamax

183. .... Insufficient blood supply to meet the needs of the tissue or organ.
A. Ischemia B. Dyspepsia C. Minipress D. Ketosis

184. .... Fibric acid
A. Oxytocin B. Morphology C. Adipose Tissue D. Trilipix

185. .... Return of the electric potential across a cell membrane to its resting state following depolarization.
A. Tyzine B. Chelate C. Stroke Volume D. Repolarization

186. .... An excessive accumulation of fluid in body tissues.
A. Edema B. Inocor C. Miotic D. Lanoxin

187. .... A substance that causes constriction of the pupil or miosis.
A. Miotic B. Baycol C. Cerebellum D. Candidiasis

188. .... Suffix meaning cells.
A. Cytic B. Oligospermia C. Pharmacodynamics D. Microcilia

189. .... Clopidogrel
A. Stroke Volume B. Plavix C. Candidemia D. Schizophrenia

190. .... Tamsulosin
A. Vasoconstriction B. Flomax C. Analytic Studies D. Emollient

191. .... Estazolam
A. Penicillinase B. Tonic C. Renin D. Prosom

192. .... Diltiazem
A. Convulsion B. Cushings Disease C. Cardizem D. Prostaglandin

193. .... An arrhythmia caused by administration of an antiarrhythmic drug.
A. Cardene B. Proarrhythmia C. Mega D. Absence Seizure

194. .... Isradipine
A. Dynacirc B. Sympatholytic C. Antagonistic D. Chronic

195. .... Prazosin
A. Somatotropin B. Adipose Tissue C. Minipress D. Gabitril

196. .... Decimal fraction with a denominator of 100.
A. Evacuation B. Basal Ganglia C. Dermatophytic D. Percent

197. ____ Levetiracetam
A. Fungicidal B. Cerebellum C. Stable Plaque D. Keppra

198. ____ Medications containing iron compounds, used to increase hemoglobin production.
A. Remission B. Primacor C. Hematinic D. Lunesta

199. ____ Temazepam
A. Afferent Nerve B. Sympathetic C. Restoril D. Antihistaminic

200. ____ After childbirth.
A. Hematinic B. Mycosis C. Postpartum D. Antihistaminic

From the words provided for each clue, provide the letter of the word which best matches the clue.

201. ____ Any disease caused by a fungus.
A. Lymphopenia B. Antagonist C. Hypertrichosis D. Mycosis

202. ____ CNS depressant drug possessing the barbituric acid ring structure.
A. Lyse B. Pressor C. Hyperstat D. Barbiturate

203. ____ Inflammation of the joints.
A. Vascor B. Myalgia C. Trilipix D. Arthritis

204. ____ Beclomethasone
A. Beconase B. Leukotrienes C. Vascor D. Seizure

205. ____ An inflammation of the hair follicles of the beard or scalp caused by ringworm with swelling and pus.
A. Automatism B. Cholelithiasis C. Potency D. Kerion

206. ____ Measure of the strength, or concentration, of a drug required to produce a specific effect.
A. Cordarone B. Corgard C. Argyria D. Potency

207. ____ Diazoxide
A. Hyperstat B. Mycosis C. Atonic Seizure D. Aldomet

208. ____ Methsuximide
A. Celontin B. Pharmacology C. Sympatholytic D. Polyuria

209. ____ Nadolol
A. Anion B. Micro C. Intrathecal D. Corgard

210. ____ Chemical action of a substance to bond permanently to a metal ion.
A. Argyria B. Chelate C. Xylocaine D. Fungus

211. ____ Life-threatening; refers to growth of a cancerous tumor.
A. Corgard B. Defecation C. Diuril D. Malignant

212. ____ Negatively charged ion.
A. Limbic System B. Activase C. Salicylism D. Anion

213. ____ Pain resulting from a damaged nervous system or damaged nerve cells.
A. Depression B. Atonic Seizure C. Aphthous Ulcer D. Neuropathic Pain

214. ...... Protein in red blood cells that transports oxygen to all tissues of the body.
A. Hemoglobin B. Erythropoiesis C. Candidemia D. Norpace

215. ...... Space around the brain and spinal cord that contains the cerebrospinal fluid.
A. Virucidal B. Vasoconstriction C. Intrathecal D. Malignant

216. ...... The cytoplasm of a striated (skeletal) muscle fiber.
A. Sarcoplasm B. Micro C. Lotensin D. Beconase

217. ...... An abnormal decrease in the number of circulating white blood cells.
A. Leucopenia B. Kerion C. Lipoprotein D. Candidemia

218. ...... Fibric acid
A. Ovulation B. Trilipix C. Monopril D. Diuril

219. ...... Benazepril
A. Micro B. Lotensin C. Nephritis D. Otrivin

220. ...... A fungus infection of the nail.
A. Ulcer B. Onychomycosis C. Emphysema D. Percent

221. ...... Hormone synthesized and released by the thyroid gland.
A. Thyroxine B. Triglyceride C. Trilipix D. Ativan

222. ...... Mental state of excitement, hyperactivity, and excessive elevation of mood.
A. Mania B. Hemoglobin C. Isotonic D. Leucopenia

223. ...... Slowed body movements.
A. Bradykinesia B. Petechial C. Insulin D. Tambocor

224. ...... Tending to cause inflammation.
A. Proinflammatory B. Myalgia C. Iodophor D. Barbiturate

225. ...... Drug that attaches to a receptor, does not initiate an action, but blocks an agonist from producing an effect.
A. Vasoconstriction B. Antagonist C. Valium D. Xylocaine

226. ...... Felodipine
A. Thrombocytopenia B. Hypertrichosis C. Sterilization D. Plendil

227. ...... Decrease in the number of circulating lymphocytes.
A. Norepinephrine B. Lymphopenia C. Nephritis D. Oxyntic Cell

228. ...... A fat formed by three fatty acids into one molecule that supplies energy to muscle cells.
A. Triglyceride B. Candidemia C. Lymphopenia D. Vasoconstriction

229. ...... Drug effect other than the therapeutic effect that is usually undesirable but not harmful.
A. Side Effect B. Arteriosclerosis C. Depression D. Alkylation

230. ...... Undesirable drug effect that implies drug poisoning; can be very harmful or life-threatening.
A. Toxic Effect B. Defecation C. Malignant D. Dysentery

231. ...... A stiffness and inflexibility of movement.
A. Rigidity B. THC C. Cardene D. Mycosis

232. .... A thin membrane enclosing a striated (skeletal) muscle fiber.
A. Phlegm B. Sarcolemma C. Oligospermia D. Erythropoiesis

233. .... Indapamide
A. Depression B. Iodophor C. Synergistic D. Lozol

234. .... Process of discharging the contents of the intestines as feces.
A. Defecation B. Edecrin C. Ova D. Spasmogenic

235. .... General term for undesirable and potentially harmful drug effect.
A. Endometrium B. Seizure C. Adverse Effect D. Phlegm

236. .... Release of an egg from the ovary.
A. Homeostasis B. Ovulation C. Bradykinesia D. Phlegm

237. .... Condition in which toxic doses of salicylates are ingested, resulting in nausea, tinnitus, and delirium.
A. Celontin B. Insomnia C. Salicylism D. Bronchodilator

238. .... Tamsulosin
A. Dysentery B. Oxytocin C. Xylocaine D. Flomax

239. .... Bacteria that retain only the red stain in a gram stain.
A. Cholelithiasis B. Toxic Effect C. Questran D. Gram Negative

240. .... Carvedilol
A. Coreg B. Cordarone C. Myalgia D. Plendil

241. .... Causing a muscle to contract intermittently, resulting in a state of spasms.
A. Parietal Cell B. Spasmogenic C. Hyperalgesia D. Bradykinesia

242. .... Secretion from the respiratory tract; usually called mucus.
A. Hyperemia B. Lipitor C. Lyse D. Phlegm

243. .... Budesonide
A. Bacteria B. Rhinocort C. Trilipix D. Neutropenia

244. .... Normal state of balance among the body's internal organs.
A. Homeostasis B. Polyphagia C. Kerion D. Hyperemia

245. .... Study of the distribution and determinants of diseases in populations.
A. Keppra B. Epidemiology C. Bacteria D. Drug Compliance

246. .... Reduced sperm count.
A. Anion B. Aphthous Ulcer C. Oligospermia D. Infarction

247. .... Pravastatin
A. Monophasic B. Pravachol C. Fungistatic D. Leucopenia

248. .... Study of drugs.
A. Pharmacology B. Epidemiology C. Parietal Cell D. Lipoprotein

249. .... Protruding eyeballs out of the socket.
A. Vascor B. Exophthalmos C. Laxative D. Apoptosis

250. .... Chlorothiazide
A. Synergistic B. Diuril C. Sectral D. Tambocor

251. .... Gemfibrozil
A. Depakene B. Lopid C. Determinant D. Lozol

252. .... Cholestyramine
A. Laxative B. Tremor C. Questran D. Gram Negative

253. .... Drug obtained from plants of the genus Digitalis.
A. Zestril B. Preload C. Cardiac Glycoside D. Rem Sleep

254. .... Prefix meaning large.
A. Mega B. Dynacirc C. Iodophor D. Exophthalmos

255. .... To disintegrate or dissolve.
A. Sectral B. Lyse C. Minipress D. Hematuria

256. .... Not able to continue drug therapy usually because of extreme sensitivity to the side effects.
A. Bioavailability B. Intolerant C. Addisons Disease D. Tremor

257. .... Hormone released from adrenal cortex that causes the retention of sodium from the kidneys.
A. Aldosterone B. THC C. Rigidity D. Biphasic

258. .... Xylometazoline
A. Rem Sleep B. Mega C. Otrivin D. Cardene

259. .... Prazosin
A. Depakene B. Isotonic C. Lozol D. Minipress

260. .... An abnormal decrease in the number of circulating platelets.
A. Vascor B. Hyponatremia C. Lactation D. Thrombocytopenia

261. .... Refers to the action of an adrenergic blocking drug or an action that decreases sympathetic activity.
A. Proarrhythmia B. Sympatholytic C. Ethmozine D. Oxytocin

262. .... Substance, chemical solution, or drug that kills viruses.
A. Incompatibility B. Virucidal C. Synergistic D. Neuropathic Pain

263. .... Part of the brain that coordinates body movements and posture and helps maintain body equilibrium.
A. Hypophosphatemia B. Cerebellum C. Xylocaine D. Erythropoiesis

264. .... Generalized-type seizure characterized by a sudden loss of muscle tone.
A. Atonic Seizure B. Osteoclasts C. Rem Sleep D. Argyria

265. .... Acebutolol
A. Sectral B. Arthritis C. Determinant D. Sterilization

266. .... Quazepam
A. Homeostasis B. Calorigenic C. Onychomycosis D. Doral

267. .... Adverse reaction which results from an exaggerated but otherwise usual pharmacological effect.
A. Dynacirc B. Type A Reaction C. Dysentery D. Lymphopenia

268. ______ Inflammation of the glomeruli often following a streptococcus infection.
A. Nephritis B. Xylocaine C. Pressor D. Creatinine

269. ______ Production of milk in female breasts.
A. Dyrenium B. Laxative C. Gastric Lavage D. Lactation

270. ______ Cell death, due to either programmed cell death or other physiological events.
A. Decimal B. Hemolytic Anemia C. Apoptosis D. Edecrin

271. ______ The uptake of nutrients and drugs from the GI tract.
A. Argyria B. THC C. Depakene D. Absorption

272. ______ Drug that relaxes bronchial smooth muscle and dilates the lower respiratory passages.
A. Sectral B. Synesthesia C. Bronchodilator D. Pluripotent

273. ______ A fixed amount of estrogen is released during the cycle.
A. Neutropenia B. Monophasic C. Gram Negative D. Lotensin

274. ______ Following drug prescription directions exactly as written.
A. Anion B. Evacuation C. Drug Compliance D. Trichomoniasis

275. ______ Nicardipine
A. Intrathecal B. Cerebellum C. Side Effect D. Cardene

276. ______ Refers to nerves of the ANS that originate from the thoracolumbar portion of the spinal cord.
A. Sympathetic B. Depakene C. Hematuria D. Vasoconstriction

277. ______ An abnormally painful response to a stimulus.
A. Tambocor B. Petechial C. Candidemia D. Hyperalgesia

278. ______ Group or island of cells.
A. Accupril B. Islets C. Evacuation D. Tremor

279. ______ A substance secreted by T cells that signals other immune cells like macrophages to aggregate.
A. Lymphokine B. Absorption C. Vasoconstriction D. Sarcoplasm

280. ______ Condition in which an arterial blood pressure is abnormally low.
A. Tremor B. Hypotension C. Norpace D. Trichomoniasis

281. ______ Increased blood flow to a body part like the eye; engorgement.
A. Gametocyte B. Gram Negative C. Hyperemia D. Hypertrichosis

282. ______ Drug used to produce mental relaxation and to reduce the desire for physical activity.
A. Sedative B. Questran C. Neutropenia D. Aphthous Ulcer

283. ______ Single-celled microorganisms, some of which cause disease.
A. Bacteria B. Seizure C. Oliguria D. Hyponatremia

284. ______ Chemical mediators involved in inflammation and asthma.
A. Monophasic B. Oligospermia C. Corgard D. Leukotrienes

285. ______ Fosinopril
A. Apoptosis B. Parietal Cell C. Seizure D. Monopril

286. ______ Lining of the uterus.
A. Endometrium B. Oliguria C. Sectral D. Isotonic

287. ______ Condition characterized by frequent watery stools (usually containing blood and mucus), tenesmus.
A. Chelate B. Sympatholytic C. Toxic Effect D. Dysentery

288. ______ Neural pathway connecting different brain areas involved in regulation of behavior and emotion.
A. Virucidal B. Limbic System C. Diuril D. Ulcer

289. ______ Active ingredient of the marijuana plant.
A. Doral B. Sarcoplasm C. THC D. Emphysema

290. ______ Drug-induced confusion that can cause increased drug consumption.
A. Epidemiology B. Apoptosis C. Automatism D. Sarcoplasm

291. ______ Tending to increase blood pressure.
A. Ulcer B. Pressor C. Lyse D. Hemolytic Anemia

292. ______ Inhibits the growth of fungi but does not kill off the fungi.
A. Determinant B. Polyuria C. Ativan D. Fungistatic

293. ______ Mature eggs
A. Ova B. Nitrostat C. Spermatogenesis D. Pressor

294. ______ A substance that promotes bowel movements.
A. Mavik B. Laxative C. Automatism D. Aphthous Ulcer

295. ______ Ethacrynic acid
A. Edecrin B. Potency C. Alkylation D. Lyse

296. ______ A molecule that contains a protein and a lipid (fat).
A. Phlegm B. Keppra C. Lipoprotein D. Nephritis

297. ______ Inhibition of the vagus nerve to the heart, causing the heart rate to increase.
A. Hyponatremia B. Norepinephrine C. Vagolytic Action D. Erythropoiesis

298. ______ A painful open sore in the mouth or upper throat; also known as a canker sore.
A. Insomnia B. Sterilization C. Creatinine D. Aphthous Ulcer

299. ______ Prazepam
A. Homeostasis B. Centrax C. Loading Dose D. Decimal

300. ______ Flushing of the stomach.
A. Salicylism B. Cardene C. Gastric Lavage D. Questran

From the words provided for each clue, provide the letter of the word which best matches the clue.

301. ______ Decrease in the number of circulating lymphocytes.
A. Lymphopenia B. Hemorrhage C. Nicobid D. Hyperacidity

302. ______ Bottom number of a fraction; shows the number of parts in a whole.
A. Thromboembolism B. Bradykinesia C. Denominator D. Hematuria

303. .... A substance that causes constriction of the pupil or miosis.
A. Incompatibility B. Mega C. Denominator D. Miotic

304. .... A type of cell formed after macrophages in the artery wall digest LDL cholesterol.
A. Foam Cells B. Antilipemic Drug C. Plavix D. Bacteria

305. .... Uncontrolled growth of abnormal cells that form a solid mass; also called a neoplasm.
A. Virucidal B. Depakene C. Acidosis D. Tumor

306. .... Spironolactone
A. Vasotec B. Ticlid C. Lipitor D. Aldactone

307. .... Undesirable interaction of drugs not suitable for combination or administration together.
A. Vasotec B. Incompatibility C. Euvolemia D. Tumor

308. .... A painful open sore in the mouth or upper throat; also known as a canker sore.
A. Broad Spectrum B. Hyperacidity C. Aphthous Ulcer D. Cardura

309. .... Cell division in which two daughter cells receive the same number of chromosomes as the parent cell.
A. Dysgeusia B. Coronary Artery C. Hyperemia D. Mitosis

310. .... Condition in which the body develops a severe allergic response; this is a medical emergency.
A. Menopause B. Tnkase C. Anaphylaxis D. Stroke

311. .... Drug that prevents mast cells from releasing histamine and other vasoactive substances.
A. Vascor B. Bradycardia C. Antiallergic D. Systemic

312. .... Initial drug dose administered to rapidly achieve therapeutic drug concentrations.
A. Limbic System B. Therapeutic Dose C. Hematuria D. Loading Dose

313. .... Organs that produce male (testes) or female (ovaries) sex cells, sperm or ova.
A. Gonads B. Gastric Lavage C. Lysosome D. Dyrenium

314. .... Having inhibition of the body's immune response.
A. Limbic System B. Immunosuppressed C. Iodophor D. Mycosis

315. .... HCTZ
A. Trilipix B. Proarrhythmia C. Dyrenium D. Hydrodiuril

316. .... The muscular layer of the heart.
A. Antiallergic B. Librium C. Myocardium D. Aldactone

317. .... Process that alters the pH to less than 7.
A. Prodrug B. Acidification C. Incompatibility D. Colestid

318. .... A substance that causes vomiting.
A. Valium B. Proportion C. Cannabinoid D. Emetogenic

319. .... Positively charged ion.
A. Serax B. Trade Name C. Cation D. Endemic

320. .... Tenecteplase
A. Tenex B. Tnkase C. Ticlid D. Buccal Absorption

321. ______ Rapid involuntary movement of eyes.
A. Bradycardia B. Nystagmus C. Virucidal D. Geriatrics

322. ______ Term used for Candida infection in the mucous membranes of the mouth and pharynx.
A. Thrush B. Intra Articular C. Mysoline D. Oliguria

323. ______ A mathematical equation that expresses the equality between two ratios.
A. Nystagmus B. Proportion C. Menstruation D. Endogenous

324. ______ Abnormally high level of chloride ions circulating in the blood.
A. Candidemia B. Serax C. Hyperchloremia D. Diplopia

325. ______ The amount of blood pumped per minute by the heart.
A. Agranulocytosis B. Cardiac Output C. Cardura D. Euphoria

326. ______ Production of milk in female breasts.
A. Anaphylaxis B. Aldactone C. Lactation D. Corgard

327. ______ Drug that inhibits the growth and proliferation of cancer cells.
A. Hyperinsulinemia B. Tumor C. Antineoplastic D. Digestion

328. ______ Dizziness often caused by a decrease in blood supply to the brain.
A. Arthritis B. Anaphylaxis C. Lightheadedness D. Argyria

329. ______ Streptokinase
A. Myocardium B. Heartburn C. Streptase D. Mitochondria

330. ______ Any cell that covers the axons in the peripheral nervous system and forms the myelin sheath.
A. Schwann Cell B. Nonbarbiturate C. Levatol D. Hematuria

331. ______ Abnormally high body temperature.
A. Isotonic B. Hyperthermia C. Acidosis D. Gastroparesis

332. ______ Loss of brain function due to a loss of blood supply.
A. Protozoan B. Osmosis C. Stroke D. Gonads

333. ______ Infection of the skin, hair, or nails caused by a fungus.
A. Dermatophytic B. Expectorant C. Lysosome D. Adverse Reaction

334. ______ Occurring in the general circulation, resulting in distribution to most organs.
A. Hemorrhage B. Arrhythmia C. Systemic D. Bradycardia

335. ______ Transmits sensory information from peripheral organs to the central nervous system).
A. Chromic B. Schwann Cell C. Afferent Nerve D. Hyperemia

336. ______ Slowed body movements.
A. Meiosis B. Digestion C. Midamor D. Bradykinesia

337. ______ Increase in the amount of drug metabolizing enzymes after repeated administration of certain drugs.
A. Sterilization B. Insomnia C. Hypokalemia D. Enzyme Induction

338. ______ Increased blood flow to a body part like the eye; engorgement.
A. Islets B. Welchol C. Mixed Number D. Hyperemia

339. .... Chlordiazepoxide
A. Flonase B. Sterilization C. Librium D. Sedative

340. .... Condition in which monthly menstruation (menses) no longer occurs.
A. Trilipix B. Amenorrhea C. Norvasc D. Chronic

341. .... Refers to sedative-hypnotic drugs that do not possess the barbituric acid structure.
A. Nonbarbiturate B. Plavix C. Vasotec D. Menstruation

342. .... Slowing down of heart rate.
A. Incompatibility B. Euvolemia C. Bradycardia D. Enzyme Induction

343. .... Diazepam
A. Gonads B. Depakene C. Valium D. Endemic

344. .... Losartan
A. Trade Name B. Klonopin C. Cozaar D. Abortifacient

345. .... Specialized cells in the hypothalamus that respond to changes in sodium concentration in the blood.
A. Tropic Hormone B. Osmoreceptors C. Tnkase D. Corgard

346. .... Enalapril
A. Zaroxolyn B. Vasotec C. Nystagmus D. Thrush

347. .... State of normal body fluid volume.
A. Euphoria B. Endogenous C. Osmoreceptors D. Euvolemia

348. .... Medical specialty that deals with individuals over 65 years of age.
A. Welchol B. Epidemiology C. Antitussive D. Geriatrics

349. .... Compound containing iodine.
A. Iodophor B. Gastroparesis C. Valium D. Oliguria

350. .... Chlorothiazide
A. Diuril B. Cryoanesthesia C. Nicobid D. Nonbarbiturate

351. .... Flushing of the stomach.
A. Stroke B. Aldactone C. Lyse D. Gastric Lavage

352. .... Amlodipine
A. Ova B. Enzyme Induction C. Norvasc D. Gonads

353. .... Prefix meaning large.
A. Nicobid B. Protozoan C. Renin D. Mega

354. .... Error introduced into a study by its design rather than due to random variation.
A. Antigen B. Drug Compliance C. Lysosome D. Systematic Error

355. .... An arrhythmia caused by administration of an antiarrhythmic drug.
A. Proarrhythmia B. Myocardium C. Aldactone D. Loading Dose

356. .... Oxazepam
A. Sedative B. Coronary Artery C. Serax D. Euphoria

357. ______ A fixed amount of estrogen is released during the cycle.
A. Expectorant B. Cardura C. Systematic Error D. Monophasic

358. ______ Part of a cell that contains enzymes capable of digesting or destroying tissue
A. Trilipix B. Monophasic C. Lysosome D. Mega

359. ______ Condition, also called delayed gastric emptying, in which the stomach muscles do not function properly.
A. Gastroparesis B. Topamax C. Trilipix D. Hyperkalemia

360. ______ Twitchings of muscle fiber groups.
A. Cation B. Tropic Hormone C. Fasciculation D. Exophthalmos

361. ______ Nadolol
A. Diplopia B. Levatol C. Corgard D. Osmoreceptors

362. ______ Return of the electric potential across a cell membrane to its resting state following depolarization.
A. Osmoreceptors B. Repolarization C. Arthritis D. Aphthous Ulcer

363. ______ Mechanical and chemical breakdown of foods into smaller units.
A. Chronic B. Nephritis C. Digestion D. Lyse

364. ______ A lipid substance secreted by glands in the skin to lubricate the skin everywhere but the palms and soles.
A. Loading Dose B. Cardizem C. Sebum D. Iodophor

365. ______ Mature eggs
A. Ova B. Absorption C. Mitochondria D. Decubitis Ulcer

366. ______ Action that causes the decomposition or destruction of proteins.
A. Absorption B. Dyrenium C. Proteolytic D. Expectorant

367. ______ Type of bacteria that cause disease; a microorganism that causes disease.
A. Pathogen B. Flonase C. Cutaneous D. Sedative

368. ______ When there is an acute deficiency of granulocytes in blood.
A. Agranulocytosis B. Hypertension C. Lysosome D. Insomnia

369. ______ Joint space into which drug is injected.
A. Lactation B. Proteolytic C. Intra Articular D. Calorigenic

370. ______ Permanent black discoloration of skin and mucous membranes caused by prolonged use of silver protein.
A. Argyria B. Keratinized C. Miotic D. Schizophrenia

371. ______ Study of the distribution and determinants of diseases in populations.
A. Radical Cure B. Proper Fraction C. Midamor D. Epidemiology

372. ______ Method of dosage with cardiac glycosides that rapidly produces effective drug levels.
A. Hyperemia B. Stroke C. Abortifacient D. Digitalization

373. ______ Drug used to produce mental relaxation and to reduce the desire for physical activity.
A. Emetogenic B. Phlebitis C. Insomnia D. Sedative

374. ______ Single-celled microorganisms, some of which cause disease.
A. Lanoxin B. Bacteria C. Loading Dose D. Welchol

375. .... Clopidogrel
A. Therapeutic Dose B. Nephritis C. Plavix D. Coronary Artery

376. .... Guanabenz
A. Morphology B. Meiosis C. Flomax D. Wytensin

377. .... Neural pathway connecting different brain areas involved in regulation of behavior and emotion.
A. Limbic System B. Oliguria C. Morphology D. Norvasc

378. .... To disintegrate or dissolve.
A. Tnkase B. Lyse C. Systemic D. Antiallergic

379. .... A heart rate that exceeds the normal range for a resting heartrate.
A. Otrivin B. Abortifacient C. Tachycardia D. Ticlid

380. .... Chemically altered form of an approved drug that produces similar effects and that is sold illegally.
A. Radical Cure B. Designer Drug C. Phlebitis D. Sebum

381. .... Fluticasone
A. Foam Cells B. Denominator C. Arrhythmia D. Flonase

382. .... High levels of insulin in the blood often associated with type 2 diabetes mellitus and insulin resistance.
A. Mevacor B. Hyperinsulinemia C. Endogenous D. Decimal

383. .... Composed of a protein substance largely found in hair and nails.
A. Mitosis B. Plavix C. Keratinized D. Decubitis Ulcer

384. .... Removing the sensation of touch or pain by applying extreme cold to the nerve endings.
A. Virucidal B. Proper Fraction C. Systematic Error D. Cryoanesthesia

385. .... Infection in the blood caused by the yeast Candida.
A. Uroxatral B. Candidemia C. Calorigenic D. Denominator

386. .... Cells that become the reproductive cells eggs (in ovary) or sperm (in testes).
A. Osteoclasts B. Aphthous Ulcer C. Germ Cells D. Tenex

387. .... Topiramate
A. Topamax B. Hemorrhage C. Cardizem D. Euvolemia

388. .... Present continually in a particular geographic region, often in spite of control measures.
A. Nephritis B. Emetogenic C. Lanoxin D. Endemic

389. .... A drug that suppresses coughing.
A. Proarrhythmia B. Hyperinsulinemia C. Pepsin D. Antitussive

390. .... Nicotinic acid
A. Coronary Artery B. Chromic C. Thromboembolism D. Nicobid

391. .... Simvastatin
A. Absorption B. Virucidal C. Zocor D. Candidemia

392. .... Drug used to treat anxiety; these drugs are also referred to as anxiolytics.
A. Antianxiety Drug B. Mega C. Osmoreceptors D. Isotonic

393. ______ The probability that an event will occur.
A. Renin B. Denominator C. Klonopin D. Risk

394. ______ Condition in which a single object is seen (perceived) as two objects; double vision.
A. Hydrodiuril B. Librium C. Diplopia D. Otrivin

395. ______ Arresting of malaria, in which protozoal parasites are eliminated from all tissues.
A. Keratinized B. Radical Cure C. Miotic D. Arthritis

396. ______ Process in which water moves across membranes following the movement of sodium ions.
A. Immunosuppressed B. Expectorant C. Osmosis D. Hemolytic Anemia

397. ______ Patented proprietary name of drug sold by a specific drug manufacturer; also referred to as the brand name.
A. Aphthous Ulcer B. Proper Fraction C. Trade Name D. Cardura

398. ______ Substance, chemical solution, or drug that kills viruses.
A. Phlebitis B. Hypotension C. Afrin D. Virucidal

399. ______ Drug that is effective against a wide variety of both gram-positive and gram-negative pathogenic bacteria.
A. Abortifacient B. Restoril C. Broad Spectrum D. Cardizem

400. ______ Fibric acid
A. Levatol B. Nystagmus C. Proteolytic D. Trilipix

From the words provided for each clue, provide the letter of the word which best matches the clue.

401. ______ A substance that promotes bowel movements.
A. Goiter B. Laxative C. Proarrhythmia D. Antacid

402. ______ Cell that synthesizes and releases hydrochloric acid into the stomach lumen.
A. Tambocor B. Parietal Cell C. Gametocyte D. Urticarial

403. ______ A strong sustained muscle contraction.
A. Tetany B. Zarontin C. Naphcon D. Aldomet

404. ______ Fluticasone
A. Flonase B. Hyperacidity C. Tetany D. Restoril

405. ______ Substance that relaxes the muscles controlling blood vessels, leading to increased blood flow.
A. Hematuria B. Creatinine C. Schizophrenia D. Vasodilator

406. ______ Refers to drugs or effects that reduce the activity of the parasympathetic nervous system.
A. Electrolyte B. Aneurysm C. Anticholinergic D. Bronchodilator

407. ______ An abnormally painful response to a stimulus.
A. Hyperalgesia B. Germ Cells C. Baycol D. Bronchial Muscles

408. ______ Bottom number of a fraction; shows the number of parts in a whole.
A. Biphasic B. Phagocyte C. Tropic D. Denominator

409. ______ When there is an acute deficiency of granulocytes in blood.
A. Agranulocytosis B. Oliguria C. Wheal D. Stroke

410. .... When drugs (substances) produce the same intensity or spectrum of activity.
A. Coreg B. Hypoxia C. Argyria D. Equipotent

411. .... Reduction of oxygen supply to tissues below the amount required for normal physiological function.
A. Streptase B. Neurontin C. Hypoxia D. Aneurysm

412. .... Space around the brain and spinal cord that contains the cerebrospinal fluid.
A. Thrombocytopenia B. Pernicious C. Flonase D. Intrathecal

413. .... Chemical mediators involved in inflammation and asthma.
A. Synaptic Knob B. Sarcolemma C. Dependency D. Leukotrienes

414. .... Oxymetazoline
A. Afrin B. Dyrenium C. Cushings Disease D. Tetany

415. .... Protozoal infection characterized by attacks of chills, fever, and sweating.
A. Blood Dyscrasia B. Native C. Malaria D. Pernicious

416. .... The amount of blood pumped per minute by the heart.
A. Cardiac Output B. Aquaresis C. Anion D. Intra Articular

417. .... Guanabenz
A. Immunosuppressed B. Wytensin C. Antitussive D. Intra Articular

418. .... Abnormally high degree of acidity (for example, pH less than 1) in the stomach.
A. Hyperacidity B. Anticholinergic C. Ulcer D. Chime

419. .... Formation of ova.
A. Interleukin B. Oxyntic Cell C. Oogenesis D. Candidiasis

420. .... Slowed body movements.
A. Retavase B. Cushings Disease C. Osmosis D. Bradykinesia

421. .... Nicotinic acid
A. Hypotonic B. Nicobid C. Thrombus D. Welchol

422. .... Carvedilol
A. Absence Seizure B. Coreg C. Phlegm D. Heart Rate

423. .... Colesevelam
A. Welchol B. Immunosuppressed C. Interferon D. Nephritis

424. .... Study of the distribution and determinants of diseases in populations.
A. Laxative B. Osmosis C. Drug Compliance D. Epidemiology

425. .... Error introduced into a study by its design rather than due to random variation.
A. Vancenase B. Sarcolemma C. Systematic Error D. Hypotension

426. .... A heart rate that exceeds the normal range for a resting heartrate.
A. Nephritis B. Geriatrics C. Wheal D. Tachycardia

427. .... Quinidine
A. Lamictal B. Doral C. Leukotrienes D. Quinidine

428. .... Nadolol
A. Baycol B. Half Life C. Corgard D. Lasix

429. .... Study of drugs.
A. Carcinoid Tumor B. Pharmacology C. Ambien D. Celontin

430. .... Cell that synthesizes and releases hydrochloric acid (HCl) into the stomach lumen.
A. Hypokalemia B. Nicobid C. Dilantin D. Oxyntic Cell

431. .... Requirement of repeated drug consumption in order to prevent onset of withdrawal symptoms.
A. Thrombus B. Proinflammatory C. Dependency D. Constipation

432. .... Cerivastatin
A. Aquaresis B. Baycol C. Hypotonic D. Osmoreceptors

433. .... Tissue containing fat cells; fat.
A. Thrombocytopenia B. Oxyntic Cell C. Synesthesia D. Adipose Tissue

434. .... Abnormality in blood.
A. Nasalide B. Blood Dyscrasia C. Aldomet D. Baycol

435. .... Abnormally high blood pressure.
A. Dyrenium B. Basal Ganglia C. Hypoxia D. Hypertension

436. .... Medical specialty that deals with individuals over 65 years of age.
A. Geriatrics B. Lipodystrophy C. Klonopin D. Denominator

437. .... Inflammation of the walls of the veins, associated with clot formation.
A. Virilization B. Thrombophlebitis C. Interferon D. Anticonvulsant

438. .... watery substance that is located behind the cornea of the eye and in front of the lens.
A. Agranulocytosis B. Aqueous Humor C. Pernicious D. Afrin

439. .... Following drug prescription directions exactly as written.
A. Acidification B. Drug Compliance C. Pravachol D. Petechial

440. .... Natural substance in the body.
A. Native B. Dilantin C. Determinant D. Restoril

441. .... Permanent black discoloration of skin and mucous membranes caused by prolonged use of silver protein.
A. Absence Seizure B. Extracellular C. Argyria D. Lanoxin

442. .... Joint space into which drug is injected.
A. Proportion B. Intra Articular C. Pernicious D. Coreg

443. .... Partially digested food and gastric secretions that moves into the duodenum from the stomach by peristalsis.
A. Chime B. Antitussive C. Intolerant D. Proarrhythmia

444. .... Name that defines the chemical composition of a drug.
A. Insulin B. Tnkase C. Uroxatral D. Chemical Name

445. .... Diazepam
A. Endorphins B. Parietal Cell C. Valium D. Bronchodilator

446. ..... Excess secretion of adenocorticotropic hormone (ACTH).
A. Hypoxia B. Ulcer C. Cushings Disease D. Remission

447. ..... Male sex hormone responsible for the development of male characteristics.
A. Antimicrobial B. Androgen C. Cannabinoid D. Pharmacology

448. ..... Intensely itching raised areas of skin caused by an allergic reaction; hives.
A. Zocor B. Solvent C. Cardiac Output D. Urticarial

449. ..... Arresting of malaria, in which protozoal parasites are eliminated from all tissues.
A. Endometrium B. Radical Cure C. Ulcer D. Parietal Cell

450. ..... Ethosuximide
A. Anion B. Activase C. Zarontin D. Malaria

451. ..... Dipyridamole
A. Chemical Name B. Intolerant C. Tnkase D. Persantine

452. ..... Period when cancer cells are not increasing in number.
A. Remission B. Digitalization C. Dyrenium D. Radical Cure

453. ..... Coiled or folded back on itself.
A. Tachycardia B. Nicobid C. Convoluted D. Antagonistic

454. ..... Phenytoin
A. Schizophrenia B. Dilantin C. Myoclonic D. Virilization

455. ..... Drug that blocks the action of histamine at the target organ.
A. Tyzine B. Antihistaminic C. Proinflammatory D. Ambien

456. ..... Alfuzosin
A. Lotensin B. Centrax C. Phagocyte D. Uroxatral

457. ..... Composed of a protein substance largely found in hair and nails.
A. Aldomet B. Keratinized C. Norepinephrine D. Pharmacology

458. ..... Reteplase
A. Retavase B. Stroke Volume C. Oogenesis D. Dyrenium

459. ..... Counteract; oppose.
A. Afrin B. Antagonistic C. Numerator D. Stroke

460. ..... A condition where the concentration of salt (sodium, electrolytes) is less than that found inside the cells.
A. Hypotonic B. Cancer C. Keratinized D. Antiseptic

461. ..... Preparation in which undissolved solids are dispersed within a liquid.
A. Keratinized B. Streptase C. Suspension D. Aldomet

462. ..... Number of heart beats per minute.
A. Hypertension B. Anticonvulsant C. Heart Rate D. Blood Dyscrasia

463. ..... Losartan
A. Cozaar B. Sarcolemma C. Antagonistic D. Bradykinesia

464. ______ Neurotransmitter of sympathetic nerves that stimulates the adrenergic receptors.
A. Wheal B. Lavage C. Norepinephrine D. Equipotent

465. ______ Interacts with one subtype of receptor over others.
A. Biphasic B. Aplastic Anemia C. Hypokalemia D. Selective

466. ______ Pravastatin
A. Pravachol B. Solvent C. Nosocomial D. Uroxatral

467. ______ pH greater than 7.45.
A. Proper Fraction B. Sectral C. Asymptomatic D. Alkalosis

468. ______ Smooth muscles of lungs.
A. Bronchial Muscles B. Endorphins C. Altace D. Permissive

469. ______ A substance capable of producing an allergic reaction.
A. Allergen B. Creatinine C. Ova D. Drowsiness

470. ______ A mathematical equation that expresses the equality between two ratios.
A. Bradykinesia B. Proportion C. Tachycardia D. Antihistaminic

471. ______ Ion in solution, such as sodium, potassium, or chloride, that is capable of mediating conduction.
A. Hypertension B. Electrolyte C. Creatinine D. Fungistatic

472. ______ Low concentration of potassium in blood.
A. Hypokalemia B. Aquaresis C. Tambocor D. Lanoxin

473. ______ Infection caused by the yeast Candida; also known as moniliasis.
A. Oxyntic Cell B. Drug Indications C. Virilization D. Candidiasis

474. ______ Benazepril
A. Lotensin B. Corgard C. Dehiscence D. Hypertension

475. ______ The muscular layer of the heart.
A. Myocardium B. Extracellular C. Adipose Tissue D. Pravachol

476. ______ An abnormal decrease in the number of circulating platelets.
A. Lavage B. Tetany C. Sectral D. Thrombocytopenia

477. ______ Tenecteplase
A. Activase B. Tnkase C. Hyperacidity D. Hypophosphatemia

478. ______ Milrinone
A. Proper Fraction B. Primacor C. Wytensin D. Schizophrenia

479. ______ Development of masculine body (hair, muscle) characteristics in females.
A. Selective B. Virilization C. Centrax D. Bias

480. ______ Methyldopa
A. Systematic Error B. Aldomet C. Halcion D. Chime

481. ______ An element similar to sodium that is used in the treatment of mania and bipolar mood disorder.
A. Oxyntic Cell B. Lithium C. Barbiturate D. Baycol

482. .... A thick-walled structure in which parasitic protozoal sex cells develop for transfer to new hosts.
A. Malaria B. Lamictal C. Oocyst D. Aplastic Anemia

483. .... Major form of psychosis; behavior is inappropriate.
A. Antiseptic B. Quinidine C. Antagonistic D. Schizophrenia

484. .... Top number of a fraction; shows the part.
A. Drowsiness B. Persantine C. Schizophrenia D. Numerator

485. .... A metabolite of muscle metabolism that is excreted in the urine in proportion to renal function.
A. Nosocomial B. Creatinine C. Nicobid D. Quinidine

486. .... Condition in which there is no outward evidence (symptom) that an infection is present.
A. Asymptomatic B. Thrombophlebitis C. Altace D. Hypotonic

487. .... Negatively charged ion.
A. Biphasic B. Anion C. Nosocomial D. Polypharmacy

488. .... Renal excretion of water without electrolytes.
A. Nosocomial B. Aquaresis C. Tnkase D. Immunity

489. .... Hormone secreted by the beta cells of the pancreas to facilitate glucose entry into the cell.
A. Vasodilator B. Radical Cure C. Insulin D. Aquaresis

490. .... Furosemide
A. Lasix B. Oliguria C. Selective D. Lithium

491. .... Substance, chemical solution, or drug that kills microorganisms.
A. Germicidal B. Cardiac Output C. Doral D. Islets

492. .... Opening in a hollow organ, such as a break in the intestinal wall.
A. Malignant B. Thrombocytopenia C. Perforation D. Aplastic Anemia

493. .... Substance that induces abortion.
A. Parietal Cell B. Abortifacient C. Basal Ganglia D. Cardiac Output

494. .... Silodosin
A. Argyria B. Germ Cells C. Rapaflo D. Denominator

495. .... Anemia caused by defective functioning of the blood-forming organs (bone marrow).
A. Aplastic Anemia B. Interferon C. Basal Ganglia D. Synaptic Knob

496. .... Appearance of blood or red blood cells in the urine.
A. Blood Dyscrasia B. Hematuria C. Suspension D. Insulin

497. .... An antigen-presenting white blood cell that is found in the skin, mucosa, and lymphoid tissues and that
A. Hyperglycemia B. Immunosuppressed C. Zarontin D. Dendritic Cell

498. .... Condition in which the thyroid is enlarged, but not as a result of a tumor.
A. Euthyroid B. Goiter C. Persantine D. Permissive

499. .... Antibacterial drugs obtained by chemical synthesis and not from other microorganisms.
A. Synesthesia B. Ova C. Cannabinoid D. Antimicrobial

500. ____ Prazepam
A. Biphasic B. Aneurysm C. Proper Fraction D. Centrax

From the words provided for each clue, provide the letter of the word which best matches the clue.

501. ____ Open sore in the mucous membranes or mucosal linings of the body.
A. Trileptal B. Mega C. Hygroton D. Ulcer

502. ____ Chemical mediator produced by immune cells that increases immune function.
A. Xanax B. Inocor C. Interferon D. Ratio

503. ____ Mature sperm cells.
A. Fungicidal B. Spermatozoa C. Vasoconstriction D. Hypochromic

504. ____ Washing (lavage) of a wound or cavity with large volumes of fluid.
A. Irrigation B. Perimenopause C. Glycosuria D. Micardis

505. ____ Time required for the body to reduce the amount of drug in the plasma by one-half.
A. Depakene B. Leucopenia C. Flonase D. Half Life

506. ____ The presence of the plasma protein albumin in the urine.
A. Ratio B. Albuminuria C. Gabitril D. Pathogen

507. ____ Method of dosage with cardiac glycosides that rapidly produces effective drug levels.
A. Digitalization B. Hyperstat C. Celontin D. Lithium

508. ____ The muscular layer of the heart.
A. Radical Cure B. Fungistatic C. Ticlid D. Myocardium

509. ____ Difficult or painful menstruation; condition that is associated with painful and difficult menstruation.
A. Phagocyte B. Percent C. Mega D. Dysmenorrhea

510. ____ Condition in which an arterial blood pressure is abnormally low.
A. Ambien B. Spermatozoa C. Hyperkalemia D. Hypotension

511. ____ Bursting open or separation of a wound, usually along sutured line.
A. Streptase B. Dehiscence C. Colestid D. Effient

512. ____ Silodosin
A. Loading Dose B. Mega C. Rapaflo D. Interferon

513. ____ Tiagabine
A. Hirsutism B. Monophasic C. Thrombus D. Gabitril

514. ____ Beclomethasone
A. Tyzine B. Vancenase C. Myocardium D. Phagocyte

515. ____ Substance that interacts with tissues to produce most of the symptoms of allergy.
A. Histamine B. Fungistatic C. Ectopic Beat D. Spermatozoa

516. ____ Interacts with one subtype of receptor over others.
A. Lightheadedness B. Hemozoin C. Celontin D. Selective

517. .... Telmisartan
A. Potentiates B. Streptase C. Micardis D. Mutagenic

518. .... Excessive thirst; increased thirst.
A. Polydipsia B. Sympathetic C. Diovan D. Tyzine

519. .... Type of cell division where diploid parent cells divide.
A. Meiosis B. Chronic C. Ulcer D. Virucidal

520. .... Drugs that relieve, interrupt, or prevent muscle spasms.
A. Rapaflo B. Spasmolytics C. Lightheadedness D. Retavase

521. .... Return of the electric potential across a cell membrane to its resting state following depolarization.
A. Expectorate B. Diplopia C. Repolarization D. Cushings Disease

522. .... Inhibits the growth of fungi but does not kill off the fungi.
A. Immunosuppressed B. Endometrium C. Fungistatic D. Loading Dose

523. .... Secretion from the respiratory tract; usually called mucus.
A. Refractory B. Phlegm C. Diplopia D. Colestid

524. .... Appearance of blood or red blood cells in the urine.
A. Cathartic B. Hematuria C. Megaloblast D. Histamine

525. .... Causing cancer.
A. Carcinogenic B. Depression C. Dose D. Xanax

526. .... Reteplase
A. Retavase B. Sympatholytic C. Solute D. Hemoglobin

527. .... The probability that an event will occur.
A. Risk B. Virucidal C. Hemozoin D. Effient

528. .... Bisoprolol
A. Zebeta B. Anorexia C. Barbital D. Gabitril

529. .... Inadequate secretion of glucocorticoids and mineralocorticoids.
A. Addisons Disease B. Mavik C. Convoluted D. Hyperchloremia

530. .... Ethacrynic acid
A. Euvolemia B. Oxytocin C. Interferon D. Edecrin

531. .... Eject from the mouth; spit.
A. Nasacort B. Expectorate C. Colestid D. Phlegm

532. .... Presence of glucose in the urine.
A. Glycosuria B. Vancenase C. Aphthous Ulcer D. Side Effect

533. .... Undesirable interaction of drugs not suitable for combination or administration together.
A. Incompatibility B. Naphcon C. Laxative D. Excoriation

534. .... Action that causes the decomposition or destruction of proteins.
A. Rapaflo B. Akathisia C. Demadex D. Proteolytic

535. .... Feeling of well-being or elation; feeling good.
A. Dose B. Bronchial Muscles C. Euphoria D. Risk

536. .... Circulating cell that ingests waste products or bacteria in order to remove them from the body.
A. Ectopic Beat B. Coreg C. Homeostasis D. Phagocyte

537. .... Refers to nerves of the ANS that originate from the thoracolumbar portion of the spinal cord.
A. Megaloblast B. Sympathetic C. Addisons Disease D. Pressor

538. .... Tightening or contraction of muscles in the blood vessels, which decreases blood flow through the vessels.
A. Ovulation B. Vasoconstriction C. Morphology D. Hematuria

539. .... Lovastatin
A. Mevacor B. Expectorate C. Bradykinesia D. Aphthous Ulcer

540. .... Carbamazepine
A. Tegretol B. Polydipsia C. Monophasic D. Loading Dose

541. .... Prefix meaning large.
A. Diplopia B. Incretins C. Mega D. Polyphagia

542. .... Hardening or fibrosis of the arteries; accumulation of fatty deposits in the walls of arteries.
A. Asthma B. Arteriosclerosis C. Megaloblast D. Site of Action

543. .... Normal salt concentration of most body fluids; a salt concentration of 0.9 percent.
A. Extracellular B. Isotonic C. Equipotent D. Aphthous Ulcer

544. .... Propranolol
A. Histamine B. Hemozoin C. Milontin D. Inderal

545. .... The cytoplasm of a striated (skeletal) muscle fiber.
A. Virucidal B. Chemical Name C. Sympatholytic D. Sarcoplasm

546. .... Condition in which the color of red blood cells is less than the normal index.
A. Aqueous Humor B. Extracellular C. Potentiates D. Hypochromic

547. .... Abnormally high degree of acidity (for example, pH less than 1) in the stomach.
A. Spermatozoa B. Fungistatic C. Hyperacidity D. Cushings Disease

548. .... The relationship of one number to another expressed by whole numbers.
A. Addisons Disease B. Ketosis C. Wheal D. Ratio

549. .... Partially digested food and gastric secretions that moves into the duodenum from the stomach by peristalsis.
A. Micardis B. Diovan C. Immunity D. Chime

550. .... Produces an action that is greater than either of the components can produce alone; synergy.
A. Potentiates B. Albuminuria C. Spasmolytics D. Inocor

551. .... Active ingredient of the marijuana plant.
A. THC B. Polydipsia C. Hemozoin D. Edema

552. .... Inflammation of the glomeruli often following a streptococcus infection.
A. Nephritis B. Isotonic C. Phlegm D. Dose

553. .... Period when cancer cells are not increasing in number.
A. Dysgeusia B. Drug Dependence C. Polydipsia D. Remission

554. .... Initial drug dose administered to rapidly achieve therapeutic drug concentrations.
A. Chemical Name B. Atromid C. Dilantin D. Loading Dose

555. .... Intended or indicated uses for any drug.
A. Virucidal B. Tranxene C. Drug Indications D. Dose

556. .... A substance that promotes bowel movements.
A. Fungicidal B. Akathisia C. Laxative D. Emesis

557. .... Condition that causes individuals to resist acquiring or developing a disease or infection.
A. Lymphopenia B. Immunity C. Irrigation D. Calan

558. .... Clofibrate
A. Polyphagia B. Oxytocin C. Xanax D. Atromid

559. .... Alteplase
A. Convoluted B. Activase C. Bactericidal D. Hyperacidity

560. .... Phenobarbital
A. Barbital B. Alkylation C. Sarcoplasm D. Pharmacodynamics

561. .... Vomiting.
A. Laxative B. Fungistatic C. Emesis D. Aldosterone

562. .... Clonazepam
A. Ticlid B. Morphology C. Klonopin D. Percent

563. .... Fluticasone
A. Flonase B. Immunosuppressed C. Bias D. Aquaresis

564. .... Substance dissolved in a solvent; usually present in a lesser amount.
A. Solute B. Trilipix C. Polydipsia D. Zebeta

565. .... Shape or structure of a cell.
A. Hypotension B. Morphology C. Colestid D. Flonase

566. .... Tending to increase blood pressure.
A. Ketosis B. Homeostasis C. Cardizem D. Pressor

567. .... watery substance that is located behind the cornea of the eye and in front of the lens.
A. Barbital B. Hyperacidity C. Aqueous Humor D. Gabitril

568. .... Renal excretion of water without electrolytes.
A. Suspension B. Lozol C. Trilipix D. Aquaresis

569. .... Flunisolide
A. Inocor B. Xanax C. Glycogen D. Nasalide

570. .... A measurement of the amount of drug that is administered.
A. Oxytocin B. Hypotension C. Dose D. Monophasic

571. .... Pharmacological substance that stimulates defecation.
A. Suspension B. Wheal C. Cathartic D. Lunesta

572. .... Amrinone
A. Inocor B. Chemical Name C. Native D. Lightheadedness

573. .... Hormone released from adrenal cortex that causes the retention of sodium from the kidneys.
A. Ratio B. Endorphins C. Addisons Disease D. Aldosterone

574. .... Refers to the action of an adrenergic blocking drug or an action that decreases sympathetic activity.
A. Drowsiness B. Sympatholytic C. Dysgeusia D. Side Effect

575. .... Diazoxide
A. Hirsutism B. Nasalide C. Hyperstat D. Carcinogenic

576. .... Condition in which a single object is seen (perceived) as two objects; double vision.
A. Diplopia B. Trileptal C. Radical Cure D. Coreg

577. .... Alprazolam
A. Drug Indications B. Hyperchloremia C. Mavik D. Xanax

578. .... Excess secretion of adenocorticotropic hormone (ACTH).
A. Hygroton B. Cushings Disease C. Loading Dose D. Xanax

579. .... Eszopiclone
A. Trileptal B. Demadex C. Norpace D. Lunesta

580. .... Inference tending to produce results that depart systematically from the true values.
A. Mega B. Bias C. Glycosuria D. Edema

581. .... Phenytoin
A. Depakene B. Interferon C. Dilantin D. Minipress

582. .... Protein in red blood cells that transports oxygen to all tissues of the body.
A. Hemoglobin B. Lopressor C. Lysosome D. Myocardium

583. .... Number written with both a whole number and a fraction.
A. Euphoria B. Bias C. Lunesta D. Mixed Number

584. .... Mental state characterized by depressed mood, with feelings of frustration and hopelessness.
A. Depression B. Atromid C. Homeostasis D. Sterilization

585. .... Metoprolol bradycardia
A. Retavase B. Minipress C. Lopressor D. Tegretol

586. .... Pertaining to the skin.
A. Incompatibility B. Solute C. Cutaneous D. Dehiscence

587. .... Ticlopidine
A. Nasacort B. Ticlid C. Hypotension D. Bactericidal

588. .... Smooth muscles of lungs.
A. Tremor B. Drug Absorption C. Irrigation D. Bronchial Muscles

589. .... Release of an egg from the ovary.
A. Mega B. Pathogen C. Ovulation D. Arrhythmia

590. .... Diltiazem
A. Hypochromic B. Alkylation C. Perimenopause D. Cardizem

591. .... An elevated concentration of potassium in blood.
A. Cathartic B. Emesis C. Chronic D. Hyperkalemia

592. .... Carvedilol
A. Diuresis B. Ambien C. Nasacort D. Coreg

593. .... Naturally occurring within the body; originating or produced within an organism, tissue, or cell.
A. Endogenous B. Mavik C. Drug Dependence D. Extracellular

594. .... A group of gastrointestinal hormones that increase the amount of insulin released.
A. Lopressor B. Trilipix C. Micardis D. Incretins

595. .... Clorazepate
A. Lozol B. Potentiates C. Tranxene D. Gabitril

596. .... Preparation in which undissolved solids are dispersed within a liquid.
A. Depakote B. Suspension C. Systematic Error D. Sarcoplasm

597. .... It refers to feeling abnormally sleepy during the day.
A. Nimotop B. Pluripotent C. Aldosterone D. Drowsiness

598. .... Valsartan
A. Anion B. Diovan C. Lysosome D. Milontin

599. .... Colestipol
A. Sympathetic B. Mavik C. Pathogen D. Colestid

600. .... Irreversible chemical bond that some cancer drugs form with nucleic acids and DNA.
A. Phagocyte B. Homeostasis C. Streptase D. Alkylation

From the words provided for each clue, provide the letter of the word which best matches the clue.

1. C An inflammation of the hair follicles of the beard or scalp caused by ringworm with swelling and pus.
A. Extracellular B. Spermatozoa C. Kerion D. Virucidal

2. C After a meal.
A. Procanbid B. Sympathomimetic C. Postprandial D. Ethmozine

3. A Intermediary kind of male germ cell in the production of spermatozoa.
A. Spermatogonia B. Centrax C. Intrathecal D. Bradykinesia

4. B The cytoplasm of a striated (skeletal) muscle fiber.
A. Cushings Disease B. Sarcoplasm C. Ethmozine D. Flonase

5. C Amlodipine
A. Virucidal B. Chronic C. Norvasc D. Incretins

6. A Protein necessary for intestinal absorption of vitamin B12.
A. Intrinsic Factor B. Intrathecal C. Cidal D. Osmosis

7. C Not able to continue drug therapy usually because of extreme sensitivity to the side effects.
A. Dermatitis B. Iodophor C. Intolerant D. THC

8. A A measure of hydration status; the amount of solute per liter of solution.
A. Osmolarity B. Infarction C. Petechial D. Polyuria

9. B Mature eggs
A. Xylocaine B. Ova C. Flonase D. Glucocorticoid

10. D Felodipine
A. Thrombophlebitis B. Gram Negative C. Opiate D. Plendil

11. D Enalapril
A. Gastric Lavage B. Oocyte C. Effient D. Vasotec

12. B Silodosin
A. Centrax B. Rapaflo C. Alopecia D. Addisons Disease

13. C Alkaloid drug in tobacco that stimulates ganglionic receptors.
A. Trileptal B. Anuria C. Nicotine D. Effient

14. B Phensuximide
A. Thromboembolism B. Milontin C. Akinesia D. Chelate

15. C Entrance of a drug into the bloodstream from its site of administration.
A. Nicotine B. Pathogen C. Drug Absorption D. Nystagmus

16. D Enzyme that digests protein in the stomach.
A. Thrombophlebitis B. Salicylism C. Unstable Plaque D. Pepsin

17. D Drug that neutralizes hydrochloric acid (HCl) secreted by the stomach.
A. Germ Cells B. Sarcoplasm C. Somatostatin D. Antacid

18. A Substance, chemical solution, or drug that kills viruses.
A. Virucidal B. Intrathecal C. Xylocaine D. Procanbid

19. A Bedsore.
A. Decubitis Ulcer B. Determinant C. Oogenesis D. Hypnotic

20. D Absorption of drug through the mucous membranes lining the oral cavity.
A. Intra Articular B. Infarction C. Polypeptide D. Buccal Absorption

21. D Substance, chemical solution, or drug that kills microorganisms.
A. Addisons Disease B. Germ Cells C. Lipitor D. Germicidal

22. A Origin of the pain is in a different location than where the individual feels the pain.
A. Referred Pain B. Emesis C. Parietal Cell D. Lotensin

23. D Rapid involuntary movement of eyes.
A. Tonic B. Penicillinase C. Rigidity D. Nystagmus

24. D Substance that induces abortion.
A. Lactation B. Barbital C. Intolerant D. Abortifacient

25. A Phenytoin
A. Dilantin B. Mixed Number C. Synesthesia D. Type B Reaction

26. C watery substance that is located behind the cornea of the eye and in front of the lens.
A. Ambien B. Sarcoplasm C. Aqueous Humor D. Chromic

27. D Flushing of the stomach.
A. Type B Reaction B. Pepsin C. Constipation D. Gastric Lavage

28. C A group of gastrointestinal hormones that increase the amount of insulin released.
A. Nitrostat B. Ambien C. Incretins D. Afrin

29. C Atorvastatin
A. Extracellular B. Chelate C. Lipitor D. Ascites

30. D Excessive urine production; increased urination.
A. Librium B. Keratinized C. Thrombophlebitis D. Polyuria

31. C Pain resulting from a damaged nervous system or damaged nerve cells.
A. Vasotec B. Osmolarity C. Neuropathic Pain D. Benzodiazepine

32. C A mathematical equation that expresses the equality between two ratios.
A. Flonase B. Nystagmus C. Proportion D. THC

33. C Excess fluid in the space between the tissues lining the abdomen and abdominal organs.
A. Akinesia B. Atonic Seizure C. Ascites D. Decubitis Ulcer

34. B Condition in which there is no outward evidence (symptom) that an infection is present.
A. Somatostatin B. Asymptomatic C. Polydipsia D. Mysoline

35. A Verapamil
A. Calan B. Infarction C. Bradykinesia D. Benzodiazepine

36. C Increased blood flow to a body part like the eye; engorgement.
A. Synesthesia B. Naphcon C. Hyperemia D. Dermatitis

37. D Slowed body movements.
A. Dyspepsia B. Cerebellum C. Polyuria D. Bradykinesia

38. A A painful open sore in the mouth or upper throat; also known as a canker sore.
A. Aphthous Ulcer B. Dyspepsia C. Barbital D. Naphcon

39. D Responsible for bone resorption by binding to bone matrix proteins and releasing enzymes to break down bone.
A. Vasotec B. Somatostatin C. Afrin D. Osteoclasts

40. D Ethosuximide
A. Gram Stain B. Diplopia C. Intrathecal D. Zarontin

41. A Enables another hormone to fully function.
A. Permissive B. Dermatitis C. Pravachol D. Potency

42. C Hormone synthesized and released by the thyroid gland.
A. Chelate B. Geriatrics C. Thyroxine D. Dermatitis

43. D Substance dissolved in a solvent; usually present in a lesser amount.
A. Immunomodulation B. Osteoclasts C. Lipitor D. Solute

44. C Drug derived from opium and producing the same pharmacological effects as opium.
A. Tenex B. Static C. Opiate D. Hypophosphatemia

45. B Oxcarbamazepine
A. Lysosome B. Trileptal C. Hypertension D. Circadian Rhythm

46. C Hormone released from adrenal cortex that causes the retention of sodium from the kidneys.
A. Hypotonic B. Geriatrics C. Aldosterone D. Gram Negative

47. B Number written with both a whole number and a fraction.
A. Gastric Lavage B. Mixed Number C. Hyperemia D. Cardiac Output

48. A Increase in muscle tone or contractions causing faster clearance of substances through the GI tract.
A. Hypermotility B. Infarction C. Gram Negative D. Ecotrin

49. A Clopidogrel
A. Plavix B. Hemolytic Anemia C. Mitochondria D. Tonic

50. B Any disease caused by a fungus.
A. Rigidity B. Mycosis C. Lipitor D. Procanbid

51. A Fluticasone
A. Flonase B. Hyperchlorhydria C. Apoptosis D. Endorphins

52. A The amount of blood pumped per minute by the heart.
A. Cardiac Output B. Circadian Rhythm C. Ascites D. Polypeptide

53. B Opening in a hollow organ, such as a break in the intestinal wall.
A. Extracellular B. Perforation C. Dyspepsia D. Static

54. B Naphazoline
A. Convulsion B. Naphcon C. Mitochondria D. Analgesia

55. A Chemical substance that produces a change in body function.
A. Drug B. Mitosis C. Iodophor D. Fraction

56. C Undesirable interaction of drugs not suitable for combination or administration together.
A. Constipation B. Carcinogenic C. Incompatibility D. Sarcoplasm

57. C Molecule that contains purine or pyrimidine bases in combination with sugar.
A. Glycogenolysis B. Hypertension C. Nucleoside D. Fungicidal

58. B Feeling of well-being or elation; feeling good.
A. Ethmozine B. Euphoria C. Hypertension D. Oocyte

59. A Inadequate secretion of glucocorticoids and mineralocorticoids.
A. Addisons Disease B. Extracellular C. Antagonist D. Virucidal

60. A Oxymetazoline
A. Afrin B. Osmolarity C. Potency D. Fungicidal

61. C Tightening or contraction of muscles in the blood vessels, which decreases blood flow through the vessels.
A. Diuril B. Designer Drug C. Vasoconstriction D. Trileptal

62. D Involuntary muscle contraction that is either tonic or clonic.
A. Oocyte B. Diuresis C. Drug D. Convulsion

63. C Levetiracetam
A. Incompatibility B. Chromic C. Keppra D. Addisons Disease

64. C Mature sperm cells.
A. Aphthous Ulcer B. Pravachol C. Spermatozoa D. Hyperchlorhydria

65. D Condition in which no urine is produced.
A. Native B. Lipitor C. Static D. Anuria

66. D Adverse reaction which is aberrant, and may be due to hypersensitivity or immunologic reactions.
A. Dyspepsia B. Synesthesia C. Carcinogenic D. Type B Reaction

67. B Active ingredient of the marijuana plant.
A. Ecotrin B. THC C. Receptor D. Ticlid

68. B Refers to the action of an adrenergic drug or an action that increases sympathetic activity.
A. Constipation B. Sympathomimetic C. Depakote D. Norepinephrine

69. D A type of cell formed after macrophages in the artery wall digest LDL cholesterol.
A. Hypoxia B. Polypeptide C. Solute D. Foam Cells

70. A Condition that causes urine to be excreted; usually associated with large volumes of urine.
A. Diuresis B. Apoptosis C. Malaria D. Spermatogonia

71. A Refers to nerves of the ANS that originate from the thoracolumbar portion of the spinal cord.
A. Sympathetic B. Glucocorticoid C. Endorphins D. Osmolarity

72. C A substance capable of producing an allergic reaction.
A. Keratinized B. Native C. Allergen D. Rigidity

73. A Neuropeptides produced within the CNS that interact with opioid receptors to produce analgesia.
A. Endorphins B. THC C. Capoten D. Analgesia

74. A Drug used to induce and maintain sleep.
A. Hypnotic B. Hypotonic C. Iodophor D. Plendil

75. C Substance, usually large, composed of an indefinite number of amino acids.
A. Vasotec B. Cidal C. Polypeptide D. Constipation

76. D Plaque formed in the artery wall that can break away and obstruct blood flow or form a clot.
A. Pravachol B. Oxyntic Cell C. Incompatibility D. Unstable Plaque

77. B Cell division in which two daughter cells receive the same number of chromosomes as the parent cell.
A. Decubitis Ulcer B. Mitosis C. Osmosis D. Gram Stain

78. A Disease of severe symptoms, which could be fatal if left untreated.
A. Pernicious B. Fraction C. Benzodiazepine D. Immunomodulation

79. B Convulsive muscle contraction characterized by sustained muscular contractions.
A. Aqueous Humor B. Tonic C. Dystonia D. Drug Absorption

80. A The presence of the plasma protein albumin in the urine.
A. Albuminuria B. Ecotrin C. Somatostatin D. Spermatogonia

81. C Method of staining and identifying bacteria.
A. Unstable Plaque B. Plavix C. Gram Stain D. Oxytocin

82. C Condition of long duration, usually months or years.
A. Hypophosphatemia B. Thrombophlebitis C. Chronic D. Circadian Rhythm

83. A Baldness or hair loss.
A. Alopecia B. Spermatozoa C. Foam Cells D. Barbital

84. D Measure of the strength, or concentration, of a drug required to produce a specific effect.
A. Germicidal B. Postprandial C. Apoptosis D. Potency

85. A Refers to venous return, the amount of blood returning to the heart that must be pumped.
A. Preload B. Nitrostat C. Referred Pain D. Sympathomimetic

86. D Chlorothiazide
A. Nystagmus B. Decubitis Ulcer C. Plendil D. Diuril

87. C A decrease in stool frequency.
A. Hemolytic Anemia B. Spermatogonia C. Constipation D. Keratinized

88. B Medical specialty that deals with individuals over 65 years of age.
A. Plendil B. Geriatrics C. Antagonist D. Sympathomimetic

89. D Lidocaine
A. Androgen B. Hemolytic Anemia C. Albuminuria D. Xylocaine

90. A Abnormally high degree of acidity (for example, pH less than 1) in the stomach.
A. Hyperacidity B. Ova C. Naphcon D. Neuropathic Pain

91. C Area of tissue that has died because of a sudden lack of blood supply.
A. Cidal B. Zaroxolyn C. Infarction D. Hypophosphatemia

92. C Normal salt concentration of most body fluids; a salt concentration of 0.9 percent.
A. Preload B. Geriatrics C. Isotonic D. Ecotrin

93. C Joint space into which drug is injected.
A. Pathogen B. Addisons Disease C. Intra Articular D. Chronic

94. C Defective metabolism of fat.
A. Drug B. Akinesia C. Lipodystrophy D. Bradykinesia

95. D Abnormally high blood pressure.
A. Extracellular B. Designer Drug C. Unstable Plaque D. Hypertension

96. C Studies with control groups, namely case-control studies, cohort studies, and randomized clinical trials.
A. Osmosis B. Determinant C. Analytic Studies D. Kerion

97. C Chlordiazepoxide
A. Mitochondria B. Naphcon C. Librium D. Iodophor

98. B Area outside the cell.
A. Glycogenolysis B. Extracellular C. Pepsin D. Rapaflo

99. A Mental state characterized by depressed mood, with feelings of frustration and hopelessness.
A. Depression B. Chromic C. Mixed Number D. Geriatrics

100. A Class of drugs used to treat anxiety and sleep disorders.
A. Benzodiazepine B. Plendil C. Thromboembolism D. Cerebellum

From the words provided for each clue, provide the letter of the word which best matches the clue.

101. A A group of microorganisms with a membrane-bound nucleus that includes yeasts and molds.
A. Fungus B. Hyperstat C. Edecrin D. Vancenase

102. A Nicardipine
A. Cardene B. Hyperstat C. Somatotropin D. Allergen

103. B Permanent black discoloration of skin and mucous membranes caused by prolonged use of silver protein.
A. Cardiac Glycoside B. Argyria C. Rhinocort D. Cholelithiasis

104. A Drug usually administered IV that stops a convulsive seizure.
A. Anticonvulsant B. Triglyceride C. Topamax D. Candidiasis

105. C Candesartan
A. Ambien B. Vasoconstriction C. Atacand D. Oligospermia

106. B High levels of insulin in the blood often associated with type 2 diabetes mellitus and insulin resistance.
A. Homeostasis B. Hyperinsulinemia C. Euphoria D. Spermatogenesis

107. C Chlordiazepoxide
A. Myocardium B. Lotensin C. Librium D. Hematinic

108. D Formation of spermatozoa.
A. Sympathetic B. Digitalization C. Ulcerogenic D. Spermatogenesis

109. A Prefix meaning small.
A. Micro B. Expectorant C. Homeostasis D. Lanoxin

110. B Muscle spasms, facial grimacing, and other involuntary movements and postures.
A. Opiate B. Dystonia C. Somatotropin D. Antipyresis

111. C Atorvastatin
A. Emetogenic B. Argyria C. Lipitor D. Mysoline

112. D Digoxin
A. Lotensin B. Micro C. Cardene D. Lanoxin

113. B Specific cellular structure that a drug binds to and that produces a physiologic effect.
A. Micro B. Receptor C. Convulsion D. Bias

114. D Action that causes the decomposition or destruction of proteins.
A. Evacuation B. Pharmacology C. Alopecia D. Proteolytic

115. A Protein necessary for intestinal absorption of vitamin B12.
A. Intrinsic Factor B. Candidemia C. Hyperinsulinemia D. Lipitor

116. D Study of drugs.
A. Hypertrichosis B. Antagonistic C. Myocardium D. Pharmacology

117. A Indigestion.
A. Dyspepsia B. Electrolyte C. Cardiac Glycoside D. Analytic Studies

118. D Suffix denoting the inhibition of, as of microorganisms.
A. Automatism B. Tetany C. Spermatogenesis D. Static

119. D Amrinone
A. Acidification B. Cardene C. Tyzine D. Inocor

120. D The muscular layer of the heart.
A. Cardiac Glycoside B. Vasoconstriction C. Anticonvulsant D. Myocardium

121. B Disease of the muscles.
A. Remission B. Myopathy C. Morphology D. Bias

122. B Elimination of the drug from the body.
A. Repolarization B. Drug Excretion C. Osmoreceptors D. Chemical Name

123. C Generalized seizure that does not involve motor convulsions; also referred to as petit mal.
A. Remission B. Normodyne C. Absence Seizure D. Intrathecal

124. C Reduced sperm count.
A. Menopause B. Drug Dependence C. Oligospermia D. Solute

125. A Bacterial enzymes that inactivate penicillin antibiotics.
A. Penicillinase B. Somatotropin C. Automatism D. Analytic Studies

126. A Disease that involves the development and reproduction of abnormal cells.
A. Cancer B. Antipyresis C. Edema D. Emetogenic

127. C Plaque formed in the artery wall that remains in the wall.
A. Drug Dependence B. Absence Seizure C. Stable Plaque D. Postpartum

128. B Flushing of the stomach.
A. Immunity B. Gastric Lavage C. Remission D. Thrombophlebitis

129. A Name that defines the chemical composition of a drug.
A. Chemical Name B. Basal Ganglia C. Lipodystrophy D. Mucolytic

130. D Milrinone
A. Euthyroid B. Myocardium C. Intrathecal D. Primacor

131. A A fat formed by three fatty acids into one molecule that supplies energy to muscle cells.
A. Triglyceride B. Depakene C. Thrombophlebitis D. Prosom

132. D Excessive hair growth on the body.
A. Allergen B. Bone Mass C. Digitalization D. Hypertrichosis

133. B Substance that is soothing to mucous membranes or skin.
A. Evacuation B. Emollient C. Acidification D. Myocardium

134. A Tightening or contraction of muscles in the blood vessels, which decreases blood flow through the vessels.
A. Vasoconstriction B. Euphoria C. Keppra D. Atacand

135. A Lack of coordination of muscle movements.
A. Ataxia B. Gabitril C. Rem Sleep D. Oogenesis

136. A Pertaining to glands that secrete substances directly into the blood.
A. Endocrine B. Postpartum C. Dyspepsia D. Glycogen

137. D Azelastine
A. Topamax B. Cholelithiasis C. Hyperemia D. Astelin

138. D Prefix meaning large.
A. Allergen B. Cytic C. Micro D. Mega

139. A CNS depressant drug possessing the barbituric acid ring structure.
A. Barbiturate B. Osmoreceptors C. Intrathecal D. Hematinic

140. B Counteract; oppose.
A. Hyperglycemia B. Antagonistic C. Evacuation D. Hypertrichosis

141. A Drug-induced confusion that can cause increased drug consumption.
A. Automatism B. Incretins C. Emetogenic D. Dermatophytic

142. B Ticlopidine
A. Basal Ganglia B. Ticlid C. Librium D. Proteolytic

143. B A substance secreted by T cells that signals other immune cells like macrophages to aggregate.
A. Dermatophytic B. Lymphokine C. Dynacirc D. Myopathy

144. B Diazoxide
A. Solute B. Hyperstat C. Evacuation D. Tetany

145. A Drug obtained from plants of the genus Digitalis.
A. Cardiac Glycoside B. Analytic Studies C. Persantine D. Ulcerogenic

146. B Antibacterial drug obtained from other microorganisms.
A. Evacuation B. Antibiotic C. Convulsion D. Drug Excretion

147. C Benazepril
A. Lavage B. Synaptic Knob C. Lotensin D. Pepsin

148. B Studies with control groups, namely case-control studies, cohort studies, and randomized clinical trials.
A. Cutaneous B. Analytic Studies C. Thrombophlebitis D. Mega

149. B Part of the brain that coordinates body movements and posture and helps maintain body equilibrium.
A. Convulsion B. Cerebellum C. Stable Plaque D. Mucolytic

150. A An inflammation of the hair follicles of the beard or scalp caused by ringworm with swelling and pus.
A. Kerion B. Somatotropin C. Opiate D. Keppra

151. C Having the ability to cause mutations.
A. Dermatophytic B. Rem Sleep C. Mutagenic D. Selective

152. D Ethacrynic acid
A. Ovulation B. Cushings Disease C. Proarrhythmia D. Edecrin

153. B Doxazosin
A. Depakene B. Cardura C. Limbic System D. Isotonic

154. D Partially digested food and gastric secretions that moves into the duodenum from the stomach by peristalsis.
A. Selective B. Antibiotic C. Chelate D. Chime

155. A Alprazolam
A. Xanax B. Postpartum C. Prostaglandin D. Electrolyte

156. A Infection caused by the yeast Candida; also known as moniliasis.
A. Candidiasis B. Repolarization C. Bias D. Tyzine

157. C Any disease caused by a fungus.
A. Spasmogenic B. Hernia C. Mycosis D. Tonic

158. A Indapamide
A. Lozol B. Cancer C. Stroke Volume D. Angina

159. A Flecainide
A. Tambocor B. Expectorant C. Mysoline D. Automatism

160. B Homogeneous mixture of two or more substances.
A. Ambien B. Solution C. Cardura D. Gabitril

161. B Higher than normal level of glucose in the blood.
A. Antipyresis B. Hyperglycemia C. Restoril D. Digitalization

162. B Condition that causes individuals to resist acquiring or developing a disease or infection.
A. Halcion B. Immunity C. Solute D. Lozol

163. B Ion in solution, such as sodium, potassium, or chloride, that is capable of mediating conduction.
A. Lavage B. Electrolyte C. Argyria D. Allergen

164. A The storage form of glucose in humans and animals.
A. Glycogen B. Euphoria C. Cushings Disease D. Pharmacology

165. A Stage of sleep characterized by rapid eye movement (REM) and dreaming.
A. Rem Sleep B. Heart Rate C. Argyria D. Analytic Studies

166. A Normal state of balance among the body's internal organs.
A. Homeostasis B. Ulcerogenic C. Lipitor D. Gabitril

167. C Specialized cells in the hypothalamus that respond to changes in sodium concentration in the blood.
A. Synthetic Drug B. Cardura C. Osmoreceptors D. Astelin

168. A Inference tending to produce results that depart systematically from the true values.
A. Bias B. Lightheadedness C. Sterilization D. Oxytocin

169. C A substance that causes vomiting.
A. Mucolytic B. Tetany C. Emetogenic D. Seizure

170. A Refers to the action of an adrenergic blocking drug or an action that decreases sympathetic activity.
A. Sympatholytic B. Gabitril C. Postpartum D. Solute

171. A Beclomethasone
A. Vancenase B. Morphology C. Psychosis D. Lotensin

172. C Origin of the pain is in a different location than where the individual feels the pain.
A. Edecrin B. Incretins C. Referred Pain D. Minipress

173. B Increased blood flow to a body part like the eye; engorgement.
A. Cardene B. Hyperemia C. Cancer D. Ticlid

174. D Substance dissolved in a solvent; usually present in a lesser amount.
A. Ratio B. Cerebellum C. Alopecia D. Solute

175. B The relationship of one number to another expressed by whole numbers.
A. Intoxication B. Ratio C. Hyperinsulinemia D. Mysoline

176. A Can stimulate uterine and intestinal muscle contractions and may cause pain by stimulating nerve endings.
A. Prostaglandin B. Keppra C. Tambocor D. Afferent Nerve

177. C Valproic
A. Renin B. Basal Ganglia C. Depakene D. Lipitor

178. B Refers to nerves of the ANS that originate from the thoracolumbar portion of the spinal cord.
A. Limbic System B. Sympathetic C. Atacand D. Spermatogenesis

179. C Nitroglycerine
A. Fungus B. Sympatholytic C. Nitrostat D. Postpartum

180. A Condition associated with an increased production of ketone bodies as a result of fat metabolism.
A. Ketosis B. Argyria C. Inflammation D. Convulsion

181. D Condition of long duration, usually months or years.
A. Intrathecal B. Evacuation C. Mycosis D. Chronic

182. B Excess secretion of adenocorticotropic hormone (ACTH).
A. Cancer B. Cushings Disease C. Cathartic D. Topamax

183. A Insufficient blood supply to meet the needs of the tissue or organ.
A. Ischemia B. Dyspepsia C. Minipress D. Ketosis

184. D Fibric acid
A. Oxytocin B. Morphology C. Adipose Tissue D. Trilipix

185. D Return of the electric potential across a cell membrane to its resting state following depolarization.
A. Tyzine B. Chelate C. Stroke Volume D. Repolarization

186. A An excessive accumulation of fluid in body tissues.
A. Edema B. Inocor C. Miotic D. Lanoxin

187. A A substance that causes constriction of the pupil or miosis.
A. Miotic B. Baycol C. Cerebellum D. Candidiasis

188. A Suffix meaning cells.
A. Cytic B. Oligospermia C. Pharmacodynamics D. Microcilia

189. B Clopidogrel
A. Stroke Volume B. Plavix C. Candidemia D. Schizophrenia

190. B Tamsulosin
A. Vasoconstriction B. Flomax C. Analytic Studies D. Emollient

191. D Estazolam
A. Penicillinase B. Tonic C. Renin D. Prosom

192. C Diltiazem
A. Convulsion B. Cushings Disease C. Cardizem D. Prostaglandin

193. B An arrhythmia caused by administration of an antiarrhythmic drug.
A. Cardene B. Proarrhythmia C. Mega D. Absence Seizure

194. A Isradipine
A. Dynacirc B. Sympatholytic C. Antagonistic D. Chronic

195. C Prazosin
A. Somatotropin B. Adipose Tissue C. Minipress D. Gabitril

196. D Decimal fraction with a denominator of 100.
A. Evacuation B. Basal Ganglia C. Dermatophytic D. Percent

197. D Levetiracetam
A. Fungicidal B. Cerebellum C. Stable Plaque D. Keppra

198. C Medications containing iron compounds, used to increase hemoglobin production.
A. Remission B. Primacor C. Hematinic D. Lunesta

199. C Temazepam
A. Afferent Nerve B. Sympathetic C. Restoril D. Antihistaminic

200. C After childbirth.
A. Hematinic B. Mycosis C. Postpartum D. Antihistaminic

From the words provided for each clue, provide the letter of the word which best matches the clue.

201. D Any disease caused by a fungus.
A. Lymphopenia B. Antagonist C. Hypertrichosis D. Mycosis

202. D CNS depressant drug possessing the barbituric acid ring structure.
A. Lyse B. Pressor C. Hyperstat D. Barbiturate

203. D Inflammation of the joints.
A. Vascor B. Myalgia C. Trilipix D. Arthritis

204. A Beclomethasone
A. Beconase B. Leukotrienes C. Vascor D. Seizure

205. D An inflammation of the hair follicles of the beard or scalp caused by ringworm with swelling and pus.
A. Automatism B. Cholelithiasis C. Potency D. Kerion

206. D Measure of the strength, or concentration, of a drug required to produce a specific effect.
A. Cordarone B. Corgard C. Argyria D. Potency

207. A Diazoxide
A. Hyperstat B. Mycosis C. Atonic Seizure D. Aldomet

208. A Methsuximide
A. Celontin B. Pharmacology C. Sympatholytic D. Polyuria

209. D Nadolol
A. Anion B. Micro C. Intrathecal D. Corgard

210. B Chemical action of a substance to bond permanently to a metal ion.
A. Argyria B. Chelate C. Xylocaine D. Fungus

211. D Life-threatening; refers to growth of a cancerous tumor.
A. Corgard B. Defecation C. Diuril D. Malignant

212. D Negatively charged ion.
A. Limbic System B. Activase C. Salicylism D. Anion

213. D Pain resulting from a damaged nervous system or damaged nerve cells.
A. Depression B. Atonic Seizure C. Aphthous Ulcer D. Neuropathic Pain

214. A Protein in red blood cells that transports oxygen to all tissues of the body.
A. Hemoglobin B. Erythropoiesis C. Candidemia D. Norpace

215. C Space around the brain and spinal cord that contains the cerebrospinal fluid.
A. Virucidal B. Vasoconstriction C. Intrathecal D. Malignant

216. A The cytoplasm of a striated (skeletal) muscle fiber.
A. Sarcoplasm B. Micro C. Lotensin D. Beconase

217. A An abnormal decrease in the number of circulating white blood cells.
A. Leucopenia B. Kerion C. Lipoprotein D. Candidemia

218. B Fibric acid
A. Ovulation B. Trilipix C. Monopril D. Diuril

219. B Benazepril
A. Micro B. Lotensin C. Nephritis D. Otrivin

220. B A fungus infection of the nail.
A. Ulcer B. Onychomycosis C. Emphysema D. Percent

221. A Hormone synthesized and released by the thyroid gland.
A. Thyroxine B. Triglyceride C. Trilipix D. Ativan

222. A Mental state of excitement, hyperactivity, and excessive elevation of mood.
A. Mania B. Hemoglobin C. Isotonic D. Leucopenia

223. A Slowed body movements.
A. Bradykinesia B. Petechial C. Insulin D. Tambocor

224. A Tending to cause inflammation.
A. Proinflammatory B. Myalgia C. Iodophor D. Barbiturate

225. B Drug that attaches to a receptor, does not initiate an action, but blocks an agonist from producing an effect.
A. Vasoconstriction B. Antagonist C. Valium D. Xylocaine

226. D Felodipine
A. Thrombocytopenia B. Hypertrichosis C. Sterilization D. Plendil

227. B Decrease in the number of circulating lymphocytes.
A. Norepinephrine B. Lymphopenia C. Nephritis D. Oxyntic Cell

228. A A fat formed by three fatty acids into one molecule that supplies energy to muscle cells.
A. Triglyceride B. Candidemia C. Lymphopenia D. Vasoconstriction

229. A Drug effect other than the therapeutic effect that is usually undesirable but not harmful.
A. Side Effect B. Arteriosclerosis C. Depression D. Alkylation

230. A Undesirable drug effect that implies drug poisoning; can be very harmful or life-threatening.
A. Toxic Effect B. Defecation C. Malignant D. Dysentery

231. A A stiffness and inflexibility of movement.
A. Rigidity B. THC C. Cardene D. Mycosis

232. B A thin membrane enclosing a striated (skeletal) muscle fiber.
A. Phlegm B. Sarcolemma C. Oligospermia D. Erythropoiesis

233. D Indapamide
A. Depression B. Iodophor C. Synergistic D. Lozol

234. A Process of discharging the contents of the intestines as feces.
A. Defecation B. Edecrin C. Ova D. Spasmogenic

235. C General term for undesirable and potentially harmful drug effect.
A. Endometrium B. Seizure C. Adverse Effect D. Phlegm

236. B Release of an egg from the ovary.
A. Homeostasis B. Ovulation C. Bradykinesia D. Phlegm

237. C Condition in which toxic doses of salicylates are ingested, resulting in nausea, tinnitus, and delirium.
A. Celontin B. Insomnia C. Salicylism D. Bronchodilator

238. D Tamsulosin
A. Dysentery B. Oxytocin C. Xylocaine D. Flomax

239. D Bacteria that retain only the red stain in a gram stain.
A. Cholelithiasis B. Toxic Effect C. Questran D. Gram Negative

240. A Carvedilol
A. Coreg B. Cordarone C. Myalgia D. Plendil

241. B Causing a muscle to contract intermittently, resulting in a state of spasms.
A. Parietal Cell B. Spasmogenic C. Hyperalgesia D. Bradykinesia

242. D Secretion from the respiratory tract; usually called mucus.
A. Hyperemia B. Lipitor C. Lyse D. Phlegm

243. B Budesonide
A. Bacteria B. Rhinocort C. Trilipix D. Neutropenia

244. A Normal state of balance among the body's internal organs.
A. Homeostasis B. Polyphagia C. Kerion D. Hyperemia

245. B Study of the distribution and determinants of diseases in populations.
A. Keppra B. Epidemiology C. Bacteria D. Drug Compliance

246. C Reduced sperm count.
A. Anion B. Aphthous Ulcer C. Oligospermia D. Infarction

247. B Pravastatin
A. Monophasic B. Pravachol C. Fungistatic D. Leucopenia

248. A Study of drugs.
A. Pharmacology B. Epidemiology C. Parietal Cell D. Lipoprotein

249. B Protruding eyeballs out of the socket.
A. Vascor B. Exophthalmos C. Laxative D. Apoptosis

250. B Chlorothiazide
A. Synergistic B. Diuril C. Sectral D. Tambocor

251. B Gemfibrozil
A. Depakene B. Lopid C. Determinant D. Lozol

252. C Cholestyramine
A. Laxative B. Tremor C. Questran D. Gram Negative

253. C Drug obtained from plants of the genus Digitalis.
A. Zestril B. Preload C. Cardiac Glycoside D. Rem Sleep

254. A Prefix meaning large.
A. Mega B. Dynacirc C. Iodophor D. Exophthalmos

255. B To disintegrate or dissolve.
A. Sectral B. Lyse C. Minipress D. Hematuria

256. B Not able to continue drug therapy usually because of extreme sensitivity to the side effects.
A. Bioavailability B. Intolerant C. Addisons Disease D. Tremor

257. A Hormone released from adrenal cortex that causes the retention of sodium from the kidneys.
A. Aldosterone B. THC C. Rigidity D. Biphasic

258. C Xylometazoline
A. Rem Sleep B. Mega C. Otrivin D. Cardene

259. D Prazosin
A. Depakene B. Isotonic C. Lozol D. Minipress

260. D An abnormal decrease in the number of circulating platelets.
A. Vascor B. Hyponatremia C. Lactation D. Thrombocytopenia

261. B Refers to the action of an adrenergic blocking drug or an action that decreases sympathetic activity.
A. Proarrhythmia B. Sympatholytic C. Ethmozine D. Oxytocin

262. B Substance, chemical solution, or drug that kills viruses.
A. Incompatibility B. Virucidal C. Synergistic D. Neuropathic Pain

263. B Part of the brain that coordinates body movements and posture and helps maintain body equilibrium.
A. Hypophosphatemia B. Cerebellum C. Xylocaine D. Erythropoiesis

264. A Generalized-type seizure characterized by a sudden loss of muscle tone.
A. Atonic Seizure B. Osteoclasts C. Rem Sleep D. Argyria

265. A Acebutolol
A. Sectral B. Arthritis C. Determinant D. Sterilization

266. D Quazepam
A. Homeostasis B. Calorigenic C. Onychomycosis D. Doral

267. B Adverse reaction which results from an exaggerated but otherwise usual pharmacological effect.
A. Dynacirc B. Type A Reaction C. Dysentery D. Lymphopenia

268. A Inflammation of the glomeruli often following a streptococcus infection.
A. Nephritis B. Xylocaine C. Pressor D. Creatinine

269. D Production of milk in female breasts.
A. Dyrenium B. Laxative C. Gastric Lavage D. Lactation

270. C Cell death, due to either programmed cell death or other physiological events.
A. Decimal B. Hemolytic Anemia C. Apoptosis D. Edecrin

271. D The uptake of nutrients and drugs from the GI tract.
A. Argyria B. THC C. Depakene D. Absorption

272. C Drug that relaxes bronchial smooth muscle and dilates the lower respiratory passages.
A. Sectral B. Synesthesia C. Bronchodilator D. Pluripotent

273. B A fixed amount of estrogen is released during the cycle.
A. Neutropenia B. Monophasic C. Gram Negative D. Lotensin

274. C Following drug prescription directions exactly as written.
A. Anion B. Evacuation C. Drug Compliance D. Trichomoniasis

275. D Nicardipine
A. Intrathecal B. Cerebellum C. Side Effect D. Cardene

276. A Refers to nerves of the ANS that originate from the thoracolumbar portion of the spinal cord.
A. Sympathetic B. Depakene C. Hematuria D. Vasoconstriction

277. D An abnormally painful response to a stimulus.
A. Tambocor B. Petechial C. Candidemia D. Hyperalgesia

278. B Group or island of cells.
A. Accupril B. Islets C. Evacuation D. Tremor

279. A A substance secreted by T cells that signals other immune cells like macrophages to aggregate.
A. Lymphokine B. Absorption C. Vasoconstriction D. Sarcoplasm

280. B Condition in which an arterial blood pressure is abnormally low.
A. Tremor B. Hypotension C. Norpace D. Trichomoniasis

281. C Increased blood flow to a body part like the eye; engorgement.
A. Gametocyte B. Gram Negative C. Hyperemia D. Hypertrichosis

282. A Drug used to produce mental relaxation and to reduce the desire for physical activity.
A. Sedative B. Questran C. Neutropenia D. Aphthous Ulcer

283. A Single-celled microorganisms, some of which cause disease.
A. Bacteria B. Seizure C. Oliguria D. Hyponatremia

284. D Chemical mediators involved in inflammation and asthma.
A. Monophasic B. Oligospermia C. Corgard D. Leukotrienes

285. D Fosinopril
A. Apoptosis B. Parietal Cell C. Seizure D. Monopril

286. A Lining of the uterus.
A. Endometrium B. Oliguria C. Sectral D. Isotonic

287. D Condition characterized by frequent watery stools (usually containing blood and mucus), tenesmus.
A. Chelate B. Sympatholytic C. Toxic Effect D. Dysentery

288. B Neural pathway connecting different brain areas involved in regulation of behavior and emotion.
A. Virucidal B. Limbic System C. Diuril D. Ulcer

289. C Active ingredient of the marijuana plant.
A. Doral B. Sarcoplasm C. THC D. Emphysema

290. C Drug-induced confusion that can cause increased drug consumption.
A. Epidemiology B. Apoptosis C. Automatism D. Sarcoplasm

291. B Tending to increase blood pressure.
A. Ulcer B. Pressor C. Lyse D. Hemolytic Anemia

292. D Inhibits the growth of fungi but does not kill off the fungi.
A. Determinant B. Polyuria C. Ativan D. Fungistatic

293. A Mature eggs
A. Ova B. Nitrostat C. Spermatogenesis D. Pressor

294. B A substance that promotes bowel movements.
A. Mavik B. Laxative C. Automatism D. Aphthous Ulcer

295. A Ethacrynic acid
A. Edecrin B. Potency C. Alkylation D. Lyse

296. C A molecule that contains a protein and a lipid (fat).
A. Phlegm B. Keppra C. Lipoprotein D. Nephritis

297. C Inhibition of the vagus nerve to the heart, causing the heart rate to increase.
A. Hyponatremia B. Norepinephrine C. Vagolytic Action D. Erythropoiesis

298. D A painful open sore in the mouth or upper throat; also known as a canker sore.
A. Insomnia B. Sterilization C. Creatinine D. Aphthous Ulcer

299. B Prazepam
A. Homeostasis B. Centrax C. Loading Dose D. Decimal

300. C Flushing of the stomach.
A. Salicylism B. Cardene C. Gastric Lavage D. Questran

From the words provided for each clue, provide the letter of the word which best matches the clue.

301. A Decrease in the number of circulating lymphocytes.
A. Lymphopenia B. Hemorrhage C. Nicobid D. Hyperacidity

302. C Bottom number of a fraction; shows the number of parts in a whole.
A. Thromboembolism B. Bradykinesia C. Denominator D. Hematuria

303. D A substance that causes constriction of the pupil or miosis.
A. Incompatibility B. Mega C. Denominator D. Miotic

304. A A type of cell formed after macrophages in the artery wall digest LDL cholesterol.
A. Foam Cells B. Antilipemic Drug C. Plavix D. Bacteria

305. D Uncontrolled growth of abnormal cells that form a solid mass; also called a neoplasm.
A. Virucidal B. Depakene C. Acidosis D. Tumor

306. D Spironolactone
A. Vasotec B. Ticlid C. Lipitor D. Aldactone

307. B Undesirable interaction of drugs not suitable for combination or administration together.
A. Vasotec B. Incompatibility C. Euvolemia D. Tumor

308. C A painful open sore in the mouth or upper throat; also known as a canker sore.
A. Broad Spectrum B. Hyperacidity C. Aphthous Ulcer D. Cardura

309. D Cell division in which two daughter cells receive the same number of chromosomes as the parent cell.
A. Dysgeusia B. Coronary Artery C. Hyperemia D. Mitosis

310. C Condition in which the body develops a severe allergic response; this is a medical emergency.
A. Menopause B. Tnkase C. Anaphylaxis D. Stroke

311. C Drug that prevents mast cells from releasing histamine and other vasoactive substances.
A. Vascor B. Bradycardia C. Antiallergic D. Systemic

312. D Initial drug dose administered to rapidly achieve therapeutic drug concentrations.
A. Limbic System B. Therapeutic Dose C. Hematuria D. Loading Dose

313. A Organs that produce male (testes) or female (ovaries) sex cells, sperm or ova.
A. Gonads B. Gastric Lavage C. Lysosome D. Dyrenium

314. B Having inhibition of the body's immune response.
A. Limbic System B. Immunosuppressed C. Iodophor D. Mycosis

315. D HCTZ
A. Trilipix B. Proarrhythmia C. Dyrenium D. Hydrodiuril

316. C The muscular layer of the heart.
A. Antiallergic B. Librium C. Myocardium D. Aldactone

317. B Process that alters the pH to less than 7.
A. Prodrug B. Acidification C. Incompatibility D. Colestid

318. D A substance that causes vomiting.
A. Valium B. Proportion C. Cannabinoid D. Emetogenic

319. C Positively charged ion.
A. Serax B. Trade Name C. Cation D. Endemic

320. B Tenecteplase
A. Tenex B. Tnkase C. Ticlid D. Buccal Absorption

321. B Rapid involuntary movement of eyes.
A. Bradycardia B. Nystagmus C. Virucidal D. Geriatrics

322. A Term used for Candida infection in the mucous membranes of the mouth and pharynx.
A. Thrush B. Intra Articular C. Mysoline D. Oliguria

323. B A mathematical equation that expresses the equality between two ratios.
A. Nystagmus B. Proportion C. Menstruation D. Endogenous

324. C Abnormally high level of chloride ions circulating in the blood.
A. Candidemia B. Serax C. Hyperchloremia D. Diplopia

325. B The amount of blood pumped per minute by the heart.
A. Agranulocytosis B. Cardiac Output C. Cardura D. Euphoria

326. C Production of milk in female breasts.
A. Anaphylaxis B. Aldactone C. Lactation D. Corgard

327. C Drug that inhibits the growth and proliferation of cancer cells.
A. Hyperinsulinemia B. Tumor C. Antineoplastic D. Digestion

328. C Dizziness often caused by a decrease in blood supply to the brain.
A. Arthritis B. Anaphylaxis C. Lightheadedness D. Argyria

329. C Streptokinase
A. Myocardium B. Heartburn C. Streptase D. Mitochondria

330. A Any cell that covers the axons in the peripheral nervous system and forms the myelin sheath.
A. Schwann Cell B. Nonbarbiturate C. Levatol D. Hematuria

331. B Abnormally high body temperature.
A. Isotonic B. Hyperthermia C. Acidosis D. Gastroparesis

332. C Loss of brain function due to a loss of blood supply.
A. Protozoan B. Osmosis C. Stroke D. Gonads

333. A Infection of the skin, hair, or nails caused by a fungus.
A. Dermatophytic B. Expectorant C. Lysosome D. Adverse Reaction

334. C Occurring in the general circulation, resulting in distribution to most organs.
A. Hemorrhage B. Arrhythmia C. Systemic D. Bradycardia

335. C Transmits sensory information from peripheral organs to the central nervous system).
A. Chromic B. Schwann Cell C. Afferent Nerve D. Hyperemia

336. D Slowed body movements.
A. Meiosis B. Digestion C. Midamor D. Bradykinesia

337. D Increase in the amount of drug metabolizing enzymes after repeated administration of certain drugs.
A. Sterilization B. Insomnia C. Hypokalemia D. Enzyme Induction

338. D Increased blood flow to a body part like the eye; engorgement.
A. Islets B. Welchol C. Mixed Number D. Hyperemia

339. C Chlordiazepoxide
A. Flonase B. Sterilization C. Librium D. Sedative

340. B Condition in which monthly menstruation (menses) no longer occurs.
A. Trilipix B. Amenorrhea C. Norvasc D. Chronic

341. A Refers to sedative-hypnotic drugs that do not possess the barbituric acid structure.
A. Nonbarbiturate B. Plavix C. Vasotec D. Menstruation

342. C Slowing down of heart rate.
A. Incompatibility B. Euvolemia C. Bradycardia D. Enzyme Induction

343. C Diazepam
A. Gonads B. Depakene C. Valium D. Endemic

344. C Losartan
A. Trade Name B. Klonopin C. Cozaar D. Abortifacient

345. B Specialized cells in the hypothalamus that respond to changes in sodium concentration in the blood.
A. Tropic Hormone B. Osmoreceptors C. Tnkase D. Corgard

346. B Enalapril
A. Zaroxolyn B. Vasotec C. Nystagmus D. Thrush

347. D State of normal body fluid volume.
A. Euphoria B. Endogenous C. Osmoreceptors D. Euvolemia

348. D Medical specialty that deals with individuals over 65 years of age.
A. Welchol B. Epidemiology C. Antitussive D. Geriatrics

349. A Compound containing iodine.
A. Iodophor B. Gastroparesis C. Valium D. Oliguria

350. A Chlorothiazide
A. Diuril B. Cryoanesthesia C. Nicobid D. Nonbarbiturate

351. D Flushing of the stomach.
A. Stroke B. Aldactone C. Lyse D. Gastric Lavage

352. C Amlodipine
A. Ova B. Enzyme Induction C. Norvasc D. Gonads

353. D Prefix meaning large.
A. Nicobid B. Protozoan C. Renin D. Mega

354. D Error introduced into a study by its design rather than due to random variation.
A. Antigen B. Drug Compliance C. Lysosome D. Systematic Error

355. A An arrhythmia caused by administration of an antiarrhythmic drug.
A. Proarrhythmia B. Myocardium C. Aldactone D. Loading Dose

356. C Oxazepam
A. Sedative B. Coronary Artery C. Serax D. Euphoria

357. D A fixed amount of estrogen is released during the cycle.
A. Expectorant B. Cardura C. Systematic Error D. Monophasic

358. C Part of a cell that contains enzymes capable of digesting or destroying tissue
A. Trilipix B. Monophasic C. Lysosome D. Mega

359. A Condition, also called delayed gastric emptying, in which the stomach muscles do not function properly.
A. Gastroparesis B. Topamax C. Trilipix D. Hyperkalemia

360. C Twitchings of muscle fiber groups.
A. Cation B. Tropic Hormone C. Fasciculation D. Exophthalmos

361. C Nadolol
A. Diplopia B. Levatol C. Corgard D. Osmoreceptors

362. B Return of the electric potential across a cell membrane to its resting state following depolarization.
A. Osmoreceptors B. Repolarization C. Arthritis D. Aphthous Ulcer

363. C Mechanical and chemical breakdown of foods into smaller units.
A. Chronic B. Nephritis C. Digestion D. Lyse

364. C A lipid substance secreted by glands in the skin to lubricate the skin everywhere but the palms and soles.
A. Loading Dose B. Cardizem C. Sebum D. Iodophor

365. A Mature eggs
A. Ova B. Absorption C. Mitochondria D. Decubitis Ulcer

366. C Action that causes the decomposition or destruction of proteins.
A. Absorption B. Dyrenium C. Proteolytic D. Expectorant

367. A Type of bacteria that cause disease; a microorganism that causes disease.
A. Pathogen B. Flonase C. Cutaneous D. Sedative

368. A When there is an acute deficiency of granulocytes in blood.
A. Agranulocytosis B. Hypertension C. Lysosome D. Insomnia

369. C Joint space into which drug is injected.
A. Lactation B. Proteolytic C. Intra Articular D. Calorigenic

370. A Permanent black discoloration of skin and mucous membranes caused by prolonged use of silver protein.
A. Argyria B. Keratinized C. Miotic D. Schizophrenia

371. D Study of the distribution and determinants of diseases in populations.
A. Radical Cure B. Proper Fraction C. Midamor D. Epidemiology

372. D Method of dosage with cardiac glycosides that rapidly produces effective drug levels.
A. Hyperemia B. Stroke C. Abortifacient D. Digitalization

373. D Drug used to produce mental relaxation and to reduce the desire for physical activity.
A. Emetogenic B. Phlebitis C. Insomnia D. Sedative

374. B Single-celled microorganisms, some of which cause disease.
A. Lanoxin B. Bacteria C. Loading Dose D. Welchol

375. C Clopidogrel
A. Therapeutic Dose B. Nephritis C. Plavix D. Coronary Artery

376. D Guanabenz
A. Morphology B. Meiosis C. Flomax D. Wytensin

377. A Neural pathway connecting different brain areas involved in regulation of behavior and emotion.
A. Limbic System B. Oliguria C. Morphology D. Norvasc

378. B To disintegrate or dissolve.
A. Tnkase B. Lyse C. Systemic D. Antiallergic

379. C A heart rate that exceeds the normal range for a resting heartrate.
A. Otrivin B. Abortifacient C. Tachycardia D. Ticlid

380. B Chemically altered form of an approved drug that produces similar effects and that is sold illegally.
A. Radical Cure B. Designer Drug C. Phlebitis D. Sebum

381. D Fluticasone
A. Foam Cells B. Denominator C. Arrhythmia D. Flonase

382. B High levels of insulin in the blood often associated with type 2 diabetes mellitus and insulin resistance.
A. Mevacor B. Hyperinsulinemia C. Endogenous D. Decimal

383. C Composed of a protein substance largely found in hair and nails.
A. Mitosis B. Plavix C. Keratinized D. Decubitis Ulcer

384. D Removing the sensation of touch or pain by applying extreme cold to the nerve endings.
A. Virucidal B. Proper Fraction C. Systematic Error D. Cryoanesthesia

385. B Infection in the blood caused by the yeast Candida.
A. Uroxatral B. Candidemia C. Calorigenic D. Denominator

386. C Cells that become the reproductive cells eggs (in ovary) or sperm (in testes).
A. Osteoclasts B. Aphthous Ulcer C. Germ Cells D. Tenex

387. A Topiramate
A. Topamax B. Hemorrhage C. Cardizem D. Euvolemia

388. D Present continually in a particular geographic region, often in spite of control measures.
A. Nephritis B. Emetogenic C. Lanoxin D. Endemic

389. D A drug that suppresses coughing.
A. Proarrhythmia B. Hyperinsulinemia C. Pepsin D. Antitussive

390. D Nicotinic acid
A. Coronary Artery B. Chromic C. Thromboembolism D. Nicobid

391. C Simvastatin
A. Absorption B. Virucidal C. Zocor D. Candidemia

392. A Drug used to treat anxiety; these drugs are also referred to as anxiolytics.
A. Antianxiety Drug B. Mega C. Osmoreceptors D. Isotonic

393. D The probability that an event will occur.
A. Renin B. Denominator C. Klonopin D. Risk

394. C Condition in which a single object is seen (perceived) as two objects; double vision.
A. Hydrodiuril B. Librium C. Diplopia D. Otrivin

395. B Arresting of malaria, in which protozoal parasites are eliminated from all tissues.
A. Keratinized B. Radical Cure C. Miotic D. Arthritis

396. C Process in which water moves across membranes following the movement of sodium ions.
A. Immunosuppressed B. Expectorant C. Osmosis D. Hemolytic Anemia

397. C Patented proprietary name of drug sold by a specific drug manufacturer; also referred to as the brand name.
A. Aphthous Ulcer B. Proper Fraction C. Trade Name D. Cardura

398. D Substance, chemical solution, or drug that kills viruses.
A. Phlebitis B. Hypotension C. Afrin D. Virucidal

399. C Drug that is effective against a wide variety of both gram-positive and gram-negative pathogenic bacteria.
A. Abortifacient B. Restoril C. Broad Spectrum D. Cardizem

400. D Fibric acid
A. Levatol B. Nystagmus C. Proteolytic D. Trilipix

From the words provided for each clue, provide the letter of the word which best matches the clue.

401. B A substance that promotes bowel movements.
A. Goiter B. Laxative C. Proarrhythmia D. Antacid

402. B Cell that synthesizes and releases hydrochloric acid into the stomach lumen.
A. Tambocor B. Parietal Cell C. Gametocyte D. Urticarial

403. A A strong sustained muscle contraction.
A. Tetany B. Zarontin C. Naphcon D. Aldomet

404. A Fluticasone
A. Flonase B. Hyperacidity C. Tetany D. Restoril

405. D Substance that relaxes the muscles controlling blood vessels, leading to increased blood flow.
A. Hematuria B. Creatinine C. Schizophrenia D. Vasodilator

406. C Refers to drugs or effects that reduce the activity of the parasympathetic nervous system.
A. Electrolyte B. Aneurysm C. Anticholinergic D. Bronchodilator

407. A An abnormally painful response to a stimulus.
A. Hyperalgesia B. Germ Cells C. Baycol D. Bronchial Muscles

408. D Bottom number of a fraction; shows the number of parts in a whole.
A. Biphasic B. Phagocyte C. Tropic D. Denominator

409. A When there is an acute deficiency of granulocytes in blood.
A. Agranulocytosis B. Oliguria C. Wheal D. Stroke

410. D When drugs (substances) produce the same intensity or spectrum of activity.
A. Coreg B. Hypoxia C. Argyria D. Equipotent

411. C Reduction of oxygen supply to tissues below the amount required for normal physiological function.
A. Streptase B. Neurontin C. Hypoxia D. Aneurysm

412. D Space around the brain and spinal cord that contains the cerebrospinal fluid.
A. Thrombocytopenia B. Pernicious C. Flonase D. Intrathecal

413. D Chemical mediators involved in inflammation and asthma.
A. Synaptic Knob B. Sarcolemma C. Dependency D. Leukotrienes

414. A Oxymetazoline
A. Afrin B. Dyrenium C. Cushings Disease D. Tetany

415. C Protozoal infection characterized by attacks of chills, fever, and sweating.
A. Blood Dyscrasia B. Native C. Malaria D. Pernicious

416. A The amount of blood pumped per minute by the heart.
A. Cardiac Output B. Aquaresis C. Anion D. Intra Articular

417. B Guanabenz
A. Immunosuppressed B. Wytensin C. Antitussive D. Intra Articular

418. A Abnormally high degree of acidity (for example, pH less than 1) in the stomach.
A. Hyperacidity B. Anticholinergic C. Ulcer D. Chime

419. C Formation of ova.
A. Interleukin B. Oxyntic Cell C. Oogenesis D. Candidiasis

420. D Slowed body movements.
A. Retavase B. Cushings Disease C. Osmosis D. Bradykinesia

421. B Nicotinic acid
A. Hypotonic B. Nicobid C. Thrombus D. Welchol

422. B Carvedilol
A. Absence Seizure B. Coreg C. Phlegm D. Heart Rate

423. A Colesevelam
A. Welchol B. Immunosuppressed C. Interferon D. Nephritis

424. D Study of the distribution and determinants of diseases in populations.
A. Laxative B. Osmosis C. Drug Compliance D. Epidemiology

425. C Error introduced into a study by its design rather than due to random variation.
A. Vancenase B. Sarcolemma C. Systematic Error D. Hypotension

426. D A heart rate that exceeds the normal range for a resting heartrate.
A. Nephritis B. Geriatrics C. Wheal D. Tachycardia

427. D Quinidine
A. Lamictal B. Doral C. Leukotrienes D. Quinidine

428. C Nadolol
A. Baycol B. Half Life C. Corgard D. Lasix

429. B Study of drugs.
A. Carcinoid Tumor B. Pharmacology C. Ambien D. Celontin

430. D Cell that synthesizes and releases hydrochloric acid (HCl) into the stomach lumen.
A. Hypokalemia B. Nicobid C. Dilantin D. Oxyntic Cell

431. C Requirement of repeated drug consumption in order to prevent onset of withdrawal symptoms.
A. Thrombus B. Proinflammatory C. Dependency D. Constipation

432. B Cerivastatin
A. Aquaresis B. Baycol C. Hypotonic D. Osmoreceptors

433. D Tissue containing fat cells; fat.
A. Thrombocytopenia B. Oxyntic Cell C. Synesthesia D. Adipose Tissue

434. B Abnormality in blood.
A. Nasalide B. Blood Dyscrasia C. Aldomet D. Baycol

435. D Abnormally high blood pressure.
A. Dyrenium B. Basal Ganglia C. Hypoxia D. Hypertension

436. A Medical specialty that deals with individuals over 65 years of age.
A. Geriatrics B. Lipodystrophy C. Klonopin D. Denominator

437. B Inflammation of the walls of the veins, associated with clot formation.
A. Virilization B. Thrombophlebitis C. Interferon D. Anticonvulsant

438. B watery substance that is located behind the cornea of the eye and in front of the lens.
A. Agranulocytosis B. Aqueous Humor C. Pernicious D. Afrin

439. B Following drug prescription directions exactly as written.
A. Acidification B. Drug Compliance C. Pravachol D. Petechial

440. A Natural substance in the body.
A. Native B. Dilantin C. Determinant D. Restoril

441. C Permanent black discoloration of skin and mucous membranes caused by prolonged use of silver protein.
A. Absence Seizure B. Extracellular C. Argyria D. Lanoxin

442. B Joint space into which drug is injected.
A. Proportion B. Intra Articular C. Pernicious D. Coreg

443. A Partially digested food and gastric secretions that moves into the duodenum from the stomach by peristalsis.
A. Chime B. Antitussive C. Intolerant D. Proarrhythmia

444. D Name that defines the chemical composition of a drug.
A. Insulin B. Tnkase C. Uroxatral D. Chemical Name

445. C Diazepam
A. Endorphins B. Parietal Cell C. Valium D. Bronchodilator

446. C Excess secretion of adenocorticotropic hormone (ACTH).
A. Hypoxia B. Ulcer C. Cushings Disease D. Remission

447. B Male sex hormone responsible for the development of male characteristics.
A. Antimicrobial B. Androgen C. Cannabinoid D. Pharmacology

448. D Intensely itching raised areas of skin caused by an allergic reaction; hives.
A. Zocor B. Solvent C. Cardiac Output D. Urticarial

449. B Arresting of malaria, in which protozoal parasites are eliminated from all tissues.
A. Endometrium B. Radical Cure C. Ulcer D. Parietal Cell

450. C Ethosuximide
A. Anion B. Activase C. Zarontin D. Malaria

451. D Dipyridamole
A. Chemical Name B. Intolerant C. Tnkase D. Persantine

452. A Period when cancer cells are not increasing in number.
A. Remission B. Digitalization C. Dyrenium D. Radical Cure

453. C Coiled or folded back on itself.
A. Tachycardia B. Nicobid C. Convoluted D. Antagonistic

454. B Phenytoin
A. Schizophrenia B. Dilantin C. Myoclonic D. Virilization

455. B Drug that blocks the action of histamine at the target organ.
A. Tyzine B. Antihistaminic C. Proinflammatory D. Ambien

456. D Alfuzosin
A. Lotensin B. Centrax C. Phagocyte D. Uroxatral

457. B Composed of a protein substance largely found in hair and nails.
A. Aldomet B. Keratinized C. Norepinephrine D. Pharmacology

458. A Reteplase
A. Retavase B. Stroke Volume C. Oogenesis D. Dyrenium

459. B Counteract; oppose.
A. Afrin B. Antagonistic C. Numerator D. Stroke

460. A A condition where the concentration of salt (sodium, electrolytes) is less than that found inside the cells.
A. Hypotonic B. Cancer C. Keratinized D. Antiseptic

461. C Preparation in which undissolved solids are dispersed within a liquid.
A. Keratinized B. Streptase C. Suspension D. Aldomet

462. C Number of heart beats per minute.
A. Hypertension B. Anticonvulsant C. Heart Rate D. Blood Dyscrasia

463. A Losartan
A. Cozaar B. Sarcolemma C. Antagonistic D. Bradykinesia

464. C Neurotransmitter of sympathetic nerves that stimulates the adrenergic receptors.
A. Wheal B. Lavage C. Norepinephrine D. Equipotent

465. D Interacts with one subtype of receptor over others.
A. Biphasic B. Aplastic Anemia C. Hypokalemia D. Selective

466. A Pravastatin
A. Pravachol B. Solvent C. Nosocomial D. Uroxatral

467. D pH greater than 7.45.
A. Proper Fraction B. Sectral C. Asymptomatic D. Alkalosis

468. A Smooth muscles of lungs.
A. Bronchial Muscles B. Endorphins C. Altace D. Permissive

469. A A substance capable of producing an allergic reaction.
A. Allergen B. Creatinine C. Ova D. Drowsiness

470. B A mathematical equation that expresses the equality between two ratios.
A. Bradykinesia B. Proportion C. Tachycardia D. Antihistaminic

471. B Ion in solution, such as sodium, potassium, or chloride, that is capable of mediating conduction.
A. Hypertension B. Electrolyte C. Creatinine D. Fungistatic

472. A Low concentration of potassium in blood.
A. Hypokalemia B. Aquaresis C. Tambocor D. Lanoxin

473. D Infection caused by the yeast Candida; also known as moniliasis.
A. Oxyntic Cell B. Drug Indications C. Virilization D. Candidiasis

474. A Benazepril
A. Lotensin B. Corgard C. Dehiscence D. Hypertension

475. A The muscular layer of the heart.
A. Myocardium B. Extracellular C. Adipose Tissue D. Pravachol

476. D An abnormal decrease in the number of circulating platelets.
A. Lavage B. Tetany C. Sectral D. Thrombocytopenia

477. B Tenecteplase
A. Activase B. Tnkase C. Hyperacidity D. Hypophosphatemia

478. B Milrinone
A. Proper Fraction B. Primacor C. Wytensin D. Schizophrenia

479. B Development of masculine body (hair, muscle) characteristics in females.
A. Selective B. Virilization C. Centrax D. Bias

480. B Methyldopa
A. Systematic Error B. Aldomet C. Halcion D. Chime

481. B An element similar to sodium that is used in the treatment of mania and bipolar mood disorder.
A. Oxyntic Cell B. Lithium C. Barbiturate D. Baycol

482. C A thick-walled structure in which parasitic protozoal sex cells develop for transfer to new hosts.
A. Malaria B. Lamictal C. Oocyst D. Aplastic Anemia

483. D Major form of psychosis; behavior is inappropriate.
A. Antiseptic B. Quinidine C. Antagonistic D. Schizophrenia

484. D Top number of a fraction; shows the part.
A. Drowsiness B. Persantine C. Schizophrenia D. Numerator

485. B A metabolite of muscle metabolism that is excreted in the urine in proportion to renal function.
A. Nosocomial B. Creatinine C. Nicobid D. Quinidine

486. A Condition in which there is no outward evidence (symptom) that an infection is present.
A. Asymptomatic B. Thrombophlebitis C. Altace D. Hypotonic

487. B Negatively charged ion.
A. Biphasic B. Anion C. Nosocomial D. Polypharmacy

488. B Renal excretion of water without electrolytes.
A. Nosocomial B. Aquaresis C. Tnkase D. Immunity

489. C Hormone secreted by the beta cells of the pancreas to facilitate glucose entry into the cell.
A. Vasodilator B. Radical Cure C. Insulin D. Aquaresis

490. A Furosemide
A. Lasix B. Oliguria C. Selective D. Lithium

491. A Substance, chemical solution, or drug that kills microorganisms.
A. Germicidal B. Cardiac Output C. Doral D. Islets

492. C Opening in a hollow organ, such as a break in the intestinal wall.
A. Malignant B. Thrombocytopenia C. Perforation D. Aplastic Anemia

493. B Substance that induces abortion.
A. Parietal Cell B. Abortifacient C. Basal Ganglia D. Cardiac Output

494. C Silodosin
A. Argyria B. Germ Cells C. Rapaflo D. Denominator

495. A Anemia caused by defective functioning of the blood-forming organs (bone marrow).
A. Aplastic Anemia B. Interferon C. Basal Ganglia D. Synaptic Knob

496. B Appearance of blood or red blood cells in the urine.
A. Blood Dyscrasia B. Hematuria C. Suspension D. Insulin

497. D An antigen-presenting white blood cell that is found in the skin, mucosa, and lymphoid tissues and that
A. Hyperglycemia B. Immunosuppressed C. Zarontin D. Dendritic Cell

498. B Condition in which the thyroid is enlarged, but not as a result of a tumor.
A. Euthyroid B. Goiter C. Persantine D. Permissive

499. D Antibacterial drugs obtained by chemical synthesis and not from other microorganisms.
A. Synesthesia B. Ova C. Cannabinoid D. Antimicrobial

500. D Prazepam
A. Biphasic B. Aneurysm C. Proper Fraction D. Centrax

From the words provided for each clue, provide the letter of the word which best matches the clue.

501. D Open sore in the mucous membranes or mucosal linings of the body.
A. Trileptal B. Mega C. Hygroton D. Ulcer

502. C Chemical mediator produced by immune cells that increases immune function.
A. Xanax B. Inocor C. Interferon D. Ratio

503. B Mature sperm cells.
A. Fungicidal B. Spermatozoa C. Vasoconstriction D. Hypochromic

504. A Washing (lavage) of a wound or cavity with large volumes of fluid.
A. Irrigation B. Perimenopause C. Glycosuria D. Micardis

505. D Time required for the body to reduce the amount of drug in the plasma by one-half.
A. Depakene B. Leucopenia C. Flonase D. Half Life

506. B The presence of the plasma protein albumin in the urine.
A. Ratio B. Albuminuria C. Gabitril D. Pathogen

507. A Method of dosage with cardiac glycosides that rapidly produces effective drug levels.
A. Digitalization B. Hyperstat C. Celontin D. Lithium

508. D The muscular layer of the heart.
A. Radical Cure B. Fungistatic C. Ticlid D. Myocardium

509. D Difficult or painful menstruation; condition that is associated with painful and difficult menstruation.
A. Phagocyte B. Percent C. Mega D. Dysmenorrhea

510. D Condition in which an arterial blood pressure is abnormally low.
A. Ambien B. Spermatozoa C. Hyperkalemia D. Hypotension

511. B Bursting open or separation of a wound, usually along sutured line.
A. Streptase B. Dehiscence C. Colestid D. Effient

512. C Silodosin
A. Loading Dose B. Mega C. Rapaflo D. Interferon

513. D Tiagabine
A. Hirsutism B. Monophasic C. Thrombus D. Gabitril

514. B Beclomethasone
A. Tyzine B. Vancenase C. Myocardium D. Phagocyte

515. A Substance that interacts with tissues to produce most of the symptoms of allergy.
A. Histamine B. Fungistatic C. Ectopic Beat D. Spermatozoa

516. D Interacts with one subtype of receptor over others.
A. Lightheadedness B. Hemozoin C. Celontin D. Selective

517. C Telmisartan
A. Potentiates B. Streptase C. Micardis D. Mutagenic

518. A Excessive thirst; increased thirst.
A. Polydipsia B. Sympathetic C. Diovan D. Tyzine

519. A Type of cell division where diploid parent cells divide.
A. Meiosis B. Chronic C. Ulcer D. Virucidal

520. B Drugs that relieve, interrupt, or prevent muscle spasms.
A. Rapaflo B. Spasmolytics C. Lightheadedness D. Retavase

521. C Return of the electric potential across a cell membrane to its resting state following depolarization.
A. Expectorate B. Diplopia C. Repolarization D. Cushings Disease

522. C Inhibits the growth of fungi but does not kill off the fungi.
A. Immunosuppressed B. Endometrium C. Fungistatic D. Loading Dose

523. B Secretion from the respiratory tract; usually called mucus.
A. Refractory B. Phlegm C. Diplopia D. Colestid

524. B Appearance of blood or red blood cells in the urine.
A. Cathartic B. Hematuria C. Megaloblast D. Histamine

525. A Causing cancer.
A. Carcinogenic B. Depression C. Dose D. Xanax

526. A Reteplase
A. Retavase B. Sympatholytic C. Solute D. Hemoglobin

527. A The probability that an event will occur.
A. Risk B. Virucidal C. Hemozoin D. Effient

528. A Bisoprolol
A. Zebeta B. Anorexia C. Barbital D. Gabitril

529. A Inadequate secretion of glucocorticoids and mineralocorticoids.
A. Addisons Disease B. Mavik C. Convoluted D. Hyperchloremia

530. D Ethacrynic acid
A. Euvolemia B. Oxytocin C. Interferon D. Edecrin

531. B Eject from the mouth; spit.
A. Nasacort B. Expectorate C. Colestid D. Phlegm

532. A Presence of glucose in the urine.
A. Glycosuria B. Vancenase C. Aphthous Ulcer D. Side Effect

533. A Undesirable interaction of drugs not suitable for combination or administration together.
A. Incompatibility B. Naphcon C. Laxative D. Excoriation

534. D Action that causes the decomposition or destruction of proteins.
A. Rapaflo B. Akathisia C. Demadex D. Proteolytic

535. C Feeling of well-being or elation; feeling good.
A. Dose B. Bronchial Muscles C. Euphoria D. Risk

536. D Circulating cell that ingests waste products or bacteria in order to remove them from the body.
A. Ectopic Beat B. Coreg C. Homeostasis D. Phagocyte

537. B Refers to nerves of the ANS that originate from the thoracolumbar portion of the spinal cord.
A. Megaloblast B. Sympathetic C. Addisons Disease D. Pressor

538. B Tightening or contraction of muscles in the blood vessels, which decreases blood flow through the vessels.
A. Ovulation B. Vasoconstriction C. Morphology D. Hematuria

539. A Lovastatin
A. Mevacor B. Expectorate C. Bradykinesia D. Aphthous Ulcer

540. A Carbamazepine
A. Tegretol B. Polydipsia C. Monophasic D. Loading Dose

541. C Prefix meaning large.
A. Diplopia B. Incretins C. Mega D. Polyphagia

542. B Hardening or fibrosis of the arteries; accumulation of fatty deposits in the walls of arteries.
A. Asthma B. Arteriosclerosis C. Megaloblast D. Site of Action

543. B Normal salt concentration of most body fluids; a salt concentration of 0.9 percent.
A. Extracellular B. Isotonic C. Equipotent D. Aphthous Ulcer

544. D Propranolol
A. Histamine B. Hemozoin C. Milontin D. Inderal

545. D The cytoplasm of a striated (skeletal) muscle fiber.
A. Virucidal B. Chemical Name C. Sympatholytic D. Sarcoplasm

546. D Condition in which the color of red blood cells is less than the normal index.
A. Aqueous Humor B. Extracellular C. Potentiates D. Hypochromic

547. C Abnormally high degree of acidity (for example, pH less than 1) in the stomach.
A. Spermatozoa B. Fungistatic C. Hyperacidity D. Cushings Disease

548. D The relationship of one number to another expressed by whole numbers.
A. Addisons Disease B. Ketosis C. Wheal D. Ratio

549. D Partially digested food and gastric secretions that moves into the duodenum from the stomach by peristalsis.
A. Micardis B. Diovan C. Immunity D. Chime

550. A Produces an action that is greater than either of the components can produce alone; synergy.
A. Potentiates B. Albuminuria C. Spasmolytics D. Inocor

551. A Active ingredient of the marijuana plant.
A. THC B. Polydipsia C. Hemozoin D. Edema

552. A Inflammation of the glomeruli often following a streptococcus infection.
A. Nephritis B. Isotonic C. Phlegm D. Dose

553. D Period when cancer cells are not increasing in number.
A. Dysgeusia B. Drug Dependence C. Polydipsia D. Remission

554. D Initial drug dose administered to rapidly achieve therapeutic drug concentrations.
A. Chemical Name B. Atromid C. Dilantin D. Loading Dose

555. C Intended or indicated uses for any drug.
A. Virucidal B. Tranxene C. Drug Indications D. Dose

556. C A substance that promotes bowel movements.
A. Fungicidal B. Akathisia C. Laxative D. Emesis

557. B Condition that causes individuals to resist acquiring or developing a disease or infection.
A. Lymphopenia B. Immunity C. Irrigation D. Calan

558. D Clofibrate
A. Polyphagia B. Oxytocin C. Xanax D. Atromid

559. B Alteplase
A. Convoluted B. Activase C. Bactericidal D. Hyperacidity

560. A Phenobarbital
A. Barbital B. Alkylation C. Sarcoplasm D. Pharmacodynamics

561. C Vomiting.
A. Laxative B. Fungistatic C. Emesis D. Aldosterone

562. C Clonazepam
A. Ticlid B. Morphology C. Klonopin D. Percent

563. A Fluticasone
A. Flonase B. Immunosuppressed C. Bias D. Aquaresis

564. A Substance dissolved in a solvent; usually present in a lesser amount.
A. Solute B. Trilipix C. Polydipsia D. Zebeta

565. B Shape or structure of a cell.
A. Hypotension B. Morphology C. Colestid D. Flonase

566. D Tending to increase blood pressure.
A. Ketosis B. Homeostasis C. Cardizem D. Pressor

567. C watery substance that is located behind the cornea of the eye and in front of the lens.
A. Barbital B. Hyperacidity C. Aqueous Humor D. Gabitril

568. D Renal excretion of water without electrolytes.
A. Suspension B. Lozol C. Trilipix D. Aquaresis

569. D Flunisolide
A. Inocor B. Xanax C. Glycogen D. Nasalide

570. C A measurement of the amount of drug that is administered.
A. Oxytocin B. Hypotension C. Dose D. Monophasic

571. C Pharmacological substance that stimulates defecation.
A. Suspension B. Wheal C. Cathartic D. Lunesta

572. A Amrinone
A. Inocor B. Chemical Name C. Native D. Lightheadedness

573. D Hormone released from adrenal cortex that causes the retention of sodium from the kidneys.
A. Ratio B. Endorphins C. Addisons Disease D. Aldosterone

574. B Refers to the action of an adrenergic blocking drug or an action that decreases sympathetic activity.
A. Drowsiness B. Sympatholytic C. Dysgeusia D. Side Effect

575. C Diazoxide
A. Hirsutism B. Nasalide C. Hyperstat D. Carcinogenic

576. A Condition in which a single object is seen (perceived) as two objects; double vision.
A. Diplopia B. Trileptal C. Radical Cure D. Coreg

577. D Alprazolam
A. Drug Indications B. Hyperchloremia C. Mavik D. Xanax

578. B Excess secretion of adenocorticotropic hormone (ACTH).
A. Hygroton B. Cushings Disease C. Loading Dose D. Xanax

579. D Eszopiclone
A. Trileptal B. Demadex C. Norpace D. Lunesta

580. B Inference tending to produce results that depart systematically from the true values.
A. Mega B. Bias C. Glycosuria D. Edema

581. C Phenytoin
A. Depakene B. Interferon C. Dilantin D. Minipress

582. A Protein in red blood cells that transports oxygen to all tissues of the body.
A. Hemoglobin B. Lopressor C. Lysosome D. Myocardium

583. D Number written with both a whole number and a fraction.
A. Euphoria B. Bias C. Lunesta D. Mixed Number

584. A Mental state characterized by depressed mood, with feelings of frustration and hopelessness.
A. Depression B. Atromid C. Homeostasis D. Sterilization

585. C Metoprolol bradycardia
A. Retavase B. Minipress C. Lopressor D. Tegretol

586. C Pertaining to the skin.
A. Incompatibility B. Solute C. Cutaneous D. Dehiscence

587. B Ticlopidine
A. Nasacort B. Ticlid C. Hypotension D. Bactericidal

588. D Smooth muscles of lungs.
A. Tremor B. Drug Absorption C. Irrigation D. Bronchial Muscles

589. C Release of an egg from the ovary.
A. Mega B. Pathogen C. Ovulation D. Arrhythmia

590. D Diltiazem
A. Hypochromic B. Alkylation C. Perimenopause D. Cardizem

591. D An elevated concentration of potassium in blood.
A. Cathartic B. Emesis C. Chronic D. Hyperkalemia

592. D Carvedilol
A. Diuresis B. Ambien C. Nasacort D. Coreg

593. A Naturally occurring within the body; originating or produced within an organism, tissue, or cell.
A. Endogenous B. Mavik C. Drug Dependence D. Extracellular

594. D A group of gastrointestinal hormones that increase the amount of insulin released.
A. Lopressor B. Trilipix C. Micardis D. Incretins

595. C Clorazepate
A. Lozol B. Potentiates C. Tranxene D. Gabitril

596. B Preparation in which undissolved solids are dispersed within a liquid.
A. Depakote B. Suspension C. Systematic Error D. Sarcoplasm

597. D It refers to feeling abnormally sleepy during the day.
A. Nimotop B. Pluripotent C. Aldosterone D. Drowsiness

598. B Valsartan
A. Anion B. Diovan C. Lysosome D. Milontin

599. D Colestipol
A. Sympathetic B. Mavik C. Pathogen D. Colestid

600. D Irreversible chemical bond that some cancer drugs form with nucleic acids and DNA.
A. Phagocyte B. Homeostasis C. Streptase D. Alkylation

Matching

Provide the word that best matches each clue.

1. ______________ The uptake of nutrients and drugs from the GI tract.
2. ______________ Male sex hormone responsible for the development of male characteristics.
3. ______________ Abnormally high body temperature.
4. ______________ Guanfacine
5. ______________ Pharmacological substance that stimulates defecation.
6. ______________ Area of tissue that has died because of a sudden lack of blood supply.
7. ______________ Felbamate
8. ______________ Twitchings of muscle fiber groups.
9. ______________ General term for undesirable and potentially harmful drug effect.
10. ______________ A drug that reduces the level of fats in the blood.
11. ______________ Complementary or additive.
12. ______________ Suffix meaning color.
13. ______________ Drug that prevents mast cells from releasing histamine and other vasoactive substances.
14. ______________ Clot formed by the action of coagulation factors and circulating blood cells.
15. ______________ Partially digested food and gastric secretions that moves into the duodenum from the stomach by peristalsis.
16. ______________ A thick-walled structure in which parasitic protozoal sex cells develop for transfer to new hosts.
17. ______________ Peptides in the plasma that stimulate cellular growth and have insulin-like activity.
18. ______________ Indigestion.
19. ______________ Substance, chemical solution, or drug that kills microorganisms.
20. ______________ Renal excretion of water without electrolytes.
21. ______________ A substance that causes vomiting.

22. ______________ Lidocaine

23. ______________ Condition associated with a decrease in bone density so that the bones are thin and fracture easily.

24. ______________ Substance, usually large, composed of an indefinite number of amino acids.

25. ______________ The amount of drug required to produce the desired change in the disease or condition.

A. Somatomedins
B. Synergistic
C. Xylocaine
D. Felbatol
E. Hyperthermia
F. Cathartic
G. Aquaresis
H. Adverse Effect
I. Chime
J. Emetogenic
K. Thrombus
L. Germicidal
M. Tenex
N. Infarction
O. Fasciculation
P. Oocyst
Q. Polypeptide
R. Androgen
S. Absorption
T. Antilipemic Drug
U. Chromic
V. Antiallergic
W. Dyspepsia
X. Therapeutic Dose
Y. Osteoporosis

Provide the word that best matches each clue.

26. ______________ A measurement of the amount of drug that is administered.

27. ______________ Minoxidil hypertrichosis

28. ______________ Accumulation of nitrogen waste materials (for example, urea) in the blood.

29. ______________ The presence of the plasma protein albumin in the urine.

30. ______________ Drug-induced confusion that can cause increased drug consumption.

31. ______________ Producing heat.

32. ______________ Return of the electric potential across a cell membrane to its resting state following depolarization.

33. ______________ Number written with both a whole number and a fraction.

34. ______________ Error introduced into a study by its design rather than due to random variation.

35. ______________ Substance, usually protein or carbohydrate, that is capable of stimulating an immune response.

36. ______________ Unusually high concentration of calcium in the blood.

37. ______________ Drug derived from opium and producing the same pharmacological effects as opium.

38. ______________ Inflammation of the walls of the veins, associated with clot formation.

39. ______________ Tending to increase blood pressure.

40. ______________ A substance capable of producing an allergic reaction.

41. ______________ Tocainide

42. ______________ Top number of a fraction; shows the part.

43. ______________ Inflammatory condition of the skin associated with itching, burning, and edematous vesicular formations.

44. ______________ Clopidogrel

45. ______________ Refers to the action of an adrenergic blocking drug or an action that decreases sympathetic activity.

46. ______________ Abnormal discharge of brain neurons that causes alteration of behavior and motor activity.

47. ______________ Cell death, due to either programmed cell death or other physiological events.

48. ______________ After childbirth.

49. ______________ Convulsive muscle contraction in which rigidity and relaxation alternate in rapid succession.

50. ______________ Percentage of the drug dosage that is absorbed.

A. Pressor	B. Uremia	C. Bioavailability	D. Seizure
E. Systematic Error	F. Plavix	G. Opiate	H. Dermatitis
I. Thrombophlebitis	J. Repolarization	K. Albuminuria	L. Loniten
M. Postpartum	N. Tonocard	O. Clonic	P. Allergen
Q. Sympatholytic	R. Apoptosis	S. Automatism	T. Antigen
U. Hypercalcemia	V. Mixed Number	W. Numerator	X. Calorigenic
Y. Dose			

Provide the word that best matches each clue.

51. ______________ Area of the heart from which abnormal impulses originate.

52. ______________ Hardening or fibrosis of the arteries; accumulation of fatty deposits in the walls of arteries.

53. ______________ Streptokinase

54. ______ HCTZ

55. ______ Alfuzosin

56. ______ Excessive thirst; increased thirst.

57. ______ A measurement of the amount of drug that is administered.

58. ______ High levels of insulin in the blood often associated with type 2 diabetes mellitus and insulin resistance.

59. ______ Atorvastatin

60. ______ Permanent black discoloration of skin and mucous membranes caused by prolonged use of silver protein.

61. ______ Entrance of a drug into the bloodstream from its site of administration.

62. ______ Peptides in the plasma that stimulate cellular growth and have insulin-like activity.

63. ______ Pertaining to the skin.

64. ______ Condition of long duration, usually months or years.

65. ______ Bottom number of a fraction; shows the number of parts in a whole.

66. ______ Decrease in the number of circulating lymphocytes.

67. ______ Large, immature cell that cannot yet function as a mature red blood cell (RBC).

68. ______ Release of an egg from the ovary.

69. ______ Captopril

70. ______ Lovastatin

71. ______ Type of tablet or pill with a coating that enables it to pass through the stomach without being dissolved.

72. ______ Inhibits the growth of fungi but does not kill off the fungi.

73. ______ Unusually high concentration of calcium in the blood.

74. ______ Type of bacteria that cause disease; a microorganism that causes disease.

75. ______ Disease that involves the development and reproduction of abnormal cells.

A. Megaloblast
B. Pathogen
C. Denominator
D. Somatomedins
E. Ovulation
F. Arteriosclerosis
G. Ectopic Focus
H. Hypercalcemia
I. Lipitor
J. Hyperinsulinemia
K. Chronic
L. Hydrodiuril
M. Cancer
N. Uroxatral
O. Fungistatic
P. Cutaneous
Q. Mevacor
R. Drug Absorption
S. Enteric Coated
T. Capoten
U. Argyria
V. Dose
W. Streptase
X. Polydipsia
Y. Lymphopenia

Provide the word that best matches each clue.

76. ______________ Opening in a hollow organ, such as a break in the intestinal wall.

77. ______________ Normal structures responsible for energy production in cells.

78. ______________ Distortion of sensory perception; usually associated with the use of LSD.

79. ______________ Disease of the muscles.

80. ______________ Plaque formed in the artery wall that can break away and obstruct blood flow or form a clot.

81. ______________ Tending to increase blood pressure.

82. ______________ Drug that inhibits the growth and proliferation of cancer cells.

83. ______________ Ability of a substance to produce many different biological responses.

84. ______________ Thick crust or scab that develops after skin is burned.

85. ______________ Inflammation of the joints.

86. ______________ Gabapentin

87. ______________ Drug that neutralizes hydrochloric acid (HCl) secreted by the stomach.

88. ______________ Bursting open or separation of a wound, usually along sutured line.

89. ______________ An inflammation of the hair follicles of the beard or scalp caused by ringworm with swelling and pus.

90. ______________ Primidone

91. ______________ A condition where the concentration of salt (sodium, electrolytes) is less than that found inside the cells.

92. ______________ Trandolapril

93. ______ Member of a family of hormones and drugs containing a structure similar to cortisone.

94. ______ name Nonproprietary name of a drug.

95. ______ Indapamide

96. ______ Undesirable interaction of drugs not suitable for combination or administration together.

97. ______ A strong sustained muscle contraction.

98. ______ Ethacrynic acid

99. ______ Feeling of discomfort or unpleasantness.

100. ______ Chemical substance that produces a change in body function.

A. Steroid
B. Antineoplastic
C. Hypotonic
D. Eschar
E. Mysoline
F. Synesthesia
G. Arthritis
H. Edecrin
I. Myopathy
J. Mavik
K. Neurontin
L. Pluripotent
M. Drug
N. Unstable Plaque
O. Lozol
P. Incompatibility
Q. Generic
R. Perforation
S. Dysphoria
T. Tetany
U. Antacid
V. Mitochondria
W. Pressor
X. Dehiscence
Y. Kerion

Provide the word that best matches each clue.

101. ______ Amount of blood pumped per heartbeat.

102. ______ Ion in solution, such as sodium, potassium, or chloride, that is capable of mediating conduction.

103. ______ A strong sustained muscle contraction.

104. ______ Bepridil

105. ______ Neuropeptides produced within the CNS that interact with opioid receptors to produce analgesia.

106. ______ Stage of sleep characterized by rapid eye movement (REM) and dreaming.

107. ______ Doxazosin

108. ______ Condition in which an arterial blood pressure is abnormally low.

109. ______ shedding of endometrial tissue with accompanying bleeding; the first day of the menstrual cycle.

110. ______ A painful burning feeling behind the sternum that occurs when stomach acid backs up into the esophagus.

111. ______ Felodipine

112. ______ Major form of psychosis; behavior is inappropriate.

113. ______ Cerivastatin

114. ______ Quinidine

115. ______ Shape or structure of a cell.

116. ______ Cells that become the reproductive cells eggs (in ovary) or sperm (in testes).

117. ______ Flushing of the stomach.

118. ______ Alkaloid drug in tobacco that stimulates ganglionic receptors.

119. ______ Interacts with one subtype of receptor over others.

120. ______ Drug-induced confusion that can cause increased drug consumption.

121. ______ Substance, usually protein or carbohydrate, that is capable of stimulating an immune response.

122. ______ Number written with both a whole number and a fraction.

123. ______ Following drug prescription directions exactly as written.

124. ______ Loss of blood from blood vessels.

125. ______ Moricizine

A. Heartburn
B. Tetany
C. Hemorrhage
D. Gastric Lavage
E. Ethmozine
F. Automatism
G. Baycol
H. Electrolyte
I. Quinidine
J. Morphology
K. Hypotension
L. Cardura
M. Nicotine
N. Mixed Number
O. Vascor
P. Plendil
Q. Menstruation
R. Antigen
S. Germ Cells
T. Drug Compliance
U. Schizophrenia
V. Endorphins
W. Selective
X. Rem Sleep
Y. Stroke Volume

Provide the word that best matches each clue.

126. ______ The probability that an event will occur.

127. ______ Inhibition of the vagus nerve to the heart, causing the heart rate to increase.

128. ______ Medications containing iron compounds, used to increase hemoglobin production.

129. ______ Substance that inhibits secretion of digestive enzymes, hormones, or acid.

130. ______ Eplerenone

131. ______ Requirement of repeated drug consumption in order to prevent onset of withdrawal symptoms.

132. ______ Substance that has the ability to attach other substances to its surface.

133. ______ Production of milk in female breasts.

134. ______ Uncontrolled growth of abnormal cells that form a solid mass; also called a neoplasm.

135. ______ Presence of glucose in the urine.

136. ______ Methyldopa

137. ______ Hormone secreted by the anterior pituitary that binds to a receptor on another endocrine gland.

138. ______ Eject from the mouth; spit.

139. ______ When two events occur together more often than would be expected by chance.

140. ______ Disopyramide

141. ______ Mechanical and chemical breakdown of foods into smaller units.

142. ______ Loss of voluntary muscle movement; restless leg movement.

143. ______ Ability of a substance to produce many different biological responses.

144. ______ Hormone released by the alpha cells of the pancreas to increase plasma glucose concentration.

145. ______ Pertaining to glands that secrete substances directly into the blood.

146. ______ Fluvastatin

147. ________ Abnormally high degree of acidity (for example, pH less than 1) in the stomach.

148. ________ Extra heartbeat, a type of cardiac arrhythmia.

149. ________ Shape or structure of a cell.

150. ________ Seizure originating in one area of the brain that may spread to other areas.

A. Akinesia
B. Aldomet
C. Association
D. Norpace
E. Expectorate
F. Glucagon
G. Tropic Hormone
H. Digestion
I. Ectopic Beat
J. Lescol
K. Inspra
L. Glycosuria
M. Partial Seizure
N. Hyperacidity
O. Adsorbent
P. Vagolytic Action
Q. Dependency
R. Pluripotent
S. Risk
T. Morphology
U. Tumor
V. Antisecretory
W. Hematinic
X. Lactation
Y. Endocrine

Provide the word that best matches each clue.

151. ________ Negatively charged ion.

152. ________ Tiny hairs that line the respiratory tract and continuously move, pushing secretions toward the mouth.

153. ________ Inadequate secretion of glucocorticoids and mineralocorticoids.

154. ________ Pertaining to glands that secrete substances directly into the blood.

155. ________ Dose administered to maintain drug blood levels in the therapeutic range.

156. ________ A stiffness and inflexibility of movement.

157. ________ Type of bacteria that cause disease; a microorganism that causes disease.

158. ________ Refers to venous return, the amount of blood returning to the heart that must be pumped.

159. ________ Drug-induced confusion that can cause increased drug consumption.

160. ________ Refers to sedative-hypnotic drugs that do not possess the barbituric acid structure.

161. ________ Shape or structure of a cell.

162. ________ Washing (lavage) of a wound or cavity with large volumes of fluid.

163. ________ Lining of the uterus.

164. ______________ Excess secretion of adenocorticotropic hormone (ACTH).

165. ______________ Reduced sperm count.

166. ______________ Clonazepam

167. ______________ Colesevelam

168. ______________ Class of drugs used to treat anxiety and sleep disorders.

169. ______________ Entrance of a drug into the bloodstream from its site of administration.

170. ______________ Following drug prescription directions exactly as written.

171. ______________ Cerivastatin

172. ______________ Candesartan

173. ______________ Counteract; oppose.

174. ______________ Can stimulate uterine and intestinal muscle contractions and may cause pain by stimulating nerve endings.

175. ______________ Vomiting.

A. Preload
B. Klonopin
C. Antagonistic
D. Oligospermia
E. Prostaglandin
F. Benzodiazepine
G. Addisons Disease
H. Atacand
I. Morphology
J. Automatism
K. Drug Absorption
L. Irrigation
M. Pathogen
N. Emesis
O. Maintenance Dose
P. Rigidity
Q. Microcilia
R. Cushings Disease
S. Drug Compliance
T. Baycol
U. Nonbarbiturate
V. Anion
W. Endometrium
X. Welchol
Y. Endocrine

Provide the word that best matches each clue.

176. ______________ Eplerenone

177. ______________ Quinidine

178. ______________ Inhibits the growth of fungi but does not kill off the fungi.

179. ______________ Excess secretion of adenocorticotropic hormone (ACTH).

180. ______________ An excessive accumulation of fluid in body tissues.

181. ______________ The situation in patients whose treatment involves multiple drug prescriptions.

182. ____________ Irreversible chemical bond that some cancer drugs form with nucleic acids and DNA.

183. ____________ Vomiting.

184. ____________ Torsemide

185. ____________ Joint space into which drug is injected.

186. ____________ Condition associated with an increased production of ketone bodies as a result of fat metabolism.

187. ____________ Undesirable interaction of drugs not suitable for combination or administration together.

188. ____________ Indapamide

189. ____________ Drug usually administered IV that stops a convulsive seizure.

190. ____________ Metolazone

191. ____________ Phensuximide

192. ____________ Release of an egg from the ovary.

193. ____________ Drug produced by a chemical process outside the body.

194. ____________ Bepridil

195. ____________ Levetiracetam

196. ____________ Peptides in the plasma that stimulate cellular growth and have insulin-like activity.

197. ____________ Origin of the pain is in a different location than where the individual feels the pain.

198. ____________ Excessive thirst; increased thirst.

199. ____________ Enzyme that digests protein in the stomach.

200. ____________ A substance secreted by T cells that signals other immune cells like macrophages to aggregate.

A. Lozol	B. Pepsin	C. Alkylation	D. Keppra
E. Ovulation	F. Cushings Disease	G. Quinidine	H. Referred Pain
I. Demadex	J. Ketosis	K. Lymphokine	L. Intra Articular
M. Zaroxolyn	N. Edema	O. Anticonvulsant	P. Emesis

Q. Polypharmacy
R. Fungistatic
S. Somatomedins
T. Inspra
U. Incompatibility
V. Vascor
W. Milontin
X. Synthetic Drug
Y. Polydipsia

Provide the word that best matches each clue.

201. ______________ watery substance that is located behind the cornea of the eye and in front of the lens.

202. ______________ Amount of blood pumped per heartbeat.

203. ______________ Mature eggs

204. ______________ Simvastatin

205. ______________ Patented proprietary name of drug sold by a specific drug manufacturer; also referred to as the brand name.

206. ______________ Lisinopril

207. ______________ Area of the heart from which abnormal impulses originate.

208. ______________ Formation of ova.

209. ______________ A lipid substance secreted by glands in the skin to lubricate the skin everywhere but the palms and soles.

210. ______________ Joint pain.

211. ______________ Triamterene

212. ______________ A measurement of the amount of drug that is administered.

213. ______________ Amrinone

214. ______________ Drug that blocks the action of histamine at the target organ.

215. ______________ Esmolol

216. ______________ Condition in which toxic doses of salicylates are ingested, resulting in nausea, tinnitus, and delirium.

217. ______________ Substance that inhibits the growth of microorganisms on living tissue.

218. ______________ Any cell that covers the axons in the peripheral nervous system and forms the myelin sheath.

219. ______________ Clonazepam

220. ______ Convulsive muscle contraction characterized by sustained muscular contractions.

221. ______ Number written with both a whole number and a fraction.

222. ______ Chlorothiazide

223. ______ Moricizine

224. ______ Bacteria that retain only the red stain in a gram stain.

225. ______ Procainamide

A. Dyrenium	B. Inocor	C. Klonopin	D. Ethmozine
E. Zocor	F. Diuril	G. Trade Name	H. Antihistaminic
I. Ova	J. Tonic	K. Salicylism	L. Antiseptic
M. Sebum	N. Dose	O. Gram Negative	P. Procanbid
Q. Brevibloc	R. Schwann Cell	S. Arthralgia	T. Mixed Number
U. Aqueous Humor	V. Ectopic Focus	W. Oogenesis	X. Stroke Volume
Y. Zestril			

Provide the word that best matches each clue.

226. ______ Chemical mediator produced by immune cells that increases immune function.

227. ______ Compound containing iodine.

228. ______ Drug obtained from plants of the genus Digitalis.

229. ______ Oxcarbamazepine

230. ______ Antibacterial drug obtained from other microorganisms.

231. ______ Dizziness often caused by a decrease in blood supply to the brain.

232. ______ Class of drugs used to treat anxiety and sleep disorders.

233. ______ Drug that relaxes bronchial smooth muscle and dilates the lower respiratory passages.

234. ______ Disopyramide

235. ______ Trandolapril

236. ______ Naphazoline

237. ____________ Nicardipine

238. ____________ Refers to sedative-hypnotic drugs that do not possess the barbituric acid structure.

239. ____________ Estazolam

240. ____________ An element similar to sodium that is used in the treatment of mania and bipolar mood disorder.

241. ____________ Hormone from adrenal medulla that stimulates adrenergic receptors, especially during stress.

242. ____________ State in which a substance has accumulated to potentially harmful levels in the body.

243. ____________ Pain associated with muscle injury.

244. ____________ Extra heartbeat, a type of cardiac arrhythmia.

245. ____________ Abnormal discharge of brain neurons that causes alteration of behavior and motor activity.

246. ____________ A substance that causes constriction of the pupil or miosis.

247. ____________ A decrease in stool frequency.

248. ____________ The uptake of nutrients and drugs from the GI tract.

249. ____________ A fat formed by three fatty acids into one molecule that supplies energy to muscle cells.

250. ____________ Difficult or painful menstruation; condition that is associated with painful and difficult menstruation.

A. Miotic
B. Myalgia
C. Constipation
D. Antibiotic
E. Interferon
F. Lithium
G. Naphcon
H. Mavik
I. Lightheadedness
J. Trileptal
K. Intoxication
L. Seizure
M. Norpace
N. Bronchodilator
O. Nonbarbiturate
P. Ectopic Beat
Q. Iodophor
R. Dysmenorrhea
S. Epinephrine
T. Cardene
U. Benzodiazepine
V. Absorption
W. Cardiac Glycoside
X. Triglyceride
Y. Prosom

Provide the word that best matches each clue.

251. ____________ Washing (lavage) of a wound or cavity with large volumes of fluid.

252. ________ Bacteria that retain only the purple stain in a gram stain.

253. ________ Disease that involves the development and reproduction of abnormal cells.

254. ________ Lidocaine

255. ________ Substance that inhibits the growth of microorganisms on living tissue.

256. ________ Disopyramide

257. ________ An inactive precursor of a drug, converted into its active form in the body by normal metabolic processes.

258. ________ Generalized seizure characterized by full body tonic and clonic motor convulsions and loss of consciousness.

259. ________ Coiled or folded back on itself.

260. ________ Drug effect other than the therapeutic effect that is usually undesirable but not harmful.

261. ________ Amount of time it takes for food to travel from the mouth to the anus.

262. ________ Abnormally high body temperature.

263. ________ When two events occur together more often than would be expected by chance.

264. ________ Mature sperm cells.

265. ________ Amrinone

266. ________ Phenobarbital

267. ________ The concentration of particles dissolved in a fluid.

268. ________ shedding of endometrial tissue with accompanying bleeding; the first day of the menstrual cycle.

269. ________ Drug that neutralizes hydrochloric acid (HCl) secreted by the stomach.

270. ________ Intensely itching raised areas of skin caused by an allergic reaction; hives.

271. ________ Tocainide

272. ________ Location within the body where a drug exerts its therapeutic effect, often a specific drug receptor.

273. ________ To disintegrate or dissolve.

274. ________ Excess hydrochloric acid in the stomach.

275. ________ Gabapentin

A. Association	B. Norpace	C. Xylocaine	D. Convoluted
E. Menstruation	F. Osmolality	G. Hyperthermia	H. Tonocard
I. Antiseptic	J. Inocor	K. Neurontin	L. Transit Time
M. Barbital	N. Urticarial	O. Cancer	P. Prodrug
Q. Tonic Clonic	R. Site of Action	S. Side Effect	T. Hyperchlorhydria
U. Gram Positive	V. Lyse	W. Spermatozoa	X. Antacid
Y. Irrigation			

Provide the word that best matches each clue.

276. ________ Condition of long duration, usually months or years.

277. ________ Produces an action that is greater than either of the components can produce alone; synergy.

278. ________ Study of the distribution and determinants of diseases in populations.

279. ________ When there is an acute deficiency of granulocytes in blood.

280. ________ Neural pathway connecting different brain areas involved in regulation of behavior and emotion.

281. ________ The amount of blood pumped per minute by the heart.

282. ________ Propranolol

283. ________ Beclomethasone

284. ________ Substance that has the ability to attach other substances to its surface.

285. ________ Condition associated with a decrease in bone density so that the bones are thin and fracture easily.

286. ________ Area of tissue that has died because of a sudden lack of blood supply.

287. ________ Drug that is effective against a wide variety of both gram-positive and gram-negative pathogenic bacteria.

288. ________ Clonidine

289. ________ Bacteria that retain only the purple stain in a gram stain.

290. ______ Enables another hormone to fully function.

291. ______ Disease that involves the development and reproduction of abnormal cells.

292. ______ A measure of the amount of minerals (mostly calcium and phosphorus) contained in a certain volume of bone.

293. ______ Diazepam

294. ______ Drug that liquefies bronchial secretions.

295. ______ Chemical action of a substance to bond permanently to a metal ion.

296. ______ Secretion from the respiratory tract; usually called mucus.

297. ______ Normal state of balance among the body's internal organs.

298. ______ Inflammation of the bronchioles associated with constriction of smooth muscle, wheezing, and edema.

299. ______ Alkaloid drug in tobacco that stimulates ganglionic receptors.

300. ______ Vomiting.

A. Emesis
B. Gram Positive
C. Potentiates
D. Cardiac Output
E. Asthma
F. Chronic
G. Chelate
H. Homeostasis
I. Bone Mass
J. Phlegm
K. Infarction
L. Broad Spectrum
M. Nicotine
N. Adsorbent
O. Mucolytic
P. Agranulocytosis
Q. Epidemiology
R. Limbic System
S. Permissive
T. Osteoporosis
U. Valium
V. Inderal
W. Cancer
X. Vancenase
Y. Catapres

Provide the word that best matches each clue.

301. ______ Benazepril

302. ______ A substance secreted by T cells that signals other immune cells like macrophages to aggregate.

303. ______ Infection caused by the yeast Candida; also known as moniliasis.

304. ______ Studies with control groups, namely case-control studies, cohort studies, and randomized clinical trials.

305. ______ Top number of a fraction; shows the part.

306. ______ Member of a family of hormones and drugs containing a structure similar to cortisone.

307. ______ A substance that promotes bowel movements.

308. ______ A substance capable of producing an allergic reaction.

309. ______ Male sex hormone responsible for the development of male characteristics.

310. ______ An elevated concentration of potassium in blood.

311. ______ Flushing of the stomach.

312. ______ Fibric acid

313. ______ Substance that is soothing to mucous membranes or skin.

314. ______ Felodipine

315. ______ Increased secretion of growth hormone in childhood, causing excessive growth and height.

316. ______ Abnormally high fat (lipid) levels in the plasma.

317. ______ Feeling of discomfort or unpleasantness.

318. ______ Condition in which the color of red blood cells is less than the normal index.

319. ______ Condition in which toxic doses of salicylates are ingested, resulting in nausea, tinnitus, and delirium.

320. ______ Condition of reliance on the use of a particular drug.

321. ______ Antibacterial drugs obtained by chemical synthesis and not from other microorganisms.

322. ______ Location within the body where a drug exerts its therapeutic effect, often a specific drug receptor.

323. ______ Formation of spermatozoa.

324. ______ Distortion of sensory perception; usually associated with the use of LSD.

325. ______ Disease of the muscles.

A. Synesthesia	B. Steroid	C. Analytic Studies	D. Plendil
E. Dysphoria	F. Laxative	G. Candidiasis	H. Hypochromic
I. Trilipix	J. Numerator	K. Lymphokine	L. Salicylism

M. Spermatogenesis N. Hyperkalemia O. Antimicrobial P. Emollient
Q. Lotensin R. Site of Action S. Drug Dependence T. Allergen
U. Gastric Lavage V. Hyperlipidemia W. Gigantism X. Myopathy
Y. Androgen

Provide the word that best matches each clue.

326. ______________ Two different amounts of estrogen hormone are released during the cycle.

327. ______________ Present continually in a particular geographic region, often in spite of control measures.

328. ______________ Substance dissolved in a solvent; usually present in a lesser amount.

329. ______________ Protein in red blood cells that transports oxygen to all tissues of the body.

330. ______________ Condition in which tissues have been damaged, characterized by swelling, pain, heat, and sometimes

331. ______________ General term for undesirable and potentially harmful drug effect.

332. ______________ Abnormally low level of sodium ions circulating in the blood.

333. ______________ Substance that induces abortion.

334. ______________ Alprazolam

335. ______________ Decreased response to pain; relief from pain; inhibition of the perception of pain.

336. ______________ Name that defines the chemical composition of a drug.

337. ______________ Lining of the uterus.

338. ______________ Cell that synthesizes and releases hydrochloric acid (HCl) into the stomach lumen.

339. ______________ Felbamate

340. ______________ Process in which water moves across membranes following the movement of sodium ions.

341. ______________ Disorder of cardiac conduction and electrical impulse formation.

342. ______________ Origin of the pain is in a different location than where the individual feels the pain.

343. ______________ Generalized seizures that are usually brief and often confined to one part of the body.

344. ______________ Condition in which a single object is seen (perceived) as two objects; double vision.

345. ______________ Antibacterial drug obtained from other microorganisms.

346. ______________ Low blood glucose level.

347. ______________ Felodipine

348. ______________ Eject from the mouth; spit.

349. ______________ Condition of reliance on the use of a particular drug.

350. ______________ Development of masculine body (hair, muscle) characteristics in females.

A. Plendil
B. Drug Dependence
C. Hemoglobin
D. Hyponatremia
E. Chemical Name
F. Hypoglycemia
G. Osmosis
H. Biphasic
I. Arrhythmia
J. Oxyntic Cell
K. Xanax
L. Inflammation
M. Diplopia
N. Expectorate
O. Referred Pain
P. Felbatol
Q. Antibiotic
R. Analgesia
S. Abortifacient
T. Adverse Effect
U. Endemic
V. Myoclonic
W. Virilization
X. Solute
Y. Endometrium

Provide the word that best matches each clue.

1. ABSORPTION — The uptake of nutrients and drugs from the GI tract.
2. ANDROGEN — Male sex hormone responsible for the development of male characteristics.
3. HYPERTHERMIA — Abnormally high body temperature.
4. TENEX — Guanfacine
5. CATHARTIC — Pharmacological substance that stimulates defecation.
6. INFARCTION — Area of tissue that has died because of a sudden lack of blood supply.
7. FELBATOL — Felbamate
8. FASCICULATION — Twitchings of muscle fiber groups.
9. ADVERSE EFFECT — General term for undesirable and potentially harmful drug effect.
10. ANTILIPEMIC DRUG — A drug that reduces the level of fats in the blood.
11. SYNERGISTIC — Complementary or additive.
12. CHROMIC — Suffix meaning color.
13. ANTIALLERGIC — Drug that prevents mast cells from releasing histamine and other vasoactive substances.
14. THROMBUS — Clot formed by the action of coagulation factors and circulating blood cells.
15. CHIME — Partially digested food and gastric secretions that moves into the duodenum from the stomach by peristalsis.
16. OOCYST — A thick-walled structure in which parasitic protozoal sex cells develop for transfer to new hosts.
17. SOMATOMEDINS — Peptides in the plasma that stimulate cellular growth and have insulin-like activity.
18. DYSPEPSIA — Indigestion.
19. GERMICIDAL — Substance, chemical solution, or drug that kills microorganisms.
20. AQUARESIS — Renal excretion of water without electrolytes.
21. EMETOGENIC — A substance that causes vomiting.

22. XYLOCAINE — Lidocaine

23. OSTEOPOROSIS — Condition associated with a decrease in bone density so that the bones are thin and fracture easily.

24. POLYPEPTIDE — Substance, usually large, composed of an indefinite number of amino acids.

25. THERAPEUTIC DOSE — The amount of drug required to produce the desired change in the disease or condition.

A. Somatomedins	B. Synergistic	C. Xylocaine	D. Felbatol
E. Hyperthermia	F. Cathartic	G. Aquaresis	H. Adverse Effect
I. Chime	J. Emetogenic	K. Thrombus	L. Germicidal
M. Tenex	N. Infarction	O. Fasciculation	P. Oocyst
Q. Polypeptide	R. Androgen	S. Absorption	T. Antilipemic Drug
U. Chromic	V. Antiallergic	W. Dyspepsia	X. Therapeutic Dose
Y. Osteoporosis			

Provide the word that best matches each clue.

26. DOSE — A measurement of the amount of drug that is administered.

27. LONITEN — Minoxidil hypertrichosis

28. UREMIA — Accumulation of nitrogen waste materials (for example, urea) in the blood.

29. ALBUMINURIA — The presence of the plasma protein albumin in the urine.

30. AUTOMATISM — Drug-induced confusion that can cause increased drug consumption.

31. CALORIGENIC — Producing heat.

32. REPOLARIZATION — Return of the electric potential across a cell membrane to its resting state following depolarization.

33. MIXED NUMBER — Number written with both a whole number and a fraction.

34. SYSTEMATIC ERROR — Error introduced into a study by its design rather than due to random variation.

35. ANTIGEN — Substance, usually protein or carbohydrate, that is capable of stimulating an immune response.

36. HYPERCALCEMIA — Unusually high concentration of calcium in the blood.

37. OPIATE — Drug derived from opium and producing the same pharmacological effects as opium.

38. THROMBOPHLEBITIS — Inflammation of the walls of the veins, associated with clot formation.

39. PRESSOR — Tending to increase blood pressure.

40. ALLERGEN — A substance capable of producing an allergic reaction.

41. TONOCARD — Tocainide

42. NUMERATOR — Top number of a fraction; shows the part.

43. DERMATITIS — Inflammatory condition of the skin associated with itching, burning, and edematous vesicular formations.

44. PLAVIX — Clopidogrel

45. SYMPATHOLYTIC — Refers to the action of an adrenergic blocking drug or an action that decreases sympathetic activity.

46. SEIZURE — Abnormal discharge of brain neurons that causes alteration of behavior and motor activity.

47. APOPTOSIS — Cell death, due to either programmed cell death or other physiological events.

48. POSTPARTUM — After childbirth.

49. CLONIC — Convulsive muscle contraction in which rigidity and relaxation alternate in rapid succession.

50. BIOAVAILABILITY — Percentage of the drug dosage that is absorbed.

A. Pressor
B. Uremia
C. Bioavailability
D. Seizure
E. Systematic Error
F. Plavix
G. Opiate
H. Dermatitis
I. Thrombophlebitis
J. Repolarization
K. Albuminuria
L. Loniten
M. Postpartum
N. Tonocard
O. Clonic
P. Allergen
Q. Sympatholytic
R. Apoptosis
S. Automatism
T. Antigen
U. Hypercalcemia
V. Mixed Number
W. Numerator
X. Calorigenic
Y. Dose

Provide the word that best matches each clue.

51. ECTOPIC FOCUS — Area of the heart from which abnormal impulses originate.

52. ARTERIOSCLEROSIS — Hardening or fibrosis of the arteries; accumulation of fatty deposits in the walls of arteries.

53. STREPTASE — Streptokinase

54. HYDRODIURIL — HCTZ

55. UROXATRAL — Alfuzosin

56. POLYDIPSIA — Excessive thirst; increased thirst.

57. DOSE — A measurement of the amount of drug that is administered.

58. HYPERINSULINEMIA — High levels of insulin in the blood often associated with type 2 diabetes mellitus and insulin resistance.

59. LIPITOR — Atorvastatin

60. ARGYRIA — Permanent black discoloration of skin and mucous membranes caused by prolonged use of silver protein.

61. DRUG ABSORPTION — Entrance of a drug into the bloodstream from its site of administration.

62. SOMATOMEDINS — Peptides in the plasma that stimulate cellular growth and have insulin-like activity.

63. CUTANEOUS — Pertaining to the skin.

64. CHRONIC — Condition of long duration, usually months or years.

65. DENOMINATOR — Bottom number of a fraction; shows the number of parts in a whole.

66. LYMPHOPENIA — Decrease in the number of circulating lymphocytes.

67. MEGALOBLAST — Large, immature cell that cannot yet function as a mature red blood cell (RBC).

68. OVULATION — Release of an egg from the ovary.

69. CAPOTEN — Captopril

70. MEVACOR — Lovastatin

71. ENTERIC COATED — Type of tablet or pill with a coating that enables it to pass through the stomach without being dissolved.

72. FUNGISTATIC — Inhibits the growth of fungi but does not kill off the fungi.

73. HYPERCALCEMIA — Unusually high concentration of calcium in the blood.

74. PATHOGEN — Type of bacteria that cause disease; a microorganism that causes disease.

75. CANCER — Disease that involves the development and reproduction of abnormal cells.

A. Megaloblast
B. Pathogen
C. Denominator
D. Somatomedins
E. Ovulation
F. Arteriosclerosis
G. Ectopic Focus
H. Hypercalcemia
I. Lipitor
J. Hyperinsulinemia
K. Chronic
L. Hydrodiuril
M. Cancer
N. Uroxatral
O. Fungistatic
P. Cutaneous
Q. Mevacor
R. Drug Absorption
S. Enteric Coated
T. Capoten
U. Argyria
V. Dose
W. Streptase
X. Polydipsia
Y. Lymphopenia

Provide the word that best matches each clue.

76. PERFORATION — Opening in a hollow organ, such as a break in the intestinal wall.

77. MITOCHONDRIA — Normal structures responsible for energy production in cells.

78. SYNESTHESIA — Distortion of sensory perception; usually associated with the use of LSD.

79. MYOPATHY — Disease of the muscles.

80. UNSTABLE PLAQUE — Plaque formed in the artery wall that can break away and obstruct blood flow or form a clot.

81. PRESSOR — Tending to increase blood pressure.

82. ANTINEOPLASTIC — Drug that inhibits the growth and proliferation of cancer cells.

83. PLURIPOTENT — Ability of a substance to produce many different biological responses.

84. ESCHAR — Thick crust or scab that develops after skin is burned.

85. ARTHRITIS — Inflammation of the joints.

86. NEURONTIN — Gabapentin

87. ANTACID — Drug that neutralizes hydrochloric acid (HCl) secreted by the stomach.

88. DEHISCENCE — Bursting open or separation of a wound, usually along sutured line.

89. KERION — An inflammation of the hair follicles of the beard or scalp caused by ringworm with swelling and pus.

90. MYSOLINE — Primidone

91. HYPOTONIC — A condition where the concentration of salt (sodium, electrolytes) is less than that found inside the cells.

92. MAVIK — Trandolapril

93. STEROID — Member of a family of hormones and drugs containing a structure similar to cortisone.

94. GENERIC — name Nonproprietary name of a drug.

95. LOZOL — Indapamide

96. INCOMPATIBILITY — Undesirable interaction of drugs not suitable for combination or administration together.

97. TETANY — A strong sustained muscle contraction.

98. EDECRIN — Ethacrynic acid

99. DYSPHORIA — Feeling of discomfort or unpleasantness.

100. DRUG — Chemical substance that produces a change in body function.

A. Steroid	B. Antineoplastic	C. Hypotonic	D. Eschar
E. Mysoline	F. Synesthesia	G. Arthritis	H. Edecrin
I. Myopathy	J. Mavik	K. Neurontin	L. Pluripotent
M. Drug	N. Unstable Plaque	O. Lozol	P. Incompatibility
Q. Generic	R. Perforation	S. Dysphoria	T. Tetany
U. Antacid	V. Mitochondria	W. Pressor	X. Dehiscence
Y. Kerion			

Provide the word that best matches each clue.

101. STROKE VOLUME — Amount of blood pumped per heartbeat.

102. ELECTROLYTE — Ion in solution, such as sodium, potassium, or chloride, that is capable of mediating conduction.

103. TETANY — A strong sustained muscle contraction.

104. VASCOR — Bepridil

105. ENDORPHINS — Neuropeptides produced within the CNS that interact with opioid receptors to produce analgesia.

106. REM SLEEP — Stage of sleep characterized by rapid eye movement (REM) and dreaming.

107. CARDURA — Doxazosin

108. HYPOTENSION — Condition in which an arterial blood pressure is abnormally low.

109. MENSTRUATION — shedding of endometrial tissue with accompanying bleeding; the first day of the menstrual cycle.

110. HEARTBURN — A painful burning feeling behind the sternum that occurs when stomach acid backs up into the esophagus.

111. PLENDIL — Felodipine

112. SCHIZOPHRENIA — Major form of psychosis; behavior is inappropriate.

113. BAYCOL — Cerivastatin

114. QUINIDINE — Quinidine

115. MORPHOLOGY — Shape or structure of a cell.

116. GERM CELLS — Cells that become the reproductive cells eggs (in ovary) or sperm (in testes).

117. GASTRIC LAVAGE — Flushing of the stomach.

118. NICOTINE — Alkaloid drug in tobacco that stimulates ganglionic receptors.

119. SELECTIVE — Interacts with one subtype of receptor over others.

120. AUTOMATISM — Drug-induced confusion that can cause increased drug consumption.

121. ANTIGEN — Substance, usually protein or carbohydrate, that is capable of stimulating an immune response.

122. MIXED NUMBER — Number written with both a whole number and a fraction.

123. DRUG COMPLIANCE — Following drug prescription directions exactly as written.

124. HEMORRHAGE — Loss of blood from blood vessels.

125. ETHMOZINE — Moricizine

A. Heartburn	B. Tetany	C. Hemorrhage	D. Gastric Lavage
E. Ethmozine	F. Automatism	G. Baycol	H. Electrolyte
I. Quinidine	J. Morphology	K. Hypotension	L. Cardura
M. Nicotine	N. Mixed Number	O. Vascor	P. Plendil
Q. Menstruation	R. Antigen	S. Germ Cells	T. Drug Compliance
U. Schizophrenia	V. Endorphins	W. Selective	X. Rem Sleep
Y. Stroke Volume			

Provide the word that best matches each clue.

126. RISK — The probability that an event will occur.

127. VAGOLYTIC ACTION — Inhibition of the vagus nerve to the heart, causing the heart rate to increase.

128. HEMATINIC — Medications containing iron compounds, used to increase hemoglobin production.

129. ANTISECRETORY — Substance that inhibits secretion of digestive enzymes, hormones, or acid.

130. INSPRA — Eplerenone

131. DEPENDENCY — Requirement of repeated drug consumption in order to prevent onset of withdrawal symptoms.

132. ADSORBENT — Substance that has the ability to attach other substances to its surface.

133. LACTATION — Production of milk in female breasts.

134. TUMOR — Uncontrolled growth of abnormal cells that form a solid mass; also called a neoplasm.

135. GLYCOSURIA — Presence of glucose in the urine.

136. ALDOMET — Methyldopa

137. TROPIC HORMONE — Hormone secreted by the anterior pituitary that binds to a receptor on another endocrine gland.

138. EXPECTORATE — Eject from the mouth; spit.

139. ASSOCIATION — When two events occur together more often than would be expected by chance.

140. NORPACE — Disopyramide

141. DIGESTION — Mechanical and chemical breakdown of foods into smaller units.

142. AKINESIA — Loss of voluntary muscle movement; restless leg movement.

143. PLURIPOTENT — Ability of a substance to produce many different biological responses.

144. GLUCAGON — Hormone released by the alpha cells of the pancreas to increase plasma glucose concentration.

145. ENDOCRINE — Pertaining to glands that secrete substances directly into the blood.

146. LESCOL — Fluvastatin

147. HYPERACIDITY — Abnormally high degree of acidity (for example, pH less than 1) in the stomach.

148. ECTOPIC BEAT — Extra heartbeat, a type of cardiac arrhythmia.

149. MORPHOLOGY — Shape or structure of a cell.

150. PARTIAL SEIZURE — Seizure originating in one area of the brain that may spread to other areas.

A. Akinesia	B. Aldomet	C. Association	D. Norpace
E. Expectorate	F. Glucagon	G. Tropic Hormone	H. Digestion
I. Ectopic Beat	J. Lescol	K. Inspra	L. Glycosuria
M. Partial Seizure	N. Hyperacidity	O. Adsorbent	P. Vagolytic Action
Q. Dependency	R. Pluripotent	S. Risk	T. Morphology
U. Tumor	V. Antisecretory	W. Hematinic	X. Lactation
Y. Endocrine			

Provide the word that best matches each clue.

151. ANION — Negatively charged ion.

152. MICROCILIA — Tiny hairs that line the respiratory tract and continuously move, pushing secretions toward the mouth.

153. ADDISONS DISEASE — Inadequate secretion of glucocorticoids and mineralocorticoids.

154. ENDOCRINE — Pertaining to glands that secrete substances directly into the blood.

155. MAINTENANCE DOSE — Dose administered to maintain drug blood levels in the therapeutic range.

156. RIGIDITY — A stiffness and inflexibility of movement.

157. PATHOGEN — Type of bacteria that cause disease; a microorganism that causes disease.

158. PRELOAD — Refers to venous return, the amount of blood returning to the heart that must be pumped.

159. AUTOMATISM — Drug-induced confusion that can cause increased drug consumption.

160. NONBARBITURATE — Refers to sedative-hypnotic drugs that do not possess the barbituric acid structure.

161. MORPHOLOGY — Shape or structure of a cell.

162. IRRIGATION — Washing (lavage) of a wound or cavity with large volumes of fluid.

163. ENDOMETRIUM — Lining of the uterus.

164. CUSHINGS DISEASE — Excess secretion of adenocorticotropic hormone (ACTH).

165. OLIGOSPERMIA — Reduced sperm count.

166. KLONOPIN — Clonazepam

167. WELCHOL — Colesevelam

168. BENZODIAZEPINE — Class of drugs used to treat anxiety and sleep disorders.

169. DRUG ABSORPTION — Entrance of a drug into the bloodstream from its site of administration.

170. DRUG COMPLIANCE — Following drug prescription directions exactly as written.

171. BAYCOL — Cerivastatin

172. ATACAND — Candesartan

173. ANTAGONISTIC — Counteract; oppose.

174. PROSTAGLANDIN — Can stimulate uterine and intestinal muscle contractions and may cause pain by stimulating nerve endings.

175. EMESIS — Vomiting.

A. Preload	B. Klonopin	C. Antagonistic	D. Oligospermia
E. Prostaglandin	F. Benzodiazepine	G. Addisons Disease	H. Atacand
I. Morphology	J. Automatism	K. Drug Absorption	L. Irrigation
M. Pathogen	N. Emesis	O. Maintenance Dose	P. Rigidity
Q. Microcilia	R. Cushings Disease	S. Drug Compliance	T. Baycol
U. Nonbarbiturate	V. Anion	W. Endometrium	X. Welchol
Y. Endocrine			

Provide the word that best matches each clue.

176. INSPRA — Eplerenone

177. QUINIDINE — Quinidine

178. FUNGISTATIC — Inhibits the growth of fungi but does not kill off the fungi.

179. CUSHINGS DISEASE — Excess secretion of adenocorticotropic hormone (ACTH).

180. EDEMA — An excessive accumulation of fluid in body tissues.

181. POLYPHARMACY — The situation in patients whose treatment involves multiple drug prescriptions.

182. ALKYLATION — Irreversible chemical bond that some cancer drugs form with nucleic acids and DNA.

183. EMESIS — Vomiting.

184. DEMADEX — Torsemide

185. INTRA ARTICULAR — Joint space into which drug is injected.

186. KETOSIS — Condition associated with an increased production of ketone bodies as a result of fat metabolism.

187. INCOMPATIBILITY — Undesirable interaction of drugs not suitable for combination or administration together.

188. LOZOL — Indapamide

189. ANTICONVULSANT — Drug usually administered IV that stops a convulsive seizure.

190. ZAROXOLYN — Metolazone

191. MILONTIN — Phensuximide

192. OVULATION — Release of an egg from the ovary.

193. SYNTHETIC DRUG — Drug produced by a chemical process outside the body.

194. VASCOR — Bepridil

195. KEPPRA — Levetiracetam

196. SOMATOMEDINS — Peptides in the plasma that stimulate cellular growth and have insulin-like activity.

197. REFERRED PAIN — Origin of the pain is in a different location than where the individual feels the pain.

198. POLYDIPSIA — Excessive thirst; increased thirst.

199. PEPSIN — Enzyme that digests protein in the stomach.

200. LYMPHOKINE — A substance secreted by T cells that signals other immune cells like macrophages to aggregate.

A. Lozol	B. Pepsin	C. Alkylation	D. Keppra
E. Ovulation	F. Cushings Disease	G. Quinidine	H. Referred Pain
I. Demadex	J. Ketosis	K. Lymphokine	L. Intra Articular
M. Zaroxolyn	N. Edema	O. Anticonvulsant	P. Emesis

Q. Polypharmacy
R. Fungistatic
S. Somatomedins
T. Inspra
U. Incompatibility
V. Vascor
W. Milontin
X. Synthetic Drug
Y. Polydipsia

Provide the word that best matches each clue.

201. AQUEOUS HUMOR — watery substance that is located behind the cornea of the eye and in front of the lens.

202. STROKE VOLUME — Amount of blood pumped per heartbeat.

203. OVA — Mature eggs

204. ZOCOR — Simvastatin

205. TRADE NAME — Patented proprietary name of drug sold by a specific drug manufacturer; also referred to as the brand name.

206. ZESTRIL — Lisinopril

207. ECTOPIC FOCUS — Area of the heart from which abnormal impulses originate.

208. OOGENESIS — Formation of ova.

209. SEBUM — A lipid substance secreted by glands in the skin to lubricate the skin everywhere but the palms and soles.

210. ARTHRALGIA — Joint pain.

211. DYRENIUM — Triamterene

212. DOSE — A measurement of the amount of drug that is administered.

213. INOCOR — Amrinone

214. ANTIHISTAMINIC — Drug that blocks the action of histamine at the target organ.

215. BREVIBLOC — Esmolol

216. SALICYLISM — Condition in which toxic doses of salicylates are ingested, resulting in nausea, tinnitus, and delirium.

217. ANTISEPTIC — Substance that inhibits the growth of microorganisms on living tissue.

218. SCHWANN CELL — Any cell that covers the axons in the peripheral nervous system and forms the myelin sheath.

219. KLONOPIN — Clonazepam

220. TONIC — Convulsive muscle contraction characterized by sustained muscular contractions.

221. MIXED NUMBER — Number written with both a whole number and a fraction.

222. DIURIL — Chlorothiazide

223. ETHMOZINE — Moricizine

224. GRAM NEGATIVE — Bacteria that retain only the red stain in a gram stain.

225. PROCANBID — Procainamide

A. Dyrenium	B. Inocor	C. Klonopin	D. Ethmozine
E. Zocor	F. Diuril	G. Trade Name	H. Antihistaminic
I. Ova	J. Tonic	K. Salicylism	L. Antiseptic
M. Sebum	N. Dose	O. Gram Negative	P. Procanbid
Q. Brevibloc	R. Schwann Cell	S. Arthralgia	T. Mixed Number
U. Aqueous Humor	V. Ectopic Focus	W. Oogenesis	X. Stroke Volume
Y. Zestril			

Provide the word that best matches each clue.

226. INTERFERON — Chemical mediator produced by immune cells that increases immune function.

227. IODOPHOR — Compound containing iodine.

228. CARDIAC GLYCOSIDE — Drug obtained from plants of the genus Digitalis.

229. TRILEPTAL — Oxcarbamazepine

230. ANTIBIOTIC — Antibacterial drug obtained from other microorganisms.

231. LIGHTHEADEDNESS — Dizziness often caused by a decrease in blood supply to the brain.

232. BENZODIAZEPINE — Class of drugs used to treat anxiety and sleep disorders.

233. BRONCHODILATOR — Drug that relaxes bronchial smooth muscle and dilates the lower respiratory passages.

234. NORPACE — Disopyramide

235. MAVIK — Trandolapril

236. NAPHCON — Naphazoline

237. CARDENE — Nicardipine

238. NONBARBITURATE — Refers to sedative-hypnotic drugs that do not possess the barbituric acid structure.

239. PROSOM — Estazolam

240. LITHIUM — An element similar to sodium that is used in the treatment of mania and bipolar mood disorder.

241. EPINEPHRINE — Hormone from adrenal medulla that stimulates adrenergic receptors, especially during stress.

242. INTOXICATION — State in which a substance has accumulated to potentially harmful levels in the body.

243. MYALGIA — Pain associated with muscle injury.

244. ECTOPIC BEAT — Extra heartbeat, a type of cardiac arrhythmia.

245. SEIZURE — Abnormal discharge of brain neurons that causes alteration of behavior and motor activity.

246. MIOTIC — A substance that causes constriction of the pupil or miosis.

247. CONSTIPATION — A decrease in stool frequency.

248. ABSORPTION — The uptake of nutrients and drugs from the GI tract.

249. TRIGLYCERIDE — A fat formed by three fatty acids into one molecule that supplies energy to muscle cells.

250. DYSMENORRHEA — Difficult or painful menstruation; condition that is associated with painful and difficult menstruation.

A. Miotic	B. Myalgia	C. Constipation	D. Antibiotic
E. Interferon	F. Lithium	G. Naphcon	H. Mavik
I. Lightheadedness	J. Trileptal	K. Intoxication	L. Seizure
M. Norpace	N. Bronchodilator	O. Nonbarbiturate	P. Ectopic Beat
Q. Iodophor	R. Dysmenorrhea	S. Epinephrine	T. Cardene
U. Benzodiazepine	V. Absorption	W. Cardiac Glycoside	X. Triglyceride
Y. Prosom			

Provide the word that best matches each clue.

251. IRRIGATION — Washing (lavage) of a wound or cavity with large volumes of fluid.

252. GRAM POSITIVE — Bacteria that retain only the purple stain in a gram stain.

253. CANCER — Disease that involves the development and reproduction of abnormal cells.

254. XYLOCAINE — Lidocaine

255. ANTISEPTIC — Substance that inhibits the growth of microorganisms on living tissue.

256. NORPACE — Disopyramide

257. PRODRUG — An inactive precursor of a drug, converted into its active form in the body by normal metabolic processes.

258. TONIC CLONIC — Generalized seizure characterized by full body tonic and clonic motor convulsions and loss of consciousness.

259. CONVOLUTED — Coiled or folded back on itself.

260. SIDE EFFECT — Drug effect other than the therapeutic effect that is usually undesirable but not harmful.

261. TRANSIT TIME — Amount of time it takes for food to travel from the mouth to the anus.

262. HYPERTHERMIA — Abnormally high body temperature.

263. ASSOCIATION — When two events occur together more often than would be expected by chance.

264. SPERMATOZOA — Mature sperm cells.

265. INOCOR — Amrinone

266. BARBITAL — Phenobarbital

267. OSMOLALITY — The concentration of particles dissolved in a fluid.

268. MENSTRUATION — shedding of endometrial tissue with accompanying bleeding; the first day of the menstrual cycle.

269. ANTACID — Drug that neutralizes hydrochloric acid (HCl) secreted by the stomach.

270. URTICARIAL — Intensely itching raised areas of skin caused by an allergic reaction; hives.

271. TONOCARD — Tocainide

272. SITE OF ACTION — Location within the body where a drug exerts its therapeutic effect, often a specific drug receptor.

273. LYSE — To disintegrate or dissolve.

274. HYPERCHLORHYDRIA — Excess hydrochloric acid in the stomach.

275. NEURONTIN — Gabapentin

A. Association
B. Norpace
C. Xylocaine
D. Convoluted
E. Menstruation
F. Osmolality
G. Hyperthermia
H. Tonocard
I. Antiseptic
J. Inocor
K. Neurontin
L. Transit Time
M. Barbital
N. Urticarial
O. Cancer
P. Prodrug
Q. Tonic Clonic
R. Site of Action
S. Side Effect
T. Hyperchlorhydria
U. Gram Positive
V. Lyse
W. Spermatozoa
X. Antacid
Y. Irrigation

Provide the word that best matches each clue.

276. CHRONIC — Condition of long duration, usually months or years.

277. POTENTIATES — Produces an action that is greater than either of the components can produce alone; synergy.

278. EPIDEMIOLOGY — Study of the distribution and determinants of diseases in populations.

279. AGRANULOCYTOSIS — When there is an acute deficiency of granulocytes in blood.

280. LIMBIC SYSTEM — Neural pathway connecting different brain areas involved in regulation of behavior and emotion.

281. CARDIAC OUTPUT — The amount of blood pumped per minute by the heart.

282. INDERAL — Propranolol

283. VANCENASE — Beclomethasone

284. ADSORBENT — Substance that has the ability to attach other substances to its surface.

285. OSTEOPOROSIS — Condition associated with a decrease in bone density so that the bones are thin and fracture easily.

286. INFARCTION — Area of tissue that has died because of a sudden lack of blood supply.

287. BROAD SPECTRUM — Drug that is effective against a wide variety of both gram-positive and gram-negative pathogenic bacteria.

288. CATAPRES — Clonidine

289. GRAM POSITIVE — Bacteria that retain only the purple stain in a gram stain.

290. PERMISSIVE — Enables another hormone to fully function.

291. CANCER — Disease that involves the development and reproduction of abnormal cells.

292. BONE MASS — A measure of the amount of minerals (mostly calcium and phosphorus) contained in a certain volume of bone.

293. VALIUM — Diazepam

294. MUCOLYTIC — Drug that liquefies bronchial secretions.

295. CHELATE — Chemical action of a substance to bond permanently to a metal ion.

296. PHLEGM — Secretion from the respiratory tract; usually called mucus.

297. HOMEOSTASIS — Normal state of balance among the body's internal organs.

298. ASTHMA — Inflammation of the bronchioles associated with constriction of smooth muscle, wheezing, and edema.

299. NICOTINE — Alkaloid drug in tobacco that stimulates ganglionic receptors.

300. EMESIS — Vomiting.

A. Emesis	B. Gram Positive	C. Potentiates	D. Cardiac Output
E. Asthma	F. Chronic	G. Chelate	H. Homeostasis
I. Bone Mass	J. Phlegm	K. Infarction	L. Broad Spectrum
M. Nicotine	N. Adsorbent	O. Mucolytic	P. Agranulocytosis
Q. Epidemiology	R. Limbic System	S. Permissive	T. Osteoporosis
U. Valium	V. Inderal	W. Cancer	X. Vancenase
Y. Catapres			

Provide the word that best matches each clue.

301. LOTENSIN — Benazepril

302. LYMPHOKINE — A substance secreted by T cells that signals other immune cells like macrophages to aggregate.

303. CANDIDIASIS — Infection caused by the yeast Candida; also known as moniliasis.

304. ANALYTIC STUDIES — Studies with control groups, namely case-control studies, cohort studies, and randomized clinical trials.

305. NUMERATOR — Top number of a fraction; shows the part.

306. STEROID	Member of a family of hormones and drugs containing a structure similar to cortisone.
307. LAXATIVE	A substance that promotes bowel movements.
308. ALLERGEN	A substance capable of producing an allergic reaction.
309. ANDROGEN	Male sex hormone responsible for the development of male characteristics.
310. HYPERKALEMIA	An elevated concentration of potassium in blood.
311. GASTRIC LAVAGE	Flushing of the stomach.
312. TRILIPIX	Fibric acid
313. EMOLLIENT	Substance that is soothing to mucous membranes or skin.
314. PLENDIL	Felodipine
315. GIGANTISM	Increased secretion of growth hormone in childhood, causing excessive growth and height.
316. HYPERLIPIDEMIA	Abnormally high fat (lipid) levels in the plasma.
317. DYSPHORIA	Feeling of discomfort or unpleasantness.
318. HYPOCHROMIC	Condition in which the color of red blood cells is less than the normal index.
319. SALICYLISM	Condition in which toxic doses of salicylates are ingested, resulting in nausea, tinnitus, and delirium.
320. DRUG DEPENDENCE	Condition of reliance on the use of a particular drug.
321. ANTIMICROBIAL	Antibacterial drugs obtained by chemical synthesis and not from other microorganisms.
322. SITE OF ACTION	Location within the body where a drug exerts its therapeutic effect, often a specific drug receptor.
323. SPERMATOGENESIS	Formation of spermatozoa.
324. SYNESTHESIA	Distortion of sensory perception; usually associated with the use of LSD.
325. MYOPATHY	Disease of the muscles.

A. Synesthesia	B. Steroid	C. Analytic Studies	D. Plendil
E. Dysphoria	F. Laxative	G. Candidiasis	H. Hypochromic
I. Trilipix	J. Numerator	K. Lymphokine	L. Salicylism

M. Spermatogenesis	N. Hyperkalemia	O. Antimicrobial	P. Emollient
Q. Lotensin	R. Site of Action	S. Drug Dependence	T. Allergen
U. Gastric Lavage	V. Hyperlipidemia	W. Gigantism	X. Myopathy
Y. Androgen			

Provide the word that best matches each clue.

326. BIPHASIC — Two different amounts of estrogen hormone are released during the cycle.

327. ENDEMIC — Present continually in a particular geographic region, often in spite of control measures.

328. SOLUTE — Substance dissolved in a solvent; usually present in a lesser amount.

329. HEMOGLOBIN — Protein in red blood cells that transports oxygen to all tissues of the body.

330. INFLAMMATION — Condition in which tissues have been damaged, characterized by swelling, pain, heat, and sometimes

331. ADVERSE EFFECT — General term for undesirable and potentially harmful drug effect.

332. HYPONATREMIA — Abnormally low level of sodium ions circulating in the blood.

333. ABORTIFACIENT — Substance that induces abortion.

334. XANAX — Alprazolam

335. ANALGESIA — Decreased response to pain; relief from pain; inhibition of the perception of pain.

336. CHEMICAL NAME — Name that defines the chemical composition of a drug.

337. ENDOMETRIUM — Lining of the uterus.

338. OXYNTIC CELL — Cell that synthesizes and releases hydrochloric acid (HCl) into the stomach lumen.

339. FELBATOL — Felbamate

340. OSMOSIS — Process in which water moves across membranes following the movement of sodium ions.

341. ARRHYTHMIA — Disorder of cardiac conduction and electrical impulse formation.

342. REFERRED PAIN — Origin of the pain is in a different location than where the individual feels the pain.

343. MYOCLONIC — Generalized seizures that are usually brief and often confined to one part of the body.

344. DIPLOPIA — Condition in which a single object is seen (perceived) as two objects; double vision.

345. ANTIBIOTIC — Antibacterial drug obtained from other microorganisms.

346. HYPOGLYCEMIA — Low blood glucose level.

347. PLENDIL — Felodipine

348. EXPECTORATE — Eject from the mouth; spit.

349. DRUG DEPENDENCE — Condition of reliance on the use of a particular drug.

350. VIRILIZATION — Development of masculine body (hair, muscle) characteristics in females.

A. Plendil
B. Drug Dependence
C. Hemoglobin
D. Hyponatremia
E. Chemical Name
F. Hypoglycemia
G. Osmosis
H. Biphasic
I. Arrhythmia
J. Oxyntic Cell
K. Xanax
L. Inflammation
M. Diplopia
N. Expectorate
O. Referred Pain
P. Felbatol
Q. Antibiotic
R. Analgesia
S. Abortifacient
T. Adverse Effect
U. Endemic
V. Myoclonic
W. Virilization
X. Solute
Y. Endometrium

Word Search

1. Find the hidden words. The words have been placed horizontally, vertically, or diagonally. When you locate a word, draw an ellipse around it.

T	H	I	R	S	U	T	I	S	M	I	O	W	A	N	E	U	R	Y	S	M	L	W
H	Z	V	M	O	F	X	V	C	D	Z	L	Z	D	A	Z	I	I	N	O	C	O	R
B	P	E	C	T	O	P	I	C	F	O	C	U	S	F	J	D	Q	Z	H	V	T	K
B	I	S	P	A	S	M	O	L	Y	T	I	C	S	P	F	O	N	F	F	A	P	H
L	S	J	I	I	C	C	A	L	O	R	I	G	E	N	I	C	D	V	U	S	I	Y
Y	X	J	T	T	A	M	G	G	N	E	J	V	E	U	V	V	I	M	M	O	X	P
E	V	A	C	U	A	T	I	O	N	P	R	E	L	O	A	D	L	K	P	D	Y	E
T	Y	L	S	Y	N	A	P	T	I	C	K	N	O	B	N	P	A	R	E	I	G	R
W	G	I	V	R	J	W	A	H	E	M	A	T	U	R	I	A	N	I	R	L	P	G
L	O	A	D	I	N	G	D	O	S	E	P	S	H	G	R	A	T	G	N	A	Q	L
N	P	N	M	M	A	L	A	B	S	O	R	P	T	I	O	N	I	P	I	T	I	Y
W	X	L	O	N	I	T	E	N	Z	D	D	K	I	G	K	U	N	Z	C	O	J	C
G	W	N	B	D	V	Y	U	N	A	C	R	O	M	E	G	A	L	Y	I	R	X	E
W	F	D	I	R	C	Y	E	X	B	C	U	T	K	Q	Z	Y	U	K	O	S	Q	M
A	I	F	A	Y	H	X	K	E	S	M	G	S	Q	T	Y	S	M	R	U	U	H	I
B	M	D	S	I	I	R	G	Z	P	W	O	J	L	F	E	N	O	R	S	G	V	A

1. Amrinone
2. Minoxidil hypertrichosis
3. Process of removal of waste material from the bowel.
4. Phenytoin
5. Disease of severe symptoms, which could be fatal if left untreated.
6. Inadequate ability to take in nutrients through the intestine.
7. Chemical substance that produces a change in body function.
8. Producing heat.
9. Appearance of blood or red blood cells in the urine.
10. Refers to venous return, the amount of blood returning to the heart that must be pumped.
11. Area of the heart from which abnormal impulses originate.
12. Initial drug dose administered to rapidly achieve therapeutic drug concentrations.
13. Higher than normal level of glucose in the blood.
14. Inference tending to produce results that depart systematically from the true values.
15. An abnormal widening or ballooning of a portion of an artery due to weakness in the wall of the blood vessel.
16. Condition usually in middle-aged adults from hyper-secretion of growth hormone.
17. Substance that relaxes the muscles controlling blood vessels, leading to increased blood flow.
18. Condition usually in women in which body and facial hair is excessive.
19. Drugs that relieve, interrupt, or prevent muscle spasms.
20. Contains vesicles that store and release neurotransmitters.

A. Dilantin
B. Synaptic Knob
C. Bias
D. Vasodilator
E. Inocor
F. Hirsutism
G. Evacuation
H. Calorigenic
I. Loniten
J. Pernicious
K. Acromegaly
L. Drug
M. Hyperglycemia
N. Malabsorption
O. Ectopic Focus
P. Aneurysm
Q. Preload
R. Loading Dose
S. Hematuria
T. Spasmolytics

2. Find the hidden words. The words have been placed horizontally, vertically, or diagonally. When you locate a word, draw an ellipse around it.

U	R	D	T	L	A	C	L	J	C	L	Z	O	V	U	L	A	T	I	O	N	L	Y
N	G	Y	A	L	T	A	C	R	E	D	W	A	W	G	A	Y	V	H	D	C	H	L
P	L	R	T	Y	R	N	E	U	R	K	Z	N	H	E	M	O	R	R	H	A	G	E
K	S	E	Y	M	O	D	S	X	E	A	B	O	R	T	I	F	A	C	I	E	N	T
Y	F	N	Z	P	M	I	H	N	B	R	J	I	J	I	N	A	Q	O	U	A	U	W
W	E	I	I	H	I	D	M	H	E	I	C	A	A	B	B	O	K	I	N	A	S	E
J	M	U	N	O	D	I	Z	U	L	S	I	N	T	E	R	L	E	U	K	I	N	V
B	P	M	E	P	P	A	H	L	L	E	C	X	N	I	C	O	B	I	D	A	T	K
D	H	X	V	E	T	S	Y	X	U	P	U	P	M	U	C	O	L	Y	T	I	C	Z
K	Y	E	Q	N	O	I	F	K	M	P	W	F	X	N	X	Q	M	I	T	G	P	M
L	S	W	Z	I	A	S	B	U	C	C	A	L	A	B	S	O	R	P	T	I	O	N
L	E	S	O	A	L	O	D	D	U	F	E	S	L	L	O	N	I	T	E	N	W	Y
T	M	F	U	N	B	V	V	A	B	S	E	N	C	E	S	E	I	Z	U	R	E	W
F	A	T	R	O	P	I	C	H	J	G	A	S	T	R	I	C	L	A	V	A	G	E
L	F	Q	A	I	E	C	K	D	F	V	R	Y	A	S	B	D	I	T	X	A	L	U
N	J	R	Y	K	L	O	N	O	P	I	N	V	E	F	O	M	H	C	D	Y	M	U

1. Nicotinic acid
2. Part of the brain that coordinates body movements and posture and helps maintain body equilibrium.
3. Tetrahydrazoline
4. Substance that induces abortion.
5. Release of an egg from the ovary.
6. Clofibrate
7. Clonazepam
8. Triamterene
9. Flushing of the stomach.
10. Having an affinity for the designated organ; for example, adrenotropic.
11. Drug that liquefies bronchial secretions.
12. Loss of blood from blood vessels.
13. Infection caused by the yeast Candida; also known as moniliasis.
14. Decrease in the number of circulating lymphocytes.
15. Disease process causing destruction of the walls of the alveoli.
16. Urokinase
17. Chemical mediator produced by immune cells that helps regulate and increase immune function.
18. Absorption of drug through the mucous membranes lining the oral cavity.
19. Generalized seizure that does not involve motor convulsions; also referred to as petit mal.
20. Minoxidil hypertrichosis

A. Mucolytic
B. Tyzine
C. Abbokinase
D. Klonopin
E. Candidiasis
F. Atromid
G. Gastric Lavage
H. Absence Seizure
I. Interleukin
J. Loniten
K. Tropic
L. Hemorrhage
M. Emphysema
N. Dyrenium
O. Buccal Absorption
P. Lymphopenia
Q. Cerebellum
R. Abortifacient
S. Ovulation
T. Nicobid

3. Find the hidden words. The words have been placed horizontally, vertically, or diagonally. When you locate a word, draw an ellipse around it.

W	O	Z	Q	T	A	S	T	S	X	A	N	U	R	O	X	A	T	R	A	L	H	V
G	V	N	I	H	T	S	O	T	M	N	R	J	I	Z	L	D	Q	Q	F	H	E	G
L	A	Y	P	R	Q	I	J	R	W	T	H	X	U	P	J	M	T	H	A	T	M	S
Y	A	P	E	O	V	W	L	O	A	I	A	R	M	K	M	A	A	Y	T	D	O	I
C	M	M	N	M	I	D	F	K	B	L	B	I	T	H	R	O	M	B	U	S	L	D
O	E	C	I	B	U	I	T	E	B	I	D	G	I	T	D	P	D	Y	P	O	Y	E
G	N	O	C	O	D	J	B	V	O	P	O	I	S	S	B	I	G	K	O	U	T	E
E	O	R	I	P	U	M	U	O	K	E	M	D	C	U	W	M	P	I	L	D	I	F
N	P	E	L	H	T	U	H	L	I	M	Y	I	H	P	H	F	H	Z	Z	H	C	F
O	A	G	L	L	A	C	W	U	N	I	O	T	E	O	A	T	A	X	I	A	A	E
L	U	A	I	E	R	O	X	M	A	C	L	Y	M	L	V	Y	G	D	Z	H	N	C
Y	S	W	N	B	K	L	X	E	S	D	Y	C	I	Y	T	I	K	Z	O	W	E	T
S	E	G	A	I	O	Y	G	S	E	R	S	V	A	U	W	H	W	D	U	T	M	C
I	B	G	S	T	O	T	O	D	X	U	I	Z	W	R	Q	J	D	I	U	R	I	L
S	P	B	E	I	O	I	S	W	F	G	S	N	X	I	W	Z	K	K	T	I	A	T
Z	C	Z	R	S	J	C	Z	F	N	U	J	R	O	A	F	F	N	A	S	G	X	Y

1. A stiffness and inflexibility of movement.
2. Carvedilol
3. Condition in which menstruation no longer occurs.
4. Inflammation of the walls of the veins, associated with clot formation.
5. A drug that reduces the level of fats in the blood.
6. Excessive urine production; increased urination.
7. Clot formed by the action of coagulation factors and circulating blood cells.
8. Insufficient blood supply to meet the needs of the tissue or organ.
9. Not enough red blood cells in blood due to a premature destruction of RBC's.
10. Amount of blood pumped per heartbeat.
11. Alfuzosin
12. Lack of coordination of muscle movements.
13. Hydrolysis of glycogen to yield free glucose.
14. Mature eggs
15. Urokinase
16. The rapid breakdown of skeletal muscle due to muscle injury.
17. Drug that liquefies bronchial secretions.
18. Drug effect other than the therapeutic effect that is usually undesirable but not harmful.
19. Bacterial enzymes that inactivate penicillin antibiotics.
20. Chlorothiazide

A. Menopause
B. Penicillinase
C. Rhabdomyolysis
D. Side Effect
E. Stroke Volume
F. Polyuria
G. Ataxia
H. Thrombophlebitis
I. Ischemia
J. Antilipemic Drug
K. Diuril
L. Thrombus
M. Uroxatral
N. Ova
O. Abbokinase
P. Glycogenolysis
Q. Hemolytic Anemia
R. Coreg
S. Mucolytic
T. Rigidity

4. Find the hidden words. The words have been placed horizontally, vertically, or diagonally. When you locate a word, draw an ellipse around it.

F	D	P	O	L	Y	P	H	A	G	I	A	C	Z	C	J	G	X	T	R	R	M	F
V	D	U	Z	F	G	J	K	N	U	J	F	K	R	H	R	J	Z	S	D	V	R	J
O	W	Z	Z	P	A	T	H	U	C	S	E	E	I	K	B	S	A	M	A	O	A	O
A	R	I	T	U	K	B	P	O	T	Y	N	T	R	W	G	H	U	F	A	Q	P	G
F	D	R	O	W	S	I	N	E	S	S	Q	O	C	T	R	Q	A	E	I	X	A	P
F	Q	Z	F	H	Y	P	E	R	T	E	N	S	I	O	N	E	E	R	C	H	F	U
E	W	B	R	E	V	I	B	L	O	C	N	I	G	E	E	D	N	T	Y	D	L	T
R	T	O	X	I	C	E	F	F	E	C	T	S	A	D	E	E	D	I	M	L	O	D
E	C	U	T	A	N	E	O	U	S	P	H	A	R	M	A	C	O	L	O	G	Y	U
N	X	Z	S	A	W	U	X	C	L	Y	R	C	T	B	E	R	R	I	Z	X	U	T
T	K	K	U	S	C	J	U	A	O	W	L	H	M	J	S	I	P	T	O	M	O	X
N	U	V	L	T	S	Z	I	R	I	J	I	Y	W	E	K	N	H	Y	C	U	E	V
E	F	K	A	E	U	C	J	D	P	A	T	H	O	G	E	N	I	D	T	Z	J	D
R	L	M	R	L	L	C	F	U	C	H	E	M	O	Z	O	I	N	R	Q	F	E	J
V	D	F	V	I	K	P	E	R	F	O	R	A	T	I	O	N	S	U	C	B	T	L
E	Y	J	L	N	J	N	H	A	N	M	D	S	D	O	S	E	M	G	O	A	V	I

1. Doxazosin
2. Study of drugs.
3. Drug that stimulates ovulation.
4. Ethacrynic acid
5. It refers to feeling abnormally sleepy during the day.
6. Condition associated with an increased production of ketone bodies as a result of fat metabolism.
7. Transmits sensory information from peripheral organs to the central nervous system).
8. Esmolol
9. Azelastine
10. Excessive hunger.
11. Nisoldipine
12. Undesirable drug effect that implies drug poisoning; can be very harmful or life-threatening.
13. Pertaining to the skin.
14. Neuropeptides produced within the CNS that interact with opioid receptors to produce analgesia.
15. A measurement of the amount of drug that is administered.
16. Opening in a hollow organ, such as a break in the intestinal wall.
17. Silodosin
18. Crystalline disposal product from the digestion of blood from blood-feeding parasites.
19. Abnormally high blood pressure.
20. Type of bacteria that cause disease; a microorganism that causes disease.

A. Hypertension
B. Endorphins
C. Astelin
D. Drowsiness
E. Pharmacology
F. Polyphagia
G. Toxic Effect
H. Pathogen
I. Cardura
J. Sular
K. Fertility Drug
L. Cutaneous
M. Perforation
N. Afferent Nerve
O. Ketosis
P. Hemozoin
Q. Rapaflo
R. Brevibloc
S. Edecrin
T. Dose

5. Find the hidden words. The words have been placed horizontally, vertically, or diagonally. When you locate a word, draw an ellipse around it.

M	Y	O	C	L	O	N	I	C	V	X	W	O	Y	G	S	T	O	F	X	K	A	P
N	K	A	S	C	A	P	I	B	Z	S	B	X	I	Y	D	O	M	T	Z	X	T	P
A	J	I	W	I	A	A	M	F	D	N	S	Y	N	E	V	G	A	L	D	H	X	C
P	D	A	P	R	L	L	Y	R	U	I	C	T	S	W	X	U	N	R	Z	T	Q	M
H	I	A	E	C	A	D	S	S	K	N	M	O	O	X	C	Q	I	W	E	M	M	P
C	E	I	N	A	N	O	V	W	Q	R	V	C	M	X	H	R	A	S	N	O	E	X
O	D	M	I	D	T	S	Q	I	I	V	T	I	N	K	F	U	D	C	O	E	T	R
N	E	M	C	I	I	T	P	N	N	V	B	N	I	D	I	P	L	O	P	I	A	X
T	M	U	I	A	B	E	E	Q	G	B	Y	A	A	I	X	S	E	Q	I	E	S	E
R	A	N	L	N	I	R	C	O	R	O	N	A	R	Y	A	R	T	E	R	Y	T	N
E	X	I	L	R	O	O	E	P	G	W	L	Z	S	M	T	H	L	Z	G	J	A	T
M	V	T	I	H	T	N	R	Q	J	G	J	G	J	V	L	M	M	P	M	U	S	J
O	A	Y	N	Y	I	E	E	S	J	M	Y	O	P	A	T	H	Y	Y	P	E	I	L
R	F	Y	A	T	C	U	I	S	P	A	S	M	O	G	E	N	I	C	R	O	S	I
R	I	K	S	H	V	D	R	U	G	H	E	M	O	R	R	H	A	G	E	R	O	U
G	N	X	E	M	F	I	N	S	U	L	I	N	L	L	Y	M	C	Z	Z	Y	L	V

1. Spread of cancer cells throughout the body, from primary to secondary sites.
2. Generalized seizures that are usually brief and often confined to one part of the body.
3. Hormone released from adrenal cortex that causes the retention of sodium from the kidneys.
4. It is difficulty getting to sleep or staying asleep, or having non-refreshing sleep for at least 1 month.
5. An excessive accumulation of fluid in body tissues.
6. Antibacterial drug obtained from other microorganisms.
7. Disease of the muscles.
8. Bacterial enzymes that inactivate penicillin antibiotics.
9. Internal biological clock; a repeatable 24-hour cycle of physiological activity.
10. Polypeptide released within the brain that has specific functions during and after pregnancy.
11. Hormone secreted by the beta cells of the pancreas to facilitate glucose entry into the cell.
12. Condition in which a single object is seen (perceived) as two objects; double vision.
13. Causing a muscle to contract intermittently, resulting in a state of spasms.
14. A trembling and involuntary rhythmic movement.
15. Artery that supplies blood flow to the heart.
16. Chemical substance that produces a change in body function.
17. Naphazoline
18. Condition that causes individuals to resist acquiring or developing a disease or infection.
19. Mental state of excitement, hyperactivity, and excessive elevation of mood.
20. Loss of blood from blood vessels.

A. Oxytocin
B. Myoclonic
C. Circadian Rhythm
D. Aldosterone
E. Myopathy
F. Spasmogenic
G. Drug
H. Penicillinase
I. Antibiotic
J. Coronary Artery
K. Insulin
L. Mania
M. Hemorrhage
N. Metastasis
O. Diplopia
P. Immunity
Q. Tremor
R. Edema
S. Insomnia
T. Naphcon

6. Find the hidden words. The words have been placed horizontally, vertically, or diagonally. When you locate a word, draw an ellipse around it.

O	A	V	G	M	E	E	I	P	S	Y	S	H	A	C	S	V	E	F	V	R	D	U
F	X	E	M	I	C	R	O	M	T	S	E	S	N	N	Y	T	V	U	A	J	S	D
N	P	C	D	N	D	I	O	P	E	E	J	Q	A	S	N	Y	Y	Z	S	N	D	E
O	O	T	E	C	O	R	D	A	R	O	N	E	L	Y	A	J	D	I	O	X	I	C
R	L	O	P	V	D	G	X	K	I	N	C	C	G	M	P	U	R	L	D	M	V	U
E	Y	X	A	P	Z	E	P	R	L	V	Q	C	E	P	T	Y	K	P	I	Z	F	B
P	P	I	K	H	A	L	F	L	I	F	E	N	S	A	I	F	A	J	L	J	K	I
I	H	C	O	Y	M	N	P	W	Z	P	T	V	I	T	C	L	M	K	A	S	E	T
N	A	E	T	T	O	N	O	C	A	R	D	L	A	H	K	C	K	N	T	Z	T	I
E	R	F	E	L	M	H	G	F	T	X	S	P	L	E	N	D	I	L	O	Q	Y	S
P	M	F	E	A	X	Y	B	K	I	H	A	O	J	T	O	B	K	I	R	Z	Y	U
H	A	E	A	E	P	P	O	S	O	L	N	C	D	I	B	S	B	P	Y	Y	R	L
R	C	C	G	Q	W	O	F	R	N	O	M	Y	O	C	L	O	N	I	C	V	O	C
I	Y	T	L	Z	K	X	D	X	H	Y	P	O	C	H	L	O	R	E	M	I	A	E
N	T	I	D	Q	U	I	C	H	O	L	E	L	I	T	H	I	A	S	I	S	M	R
E	M	B	Q	I	Z	A	F	L	B	W	F	A	U	J	C	A	F	R	I	N	W	D

1. Reduction of oxygen supply to tissues below the amount required for normal physiological function.
2. Bedsore.
3. Oxymetazoline
4. Tocainide
5. The presence of gallstones in the gallbladder.
6. Process that results in destruction of all microorganisms.
7. Refers to nerves of the ANS that originate from the thoracolumbar portion of the spinal cord.
8. Decreased response to pain; relief from pain; inhibition of the perception of pain.
9. Generalized seizures that are usually brief and often confined to one part of the body.
10. Undesirable drug effect that implies drug poisoning; can be very harmful or life-threatening.
11. Contains vesicles that store and release neurotransmitters.
12. Felodipine
13. Prefix meaning small.
14. Abnormally low level of chloride ions circulating in the blood.
15. Amiodarone
16. Substance that relaxes the muscles controlling blood vessels, leading to increased blood flow.
17. The situation in patients whose treatment involves multiple drug prescriptions.
18. Time required for the body to reduce the amount of drug in the plasma by one-half.
19. Sodium valproate
20. Neurotransmitter of sympathetic nerves that stimulates the adrenergic receptors.

A. Depakote
B. Vasodilator
C. Myoclonic
D. Tonocard
E. Polypharmacy
F. Cordarone
G. Analgesia
H. Synaptic Knob
I. Sterilization
J. Cholelithiasis
K. Plendil
L. Sympathetic
M. Hypochloremia
N. Hypoxia
O. Afrin
P. Toxic Effect
Q. Norepinephrine
R. Micro
S. Half Life
T. Decubitis Ulcer

7. Find the hidden words. The words have been placed horizontally, vertically, or diagonally. When you locate a word, draw an ellipse around it.

L	N	C	H	K	H	Y	P	O	K	A	L	E	M	I	A	F	P	H	E	P	E	O
I	H	Q	J	V	F	U	N	G	U	S	H	P	K	V	L	G	M	Y	Q	R	V	P
H	F	U	N	G	I	C	I	D	A	L	Y	X	A	G	N	A	Y	P	J	O	A	K
E	A	B	B	Q	W	P	O	H	M	C	P	G	L	M	T	S	I	E	R	S	C	X
V	S	B	Q	Q	Z	Y	Q	Y	G	N	E	D	Q	B	B	T	N	R	T	T	U	X
G	K	E	R	I	O	N	G	D	T	K	R	H	G	O	T	R	D	C	R	A	A	Y
Z	V	I	I	F	E	D	O	R	F	C	T	L	U	W	S	O	E	A	A	G	T	U
A	B	S	O	R	P	T	I	O	N	F	H	C	K	U	C	P	R	L	N	L	I	T
Z	N	P	K	F	Z	F	S	D	J	K	E	R	G	Z	D	A	A	C	X	A	O	Q
U	C	R	R	P	L	C	K	I	P	L	R	Z	Q	C	J	R	L	E	E	N	N	N
Y	H	I	E	F	V	U	Q	U	F	A	M	I	X	C	F	E	Y	M	N	D	K	E
U	E	M	K	F	V	O	T	R	C	A	I	N	M	Z	S	S	S	I	E	I	D	N
N	L	A	U	D	Q	V	R	I	U	E	A	E	V	L	I	I	Y	A	Q	N	M	T
N	A	C	G	D	A	A	K	L	Q	A	N	I	O	N	O	S	K	E	P	P	R	A
L	T	O	G	Q	S	P	E	R	M	A	T	O	G	E	N	E	S	I	S	L	Y	R
T	E	R	H	Y	P	E	R	T	R	I	C	H	O	S	I	S	W	B	Y	B	M	U

1. Clorazepate
2. Abnormally high body temperature.
3. The uptake of nutrients and drugs from the GI tract.
4. HCTZ
5. Condition, also called delayed gastric emptying, in which the stomach muscles do not function properly.
6. Milrinone
7. Mature eggs
8. Unusually high concentration of calcium in the blood.
9. Formation of spermatozoa.
10. Negatively charged ion.
11. Levetiracetam
12. An inflammation of the hair follicles of the beard or scalp caused by ringworm with swelling and pus.
13. Chemical action of a substance to bond permanently to a metal ion.
14. A group of microorganisms with a membrane-bound nucleus that includes yeasts and molds.
15. Can stimulate uterine and intestinal muscle contractions and may cause pain by stimulating nerve endings.
16. Process of removal of waste material from the bowel.
17. Propranolol
18. Excessive hair growth on the body.
19. Substance, chemical solution, or drug that kills fungi; chemical that kills or destroys fungi.
20. Low concentration of potassium in blood.

A. Primacor
B. Fungicidal
C. Absorption
D. Hypercalcemia
E. Kerion
F. Hypertrichosis
G. Evacuation
H. Anion
I. Inderal
J. Spermatogenesis
K. Chelate
L. Fungus
M. Hypokalemia
N. Gastroparesis
O. Hydrodiuril
P. Keppra
Q. Ova
R. Tranxene
S. Prostaglandin
T. Hyperthermia

8. Find the hidden words. The words have been placed horizontally, vertically, or diagonally. When you locate a word, draw an ellipse around it.

B	V	I	R	I	L	I	Z	A	T	I	O	N	C	Z	P	H	P	B	L	E	A	Q
L	P	T	M	V	L	N	S	D	T	Z	T	P	R	T	X	Z	I	O	O	X	W	Z
O	I	T	F	W	N	L	E	R	Z	K	K	W	D	R	Q	N	R	N	A	P	V	K
O	N	R	K	A	Z	S	R	U	S	T	R	E	P	T	A	S	E	E	D	E	T	I
D	F	A	U	A	K	X	A	G	A	T	A	C	A	N	D	U	D	M	I	C	M	N
D	L	N	G	I	O	U	X	A	U	N	C	P	C	T	M	E	P	A	N	T	I	T
Y	A	S	C	Z	H	W	C	B	S	I	L	C	T	H	I	X	A	S	G	O	Q	E
S	M	I	U	L	C	E	R	S	E	C	D	F	F	L	D	Q	R	S	D	R	V	R
C	M	T	X	D	O	P	X	O	D	O	W	L	B	T	Y	Q	X	V	O	A	J	F
R	A	T	J	R	V	S	O	R	A	T	U	I	B	T	S	Z	Z	R	S	T	U	E
A	T	I	D	Z	J	X	I	P	T	I	W	M	U	K	T	Y	K	S	E	E	Z	R
S	I	M	G	A	A	Z	Q	T	I	N	K	A	U	T	O	M	A	T	I	S	M	O
I	O	E	B	R	G	L	K	I	V	E	M	X	W	I	N	U	E	E	O	Y	C	N
A	N	Z	O	C	O	R	T	O	E	L	S	W	I	B	I	J	O	Y	S	K	A	P
O	I	B	T	I	O	T	O	N	O	C	A	R	D	P	A	C	X	N	Z	K	L	Z
D	Z	A	N	T	I	S	E	C	R	E	T	O	R	Y	G	T	W	U	W	N	O	H

1. Candesartan
2. Muscle spasms, facial grimacing, and other involuntary movements and postures.
3. Amount of time it takes for food to travel from the mouth to the anus.
4. Entrance of a drug into the bloodstream from its site of administration.
5. Drug-induced confusion that can cause increased drug consumption.
6. Simvastatin
7. A measure of the amount of minerals (mostly calcium and phosphorus) contained in a certain volume of bone.
8. Streptokinase
9. Development of masculine body (hair, muscle) characteristics in females.
10. Tocainide
11. Drug used to produce mental relaxation and to reduce the desire for physical activity.
12. Open sore in the mucous membranes or mucosal linings of the body.
13. Oxazepam
14. Initial drug dose administered to rapidly achieve therapeutic drug concentrations.
15. Condition in which tissues have been damaged, characterized by swelling, pain, heat, and sometimes
16. Abnormality in blood.
17. Alkaloid drug in tobacco that stimulates ganglionic receptors.
18. Eject from the mouth; spit.
19. Chemical mediator produced by immune cells that increases immune function.
20. Substance that inhibits secretion of digestive enzymes, hormones, or acid.

A. Expectorate
B. Inflammation
C. Loading Dose
D. Dystonia
E. Streptase
F. Transit Time
G. Antisecretory
H. Bone Mass
I. Sedative
J. Atacand
K. Nicotine
L. Blood Dyscrasia
M. Tonocard
N. Ulcer
O. Serax
P. Automatism
Q. Interferon
R. Virilization
S. Drug Absorption
T. Zocor

9. Find the hidden words. The words have been placed horizontally, vertically, or diagonally. When you locate a word, draw an ellipse around it.

B	D	Y	K	G	G	A	N	T	I	A	L	L	E	R	G	I	C	E	K	T	A	U
S	V	B	J	G	H	S	O	P	E	N	I	C	I	L	L	I	N	A	S	E	E	E
I	H	T	U	M	O	R	W	E	X	C	O	D	C	O	N	V	U	L	S	I	O	N
T	G	D	B	B	E	N	Z	O	D	I	A	Z	E	P	I	N	E	C	N	F	Z	D
E	K	R	J	Q	Y	K	B	R	U	R	Z	K	E	R	I	O	N	T	A	N	S	O
O	E	U	B	G	G	Q	X	H	Q	T	D	X	F	F	L	O	N	A	S	E	V	M
F	V	G	C	I	A	D	I	G	U	P	A	T	H	O	G	E	N	U	L	R	T	E
A	H	E	W	G	R	W	K	B	Q	X	K	A	W	P	V	B	Z	E	U	L	P	T
C	Y	X	L	A	N	O	X	I	N	J	L	D	Q	G	T	I	S	P	G	O	U	R
T	N	C	Q	N	N	G	T	P	H	M	O	S	I	Y	T	A	G	K	G	D	G	I
I	M	R	J	T	G	Z	D	H	V	I	T	O	X	Q	W	S	K	V	L	Z	O	U
O	H	E	K	I	I	Q	C	A	G	X	E	R	Q	W	O	M	V	V	R	I	N	M
N	C	T	N	S	A	G	J	S	I	G	N	B	U	L	C	E	R	K	Y	F	T	W
J	I	I	M	M	B	I	K	I	M	V	S	E	C	T	R	I	L	E	P	T	A	L
Q	A	O	A	O	T	K	L	C	R	Z	I	N	A	N	G	I	O	E	D	E	M	A
M	F	N	H	J	I	I	K	S	F	Y	N	T	E	Y	R	X	M	A	G	O	C	L

1. Elimination of the drug from the body.
2. Type of bacteria that cause disease; a microorganism that causes disease.
3. Digoxin
4. An inflammation of the hair follicles of the beard or scalp caused by ringworm with swelling and pus.
5. Class of drugs used to treat anxiety and sleep disorders.
6. Uncontrolled growth of abnormal cells that form a solid mass; also called a neoplasm.
7. Location within the body where a drug exerts its therapeutic effect, often a specific drug receptor.
8. Inference tending to produce results that depart systematically from the true values.
9. Two different amounts of estrogen hormone are released during the cycle.
10. Benazepril
11. Open sore in the mucous membranes or mucosal linings of the body.
12. Oxcarbamazepine
13. Increased secretion of growth hormone in childhood, causing excessive growth and height.
14. Lining of the uterus.
15. Drug that prevents mast cells from releasing histamine and other vasoactive substances.
16. Substance that has the ability to attach other substances to its surface.
17. Involuntary muscle contraction that is either tonic or clonic.
18. Edema and swelling beneath the skin.
19. Fluticasone
20. Bacterial enzymes that inactivate penicillin antibiotics.

A. Biphasic
B. Gigantism
C. Convulsion
D. Angioedema
E. Drug Excretion
F. Lanoxin
G. Bias
H. Kerion
I. Flonase
J. Adsorbent
K. Trileptal
L. Lotensin
M. Site of Action
N. Benzodiazepine
O. Endometrium
P. Ulcer
Q. Pathogen
R. Penicillinase
S. Tumor
T. Antiallergic

10. Find the hidden words. The words have been placed horizontally, vertically, or diagonally. When you locate a word, draw an ellipse around it.

N	L	F	N	L	A	O	M	M	A	S	Q	Y	A	U	T	O	M	A	T	I	S	M
V	T	Y	S	O	S	V	P	A	Z	D	Q	P	E	N	R	E	Y	D	N	O	M	V
I	F	M	B	Z	T	U	M	E	N	A	R	C	H	E	U	Y	V	V	K	A	P	Z
I	E	T	E	Y	E	L	L	F	O	Y	V	C	E	R	E	B	E	L	L	U	M	X
G	R	V	G	O	L	A	J	M	D	D	C	M	O	D	Y	S	E	N	T	E	R	Y
L	R	O	U	C	I	T	E	I	F	C	O	N	V	O	L	U	T	E	D	O	P	N
I	Z	E	Y	P	N	I	C	G	H	K	C	A	T	A	P	R	E	S	K	P	V	N
H	Z	R	H	L	Y	O	X	M	I	T	O	C	H	O	N	D	R	I	A	L	W	I
H	Y	P	E	R	I	N	S	U	L	I	N	E	M	I	A	V	Q	H	N	J	Q	C
D	K	Q	P	I	Q	M	A	I	N	T	E	N	A	N	C	E	D	O	S	E	E	O
M	H	J	L	X	A	W	V	C	S	T	A	B	L	E	P	L	A	Q	U	E	D	T
W	W	H	P	R	O	D	R	U	G	V	L	X	W	H	R	D	Q	N	J	X	L	I
P	R	O	C	A	N	B	I	D	B	A	R	B	I	T	U	R	A	T	E	G	M	N
D	X	U	U	G	E	D	M	K	X	A	A	W	P	B	T	M	L	Q	B	V	S	E
M	T	I	R	I	N	T	E	R	F	E	R	O	N	D	Y	S	P	E	P	S	I	A
D	R	U	G	M	N	Z	A	C	E	T	Y	L	C	H	O	L	I	N	E	X	M	Z

1. Dose administered to maintain drug blood levels in the therapeutic range.
2. CNS depressant drug possessing the barbituric acid ring structure.
3. Part of the brain that coordinates body movements and posture and helps maintain body equilibrium.
4. Release of an egg from the ovary.
5. First menstruation during puberty.
6. An inactive precursor of a drug, converted into its active form in the body by normal metabolic processes.
7. Neurotransmitter of parasympathetic nerves.
8. Chemical mediator produced by immune cells that increases immune function.
9. Clonidine
10. Indigestion.
11. Procainamide
12. Alkaloid drug in tobacco that stimulates ganglionic receptors.
13. Normal structures responsible for energy production in cells.
14. Condition characterized by frequent watery stools (usually containing blood and mucus), tenesmus.
15. Coiled or folded back on itself.
16. Plaque formed in the artery wall that remains in the wall.
17. Drug-induced confusion that can cause increased drug consumption.
18. Azelastine
19. High levels of insulin in the blood often associated with type 2 diabetes mellitus and insulin resistance.
20. Chemical substance that produces a change in body function.

A. Nicotine
B. Stable Plaque
C. Astelin
D. Interferon
E. Hyperinsulinemia
F. Menarche
G. Convoluted
H. Cerebellum
I. Dyspepsia
J. Mitochondria
K. Ovulation
L. Prodrug
M. Acetylcholine
N. Procanbid
O. Catapres
P. Barbiturate
Q. Maintenance Dose
R. Dysentery
S. Drug
T. Automatism

1. Find the hidden words. The words have been placed horizontally, vertically, or diagonally. When you locate a word, draw an ellipse around it.

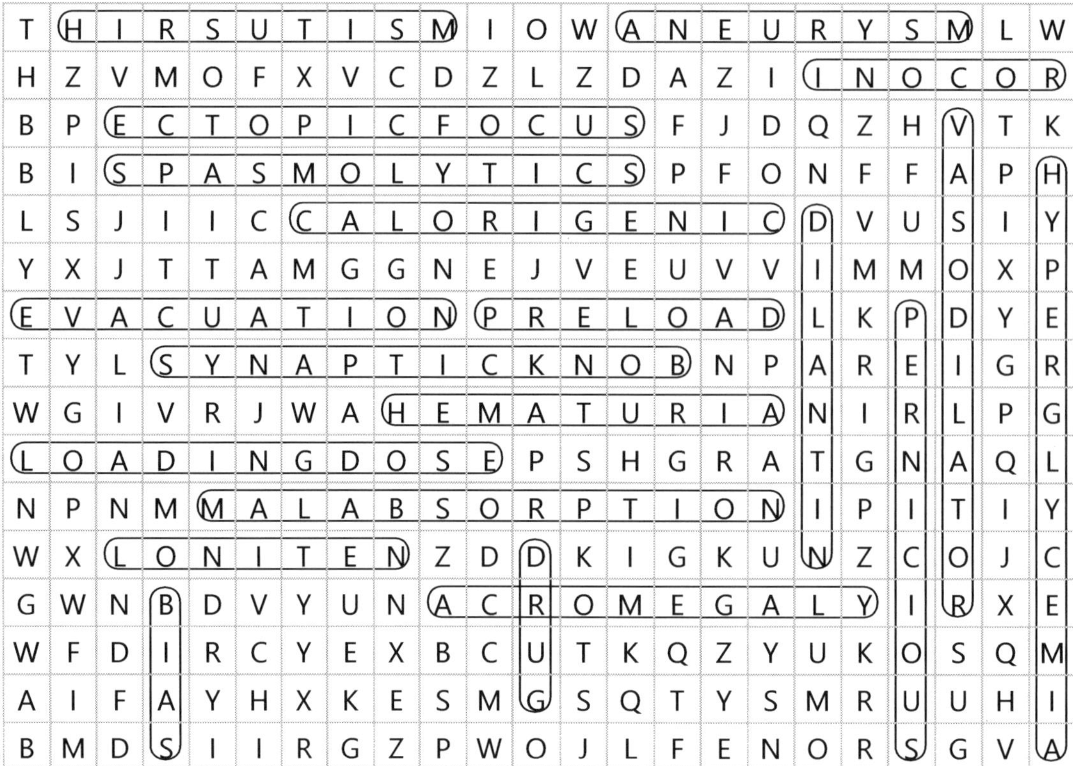

1. Amrinone
2. Minoxidil hypertrichosis
3. Process of removal of waste material from the bowel.
4. Phenytoin
5. Disease of severe symptoms, which could be fatal if left untreated.
6. Inadequate ability to take in nutrients through the intestine.
7. Chemical substance that produces a change in body function.
8. Producing heat.
9. Appearance of blood or red blood cells in the urine.
10. Refers to venous return, the amount of blood returning to the heart that must be pumped.
11. Area of the heart from which abnormal impulses originate.
12. Initial drug dose administered to rapidly achieve therapeutic drug concentrations.
13. Higher than normal level of glucose in the blood.
14. Inference tending to produce results that depart systematically from the true values.
15. An abnormal widening or ballooning of a portion of an artery due to weakness in the wall of the blood vessel.
16. Condition usually in middle-aged adults from hyper-secretion of growth hormone.
17. Substance that relaxes the muscles controlling blood vessels, leading to increased blood flow.
18. Condition usually in women in which body and facial hair is excessive.
19. Drugs that relieve, interrupt, or prevent muscle spasms.
20. Contains vesicles that store and release neurotransmitters.

A. Dilantin
B. Synaptic Knob
C. Bias
D. Vasodilator
E. Inocor
F. Hirsutism
G. Evacuation
H. Calorigenic
I. Loniten
J. Pernicious
K. Acromegaly
L. Drug
M. Hyperglycemia
N. Malabsorption
O. Ectopic Focus
P. Aneurysm
Q. Preload
R. Loading Dose
S. Hematuria
T. Spasmolytics

2. Find the hidden words. The words have been placed horizontally, vertically, or diagonally. When you locate a word, draw an ellipse around it.

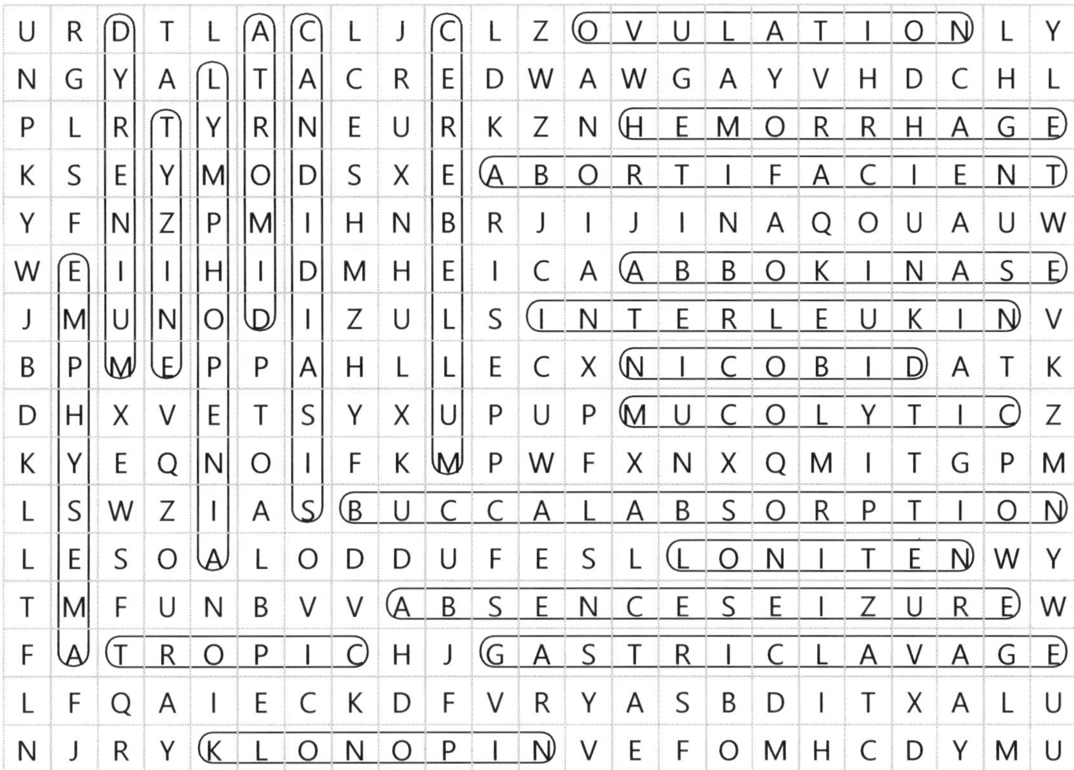

U	R	D	T	L	A	C	L	J	C	L	Z	O	V	U	L	A	T	I	O	N	L	Y
N	G	Y	A	L	T	A	C	R	E	D	W	A	W	G	A	Y	V	H	D	C	H	L
P	L	R	T	Y	R	N	E	U	R	K	Z	N	H	E	M	O	R	R	H	A	G	E
K	S	E	Y	M	O	D	S	X	E	A	B	O	R	T	I	F	A	C	I	E	N	T
Y	F	N	Z	P	M	I	H	N	B	R	J	I	J	I	N	A	Q	O	U	A	U	W
W	E	I	I	H	I	D	M	H	E	I	C	A	A	B	B	O	K	I	N	A	S	E
J	M	U	N	O	D	I	Z	U	L	S	I	N	T	E	R	L	E	U	K	I	N	V
B	P	M	E	P	P	A	H	L	L	E	C	X	N	I	C	O	B	I	D	A	T	K
D	H	X	V	E	T	S	Y	X	U	P	U	P	M	U	C	O	L	Y	T	I	C	Z
K	Y	E	Q	N	O	I	F	K	M	P	W	F	X	N	X	Q	M	I	T	G	P	M
L	S	W	Z	I	A	S	B	U	C	C	A	L	A	B	S	O	R	P	T	I	O	N
L	E	S	O	A	L	O	D	D	U	F	E	S	L	L	O	N	I	T	E	N	W	Y
T	M	F	U	N	B	V	V	A	B	S	E	N	C	E	S	E	I	Z	U	R	E	W
F	A	T	R	O	P	I	C	H	J	G	A	S	T	R	I	C	L	A	V	A	G	E
L	F	Q	A	I	E	C	K	D	F	V	R	Y	A	S	B	D	I	T	X	A	L	U
N	J	R	Y	K	L	O	N	O	P	I	N	V	E	F	O	M	H	C	D	Y	M	U

1. Nicotinic acid
2. Part of the brain that coordinates body movements and posture and helps maintain body equilibrium.
3. Tetrahydrazoline
4. Substance that induces abortion.
5. Release of an egg from the ovary.
6. Clofibrate
7. Clonazepam
8. Triamterene
9. Flushing of the stomach.
10. Having an affinity for the designated organ; for example, adrenotropic.
11. Drug that liquefies bronchial secretions.
12. Loss of blood from blood vessels.
13. Infection caused by the yeast Candida; also known as moniliasis.
14. Decrease in the number of circulating lymphocytes.
15. Disease process causing destruction of the walls of the alveoli.
16. Urokinase
17. Chemical mediator produced by immune cells that helps regulate and increase immune function.
18. Absorption of drug through the mucous membranes lining the oral cavity.
19. Generalized seizure that does not involve motor convulsions; also referred to as petit mal.
20. Minoxidil hypertrichosis

A. Mucolytic
B. Tyzine
C. Abbokinase
D. Klonopin
E. Candidiasis
F. Atromid
G. Gastric Lavage
H. Absence Seizure
I. Interleukin
J. Loniten
K. Tropic
L. Hemorrhage
M. Emphysema
N. Dyrenium
O. Buccal Absorption
P. Lymphopenia
Q. Cerebellum
R. Abortifacient
S. Ovulation
T. Nicobid

3. Find the hidden words. The words have been placed horizontally, vertically, or diagonally. When you locate a word, draw an ellipse around it.

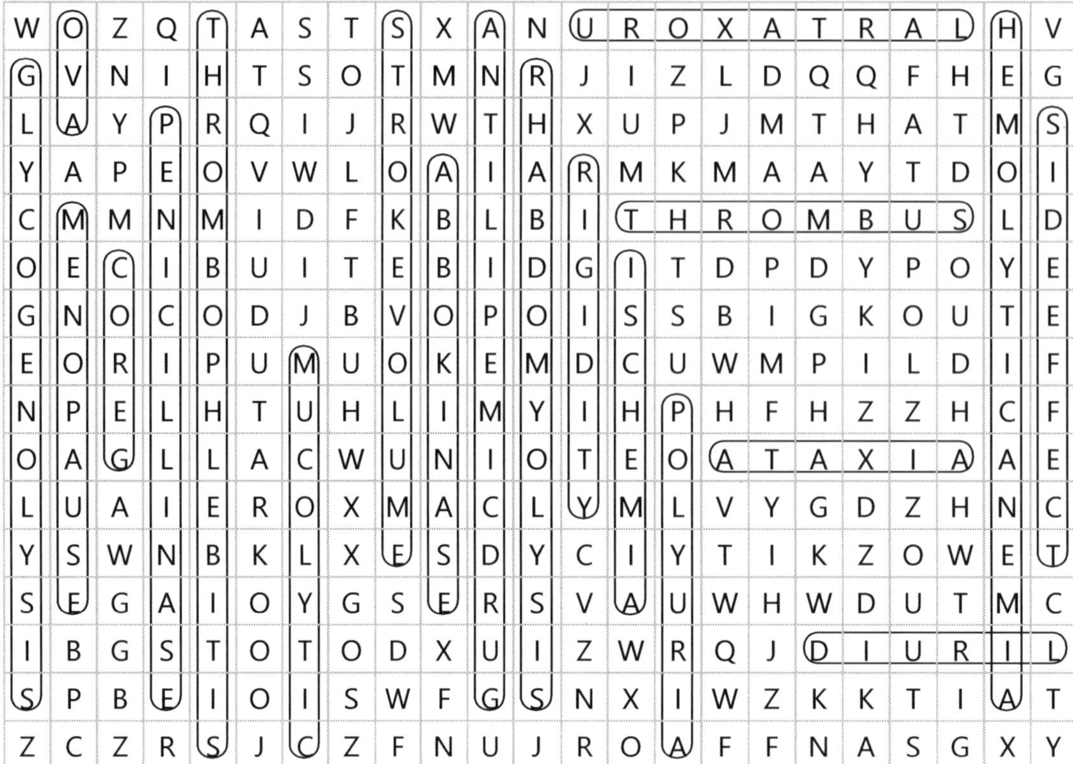

1. A stiffness and inflexibility of movement.
2. Carvedilol
3. Condition in which menstruation no longer occurs.
4. Inflammation of the walls of the veins, associated with clot formation.
5. A drug that reduces the level of fats in the blood.
6. Excessive urine production; increased urination.
7. Clot formed by the action of coagulation factors and circulating blood cells.
8. Insufficient blood supply to meet the needs of the tissue or organ.
9. Not enough red blood cells in blood due to a premature destruction of RBC's.
10. Amount of blood pumped per heartbeat.
11. Alfuzosin
12. Lack of coordination of muscle movements.
13. Hydrolysis of glycogen to yield free glucose.
14. Mature eggs
15. Urokinase
16. The rapid breakdown of skeletal muscle due to muscle injury.
17. Drug that liquefies bronchial secretions.
18. Drug effect other than the therapeutic effect that is usually undesirable but not harmful.
19. Bacterial enzymes that inactivate penicillin antibiotics.
20. Chlorothiazide

A. Menopause
B. Penicillinase
C. Rhabdomyolysis
D. Side Effect
E. Stroke Volume
F. Polyuria
G. Ataxia
H. Thrombophlebitis
I. Ischemia
J. Antilipemic Drug
K. Diuril
L. Thrombus
M. Uroxatral
N. Ova
O. Abbokinase
P. Glycogenolysis
Q. Hemolytic Anemia
R. Coreg
S. Mucolytic
T. Rigidity

4. Find the hidden words. The words have been placed horizontally, vertically, or diagonally. When you locate a word, draw an ellipse around it.

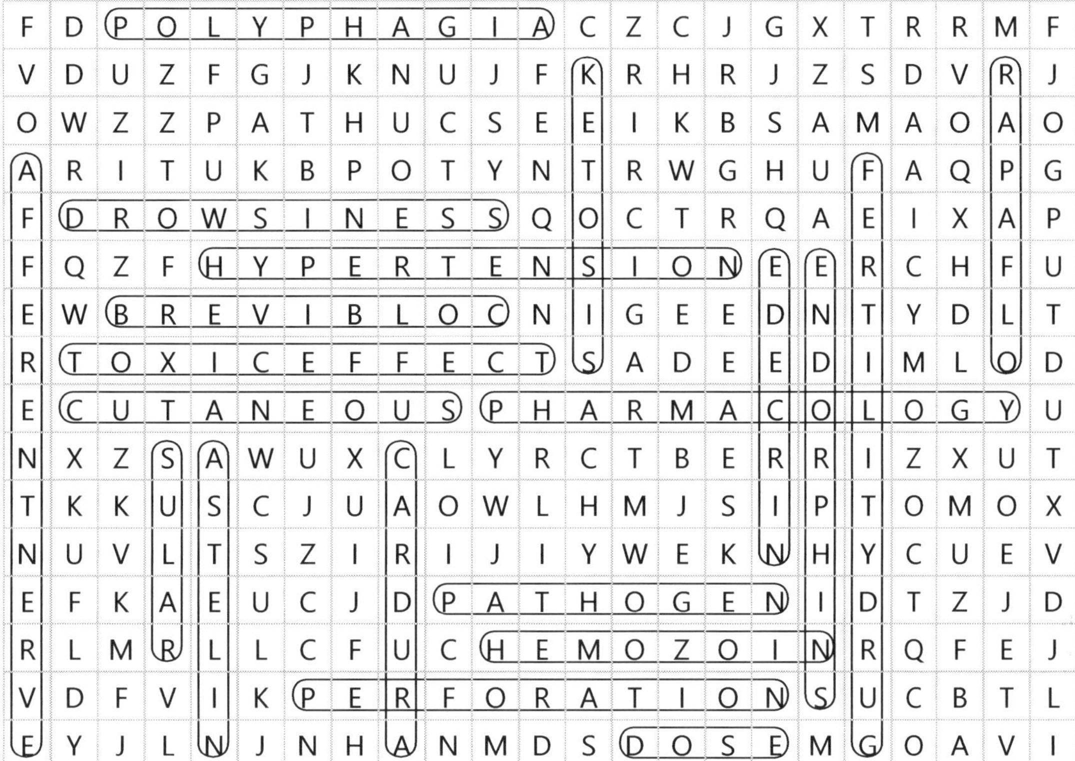

1. Doxazosin
2. Study of drugs.
3. Drug that stimulates ovulation.
4. Ethacrynic acid
5. It refers to feeling abnormally sleepy during the day.
6. Condition associated with an increased production of ketone bodies as a result of fat metabolism.
7. Transmits sensory information from peripheral organs to the central nervous system).
8. Esmolol
9. Azelastine
10. Excessive hunger.
11. Nisoldipine
12. Undesirable drug effect that implies drug poisoning; can be very harmful or life-threatening.
13. Pertaining to the skin.
14. Neuropeptides produced within the CNS that interact with opioid receptors to produce analgesia.
15. A measurement of the amount of drug that is administered.
16. Opening in a hollow organ, such as a break in the intestinal wall.
17. Silodosin
18. Crystalline disposal product from the digestion of blood from blood-feeding parasites.
19. Abnormally high blood pressure.
20. Type of bacteria that cause disease; a microorganism that causes disease.

A. Hypertension	B. Endorphins	C. Astelin	D. Drowsiness	E. Pharmacology
F. Polyphagia	G. Toxic Effect	H. Pathogen	I. Cardura	J. Sular
K. Fertility Drug	L. Cutaneous	M. Perforation	N. Afferent Nerve	O. Ketosis
P. Hemozoin	Q. Rapaflo	R. Brevibloc	S. Edecrin	T. Dose

5. Find the hidden words. The words have been placed horizontally, vertically, or diagonally. When you locate a word, draw an ellipse around it.

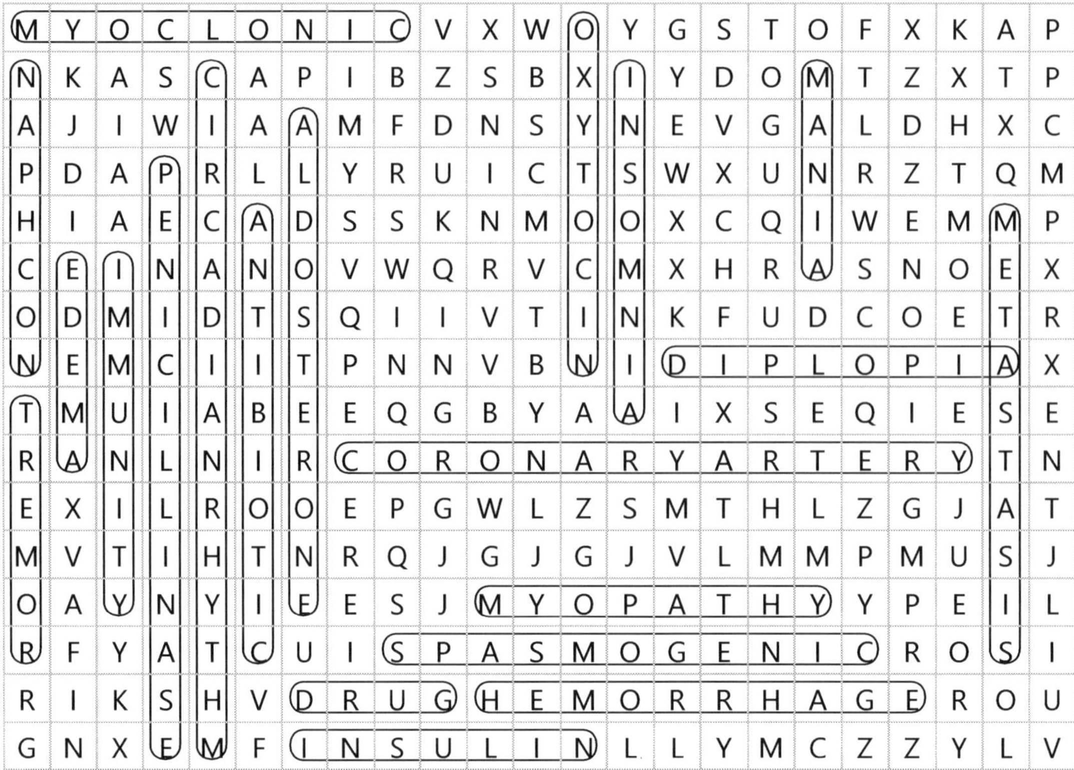

1. Spread of cancer cells throughout the body, from primary to secondary sites.
2. Generalized seizures that are usually brief and often confined to one part of the body.
3. Hormone released from adrenal cortex that causes the retention of sodium from the kidneys.
4. It is difficulty getting to sleep or staying asleep, or having non-refreshing sleep for at least 1 month.
5. An excessive accumulation of fluid in body tissues.
6. Antibacterial drug obtained from other microorganisms.
7. Disease of the muscles.
8. Bacterial enzymes that inactivate penicillin antibiotics.
9. Internal biological clock; a repeatable 24-hour cycle of physiological activity.
10. Polypeptide released within the brain that has specific functions during and after pregnancy.
11. Hormone secreted by the beta cells of the pancreas to facilitate glucose entry into the cell.
12. Condition in which a single object is seen (perceived) as two objects; double vision.
13. Causing a muscle to contract intermittently, resulting in a state of spasms.
14. A trembling and involuntary rhythmic movement.
15. Artery that supplies blood flow to the heart.
16. Chemical substance that produces a change in body function.
17. Naphazoline
18. Condition that causes individuals to resist acquiring or developing a disease or infection.
19. Mental state of excitement, hyperactivity, and excessive elevation of mood.
20. Loss of blood from blood vessels.

A. Oxytocin	B. Myoclonic	C. Circadian Rhythm	D. Aldosterone
E. Myopathy	F. Spasmogenic	G. Drug	H. Penicillinase
I. Antibiotic	J. Coronary Artery	K. Insulin	L. Mania
M. Hemorrhage	N. Metastasis	O. Diplopia	P. Immunity
Q. Tremor	R. Edema	S. Insomnia	T. Naphcon

6. Find the hidden words. The words have been placed horizontally, vertically, or diagonally. When you locate a word, draw an ellipse around it.

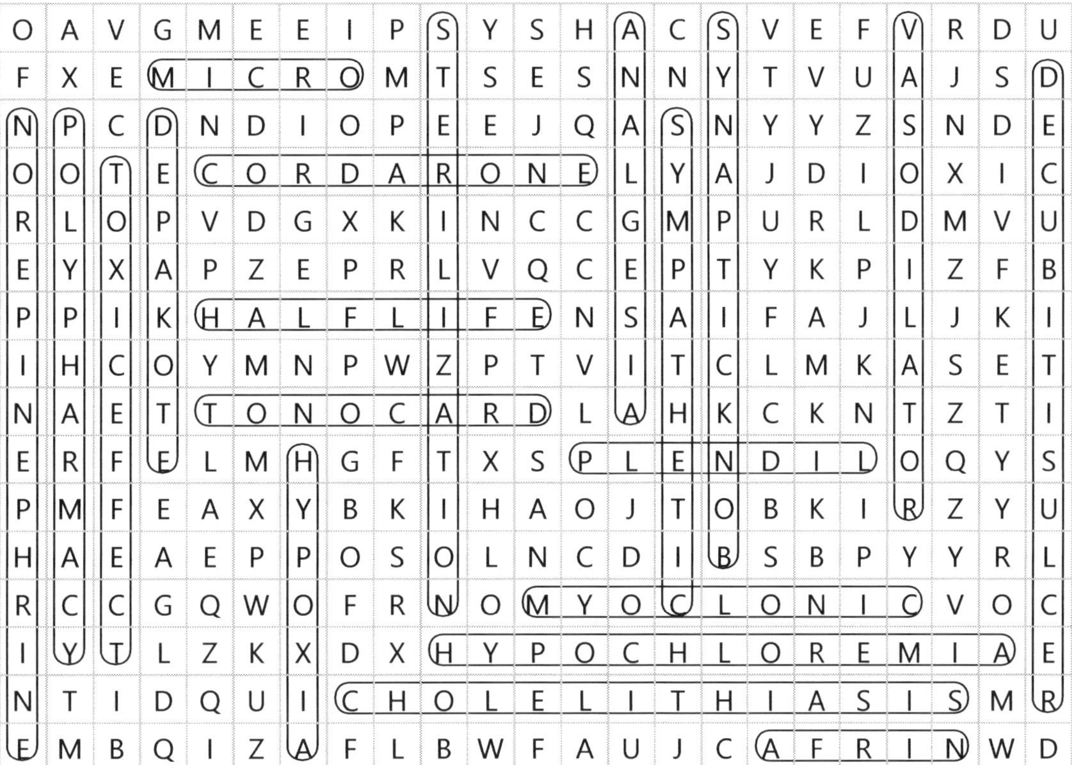

1. Reduction of oxygen supply to tissues below the amount required for normal physiological function.
2. Bedsore.
3. Oxymetazoline
4. Tocainide
5. The presence of gallstones in the gallbladder.
6. Process that results in destruction of all microorganisms.
7. Refers to nerves of the ANS that originate from the thoracolumbar portion of the spinal cord.
8. Decreased response to pain; relief from pain; inhibition of the perception of pain.
9. Generalized seizures that are usually brief and often confined to one part of the body.
10. Undesirable drug effect that implies drug poisoning; can be very harmful or life-threatening.
11. Contains vesicles that store and release neurotransmitters.
12. Felodipine
13. Prefix meaning small.
14. Abnormally low level of chloride ions circulating in the blood.
15. Amiodarone
16. Substance that relaxes the muscles controlling blood vessels, leading to increased blood flow.
17. The situation in patients whose treatment involves multiple drug prescriptions.
18. Time required for the body to reduce the amount of drug in the plasma by one-half.
19. Sodium valproate
20. Neurotransmitter of sympathetic nerves that stimulates the adrenergic receptors.

A. Depakote
B. Vasodilator
C. Myoclonic
D. Tonocard
E. Polypharmacy
F. Cordarone
G. Analgesia
H. Synaptic Knob
I. Sterilization
J. Cholelithiasis
K. Plendil
L. Sympathetic
M. Hypochloremia
N. Hypoxia
O. Afrin
P. Toxic Effect
Q. Norepinephrine
R. Micro
S. Half Life
T. Decubitis Ulcer

7. Find the hidden words. The words have been placed horizontally, vertically, or diagonally. When you locate a word, draw an ellipse around it.

L	N	C	H	K	H	Y	P	O	K	A	L	E	M	I	A	F	P	H	E	P	E	O
I	H	Q	J	V	F	U	N	G	U	S	H	P	K	V	L	G	M	Y	Q	R	V	P
H	F	U	N	G	I	C	I	D	A	L	Y	X	A	G	N	A	Y	P	J	O	A	K
E	A	B	B	Q	W	P	O	H	M	C	P	G	L	M	T	S	I	E	R	S	C	X
V	S	B	Q	Q	Z	Y	Q	Y	G	N	E	D	Q	B	B	T	N	R	T	T	U	X
G	K	E	R	I	O	N	G	D	T	K	R	H	G	O	T	R	D	C	R	A	A	Y
Z	V	I	I	F	E	D	O	R	F	C	T	L	U	W	S	O	E	A	A	G	T	U
A	B	S	O	R	P	T	I	O	N	F	H	C	K	U	C	P	R	L	N	L	I	T
Z	N	P	K	F	Z	F	S	D	J	K	E	R	G	Z	D	A	A	C	X	A	O	Q
U	C	R	R	P	L	C	K	I	P	L	R	Z	Q	C	J	R	L	E	E	N	N	N
Y	H	I	E	F	V	U	Q	U	F	A	M	I	X	C	F	E	Y	M	N	D	K	E
U	E	M	K	F	V	O	T	R	C	A	I	N	M	Z	S	S	S	I	E	I	D	N
N	L	A	U	D	Q	V	R	I	U	E	A	E	V	L	I	I	Y	A	Q	N	M	T
N	A	C	G	D	A	A	K	L	Q	A	N	I	O	N	O	S	K	E	P	P	R	A
L	T	O	G	Q	S	P	E	R	M	A	T	O	G	E	N	E	S	I	S	L	Y	R
T	E	R	H	Y	P	E	R	T	R	I	C	H	O	S	I	S	W	B	Y	B	M	U

1. Clorazepate
2. Abnormally high body temperature.
3. The uptake of nutrients and drugs from the GI tract.
4. HCTZ
5. Condition, also called delayed gastric emptying, in which the stomach muscles do not function properly.
6. Milrinone
7. Mature eggs
8. Unusually high concentration of calcium in the blood.
9. Formation of spermatozoa.
10. Negatively charged ion.
11. Levetiracetam
12. An inflammation of the hair follicles of the beard or scalp caused by ringworm with swelling and pus.
13. Chemical action of a substance to bond permanently to a metal ion.
14. A group of microorganisms with a membrane-bound nucleus that includes yeasts and molds.
15. Can stimulate uterine and intestinal muscle contractions and may cause pain by stimulating nerve endings.
16. Process of removal of waste material from the bowel.
17. Propranolol
18. Excessive hair growth on the body.
19. Substance, chemical solution, or drug that kills fungi; chemical that kills or destroys fungi.
20. Low concentration of potassium in blood.

A. Primacor
B. Fungicidal
C. Absorption
D. Hypercalcemia
E. Kerion
F. Hypertrichosis
G. Evacuation
H. Anion
I. Inderal
J. Spermatogenesis
K. Chelate
L. Fungus
M. Hypokalemia
N. Gastroparesis
O. Hydrodiuril
P. Keppra
Q. Ova
R. Tranxene
S. Prostaglandin
T. Hyperthermia

8. Find the hidden words. The words have been placed horizontally, vertically, or diagonally. When you locate a word, draw an ellipse around it.

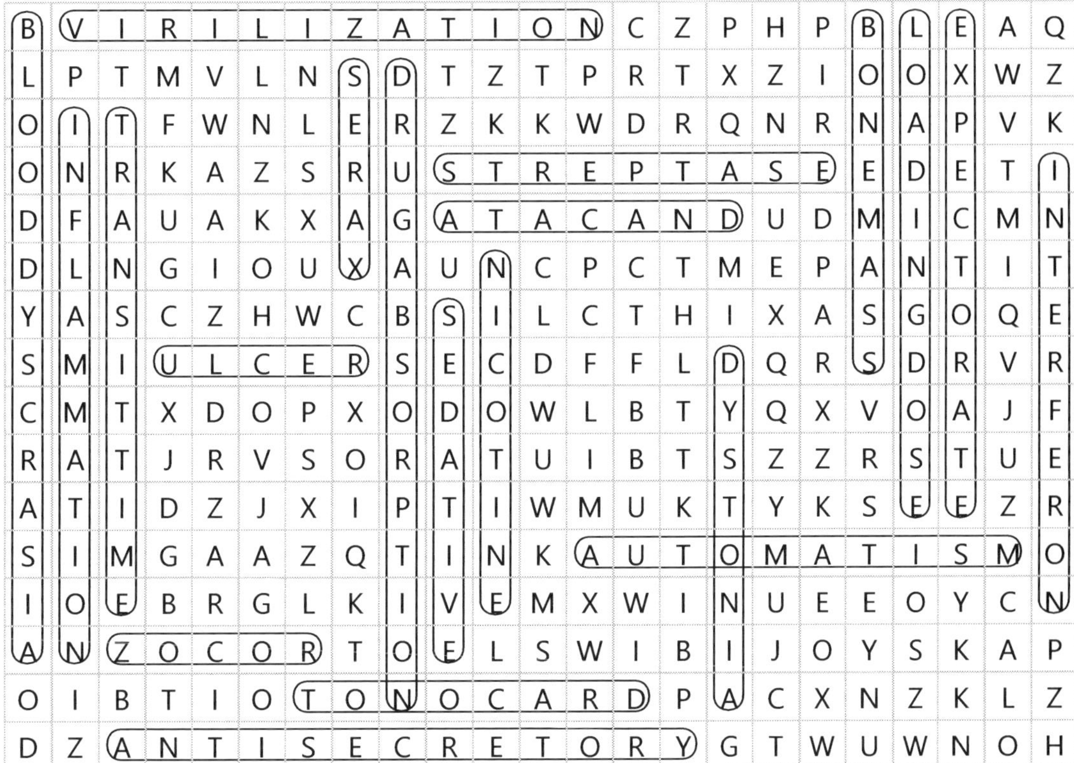

1. Candesartan
2. Muscle spasms, facial grimacing, and other involuntary movements and postures.
3. Amount of time it takes for food to travel from the mouth to the anus.
4. Entrance of a drug into the bloodstream from its site of administration.
5. Drug-induced confusion that can cause increased drug consumption.
6. Simvastatin
7. A measure of the amount of minerals (mostly calcium and phosphorus) contained in a certain volume of bone.
8. Streptokinase
9. Development of masculine body (hair, muscle) characteristics in females.
10. Tocainide
11. Drug used to produce mental relaxation and to reduce the desire for physical activity.
12. Open sore in the mucous membranes or mucosal linings of the body.
13. Oxazepam
14. Initial drug dose administered to rapidly achieve therapeutic drug concentrations.
15. Condition in which tissues have been damaged, characterized by swelling, pain, heat, and sometimes
16. Abnormality in blood.
17. Alkaloid drug in tobacco that stimulates ganglionic receptors.
18. Eject from the mouth; spit.
19. Chemical mediator produced by immune cells that increases immune function.
20. Substance that inhibits secretion of digestive enzymes, hormones, or acid.

A. Expectorate	B. Inflammation	C. Loading Dose	D. Dystonia
E. Streptase	F. Transit Time	G. Antisecretory	H. Bone Mass
I. Sedative	J. Atacand	K. Nicotine	L. Blood Dyscrasia
M. Tonocard	N. Ulcer	O. Serax	P. Automatism
Q. Interferon	R. Virilization	S. Drug Absorption	T. Zocor

nd the hidden words. The words have been placed horizontally, vertically, or diagonally. When you locate a word, draw an ellipse around it.

B	D	Y	K	G	G	A	N	T	I	A	L	L	E	R	G	I	C	E	K	T	A	U
S	V	B	J	G	H	S	O	P	E	N	I	C	I	L	L	I	N	A	S	E	E	E
I	H	T	U	M	O	R	W	E	X	C	O	D	C	O	N	V	U	L	S	I	O	N
T	G	D	B	B	E	N	Z	O	D	I	A	Z	E	P	I	N	E	C	N	F	Z	D
E	K	R	J	Q	Y	K	B	R	U	R	Z	K	E	R	I	O	N	T	A	N	S	O
O	E	U	B	G	G	Q	X	H	Q	T	D	X	F	F	L	O	N	A	S	E	V	M
F	V	G	C	I	A	D	I	G	U	P	A	T	H	O	G	E	N	U	L	R	T	E
A	H	E	W	G	R	W	K	B	Q	X	K	A	W	P	V	B	Z	E	U	L	P	T
C	Y	X	L	A	N	O	X	I	N	J	L	D	Q	G	T	I	S	P	G	O	U	R
T	N	C	Q	N	N	G	T	P	H	M	O	S	I	Y	T	A	G	K	G	D	G	I
I	M	R	J	T	G	Z	D	H	V	I	T	O	X	Q	W	S	K	V	L	Z	O	U
O	H	E	K	I	I	Q	C	A	G	X	E	R	Q	W	O	M	V	V	R	I	N	M
N	C	T	N	S	A	G	J	S	I	G	N	B	U	L	C	E	R	K	Y	F	T	W
J	I	I	M	M	B	I	K	I	M	V	S	E	C	T	R	I	L	E	P	T	A	L
Q	A	O	A	O	T	K	L	C	R	Z	I	N	A	N	G	I	O	E	D	E	M	A
M	F	N	H	J	I	I	K	S	F	Y	N	T	E	Y	R	X	M	A	G	O	C	L

1. Elimination of the drug from the body.
2. Type of bacteria that cause disease; a microorganism that causes disease.
3. Digoxin
4. An inflammation of the hair follicles of the beard or scalp caused by ringworm with swelling and pus.
5. Class of drugs used to treat anxiety and sleep disorders.
6. Uncontrolled growth of abnormal cells that form a solid mass; also called a neoplasm.
7. Location within the body where a drug exerts its therapeutic effect, often a specific drug receptor.
8. Inference tending to produce results that depart systematically from the true values.
9. Two different amounts of estrogen hormone are released during the cycle.
10. Benazepril
11. Open sore in the mucous membranes or mucosal linings of the body.
12. Oxcarbamazepine
13. Increased secretion of growth hormone in childhood, causing excessive growth and height.
14. Lining of the uterus.
15. Drug that prevents mast cells from releasing histamine and other vasoactive substances.
16. Substance that has the ability to attach other substances to its surface.
17. Involuntary muscle contraction that is either tonic or clonic.
18. Edema and swelling beneath the skin.
19. Fluticasone
20. Bacterial enzymes that inactivate penicillin antibiotics.

A. Biphasic
B. Gigantism
C. Convulsion
D. Angioedema
E. Drug Excretion
F. Lanoxin
G. Bias
H. Kerion
I. Flonase
J. Adsorbent
K. Trileptal
L. Lotensin
M. Site of Action
N. Benzodiazepine
O. Endometrium
P. Ulcer
Q. Pathogen
R. Penicillinase
S. Tumor
T. Antiallergic

10. Find the hidden words. The words have been placed horizontally, vertically, or diagonally. When you locate a word, draw an ellipse around it.

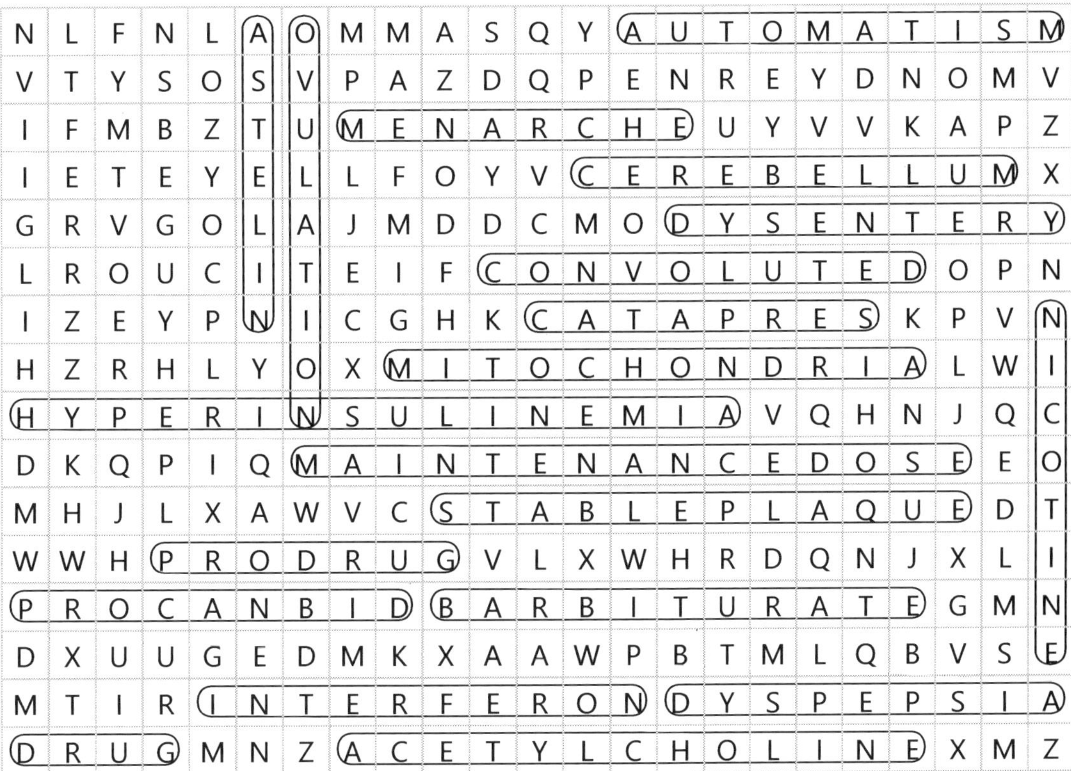

1. Dose administered to maintain drug blood levels in the therapeutic range.
2. CNS depressant drug possessing the barbituric acid ring structure.
3. Part of the brain that coordinates body movements and posture and helps maintain body equilibrium.
4. Release of an egg from the ovary.
5. First menstruation during puberty.
6. An inactive precursor of a drug, converted into its active form in the body by normal metabolic processes.
7. Neurotransmitter of parasympathetic nerves.
8. Chemical mediator produced by immune cells that increases immune function.
9. Clonidine
10. Indigestion.
11. Procainamide
12. Alkaloid drug in tobacco that stimulates ganglionic receptors.
13. Normal structures responsible for energy production in cells.
14. Condition characterized by frequent watery stools (usually containing blood and mucus), tenesmus.
15. Coiled or folded back on itself.
16. Plaque formed in the artery wall that remains in the wall.
17. Drug-induced confusion that can cause increased drug consumption.
18. Azelastine
19. High levels of insulin in the blood often associated with type 2 diabetes mellitus and insulin resistance.
20. Chemical substance that produces a change in body function.

A. Nicotine
B. Stable Plaque
C. Astelin
D. Interferon
E. Hyperinsulinemia
F. Menarche
G. Convoluted
H. Cerebellum
I. Dyspepsia
J. Mitochondria
K. Ovulation
L. Prodrug
M. Acetylcholine
N. Procanbid
O. Catapres
P. Barbiturate
Q. Maintenance Dose
R. Dysentery
S. Drug
T. Automatism

Printed in Great Britain
by Amazon

56208081R00120